# THE GENESIS OF A POLICY

DEFINING AND DEFENDING
AUSTRALIA'S NATIONAL INTEREST
IN THE ASIA-PACIFIC, 1921–57

# THE GENESIS OF A POLICY

DEFINING AND DEFENDING
AUSTRALIA'S NATIONAL INTEREST
IN THE ASIA-PACIFIC, 1921–57

## HONAE CUFFE

Published by ANU Press
The Australian National University
Acton ACT 2601, Australia
Email: anupress@anu.edu.au

Available to download for free at press.anu.edu.au

ISBN (print): 9781760464684
ISBN (online): 9781760464691

WorldCat (print): 1281752426
WorldCat (online): 1281751958

DOI: 10.22459/GP.2021

This title is published under a Creative Commons Attribution-NonCommercial-NoDerivatives 4.0 International (CC BY-NC-ND 4.0).

The full licence terms are available at creativecommons.org/licenses/by-nc-nd/4.0/legalcode

Cover design and layout by ANU Press

This book is published under the aegis of the Asia-Pacific Security Studies Editorial Committee of the ANU Press.

This edition © 2021 ANU Press

# Contents

| | |
|---|---|
| Abbreviations | vii |
| Acknowledgements | ix |
| Introduction: A unique strategic position | 1 |

**Part 1**

| | |
|---|---|
| 1. The interwar setting and Australia's strategic outlook, 1921–31 | 13 |
| 2. Increasing assertiveness in foreign and economic affairs, 1931–35 | 35 |
| 3. Expectations of the empire connection and the Trade Diversion Policy, 1936–37 | 59 |

**Part 2**

| | |
|---|---|
| 4. 'A chronic lack of self-reliance'? Australia's response to the coming Pacific War, 1937–41 | 81 |
| 5. 'An undoubted right to speak': Projecting Australia's influence in the postwar Asia-Pacific, 1942–45 | 109 |

**Part 3**

| | |
|---|---|
| 6. The new order: Australia's perspective on Commonwealth engagement with South-East Asia and the South Pacific, 1946–50 | 135 |
| 7. A confluence of interests: Australia realigns with the US, 1951–57 | 171 |
| Conclusion | 201 |
| Bibliography | 207 |
| Index | 237 |

# Abbreviations

| | |
|---|---|
| ABDACOM | American–British–Dutch–Australian Command |
| ACJ | Allied Council for Japan |
| AEM | Australian Eastern Mission |
| AGPS | Australian Government Printing Service |
| AIF | Australian Imperial Force |
| ALP | Australian Labor Party |
| AMF | Australian Military Forces |
| ANZAC Agreement | Australian–New Zealand Agreement |
| ANZAM | Australian, New Zealand and Malayan (arrangement and area) |
| ANZUS | Australia, New Zealand, United States Security Treaty |
| CID | Committee of Imperial Defence |
| COS | Chiefs of Staff Committee |
| *CPD* | *Commonwealth Parliamentary Debates* |
| *DAFP* | *Documents on Australian Foreign Policy* (book series) |
| DEA | Department of External Affairs (Australia) |
| DFAT | Department of Foreign Affairs and Trade (Australia) |
| ECOSOC | United Nations Economic and Social Commission for Asia |
| ERP | European Recovery Program |
| FESR | Far East Strategic Reserve |
| *FRUS* | *Foreign Relations of the United States* (book series) |
| GDP | gross domestic product |

| | |
|---|---|
| IJN | Imperial Japanese Navy |
| MFN | most-favoured nation |
| NAA | National Archives of Australia |
| NARA | National Archives and Records Administration (USA) |
| NEI | Netherlands East Indies |
| NLA | National Library of Australia |
| NSC | National Security Council (USA) |
| PWC | Pacific War Council |
| RAAF | Royal Australian Air Force |
| RAN | Royal Australian Navy |
| RN | Royal Navy |
| SEATO | Southeast Asia Treaty Organization |
| SPC | South Pacific Commission |
| SWPA | South West Pacific Area |
| TNA | The National Archives (United Kingdom) |
| UN | United Nations |
| US | United States |
| USJCS | United States Joint Chiefs of Staff |
| USSR | Union of Soviet Socialist Republics |

# Acknowledgements

This book was written on Ngunnawal, Ngambri and Awabakal country. I respectfully acknowledge the traditional custodians of this land, their rich history and culture, and Elders past and present. Sovereignty was never ceded, and colonisation is an ongoing project.

This book began its journey as PhD thesis. During my doctoral research, I was the fortunate beneficiary of the Australian Government Research Training Program and the University of Newcastle Provisional Research Degree Scholarship. Without this financial support, which has allowed me to travel, research and present in Australia and the United Kingdom, this project would not have come to fruition. I also wish to acknowledge the support I received as a recipient of the International Australian Studies Association 2021 Early Career Researcher Publication Subsidy Scheme and the Australian Academy of the Humanities 2021 Publication Subsidy. Finally, I am indebted to the countless archivists and librarians who guided me in my research at the National Archives of Australia, National Library of Australia, the UK's National Archives and British Library.

I am forever grateful for the supportive research community that I have been a part of at the University of Newcastle and elsewhere. I could not have completed a project of this magnitude without the guidance of my supervisors, Associate Professor Wayne Reynolds and Dr Kit Candlin. For your expertise, encouragement and attention to my emotional wellbeing, I am sincerely grateful. I am thankful for the insight and warm encouragement extended by the History Department and my fellow postgraduates. I would like to make a special note of thanks to Peter Hooker, Dr Michael Kilmister and Pearl Nunn—your kindness never failed to encourage me during moments of doubt. A very special thank you to Dr Liam Kane—your care, humour and tenacity have buoyed me through difficult months, and I am unendingly grateful to count you as a friend and peer.

I offer my most heartfelt thanks to the exceptional women and scholars of MC148—Dr Naomi Fraser, Dr Annika Herb, Dr Amy Lovat, Dr Ashleigh Mcintyre, Kerry Plunkett, Dr Di Rayson, Ella Rusak, Caroline Schneider and Dr Elicia Taylor. Before I arrived in this room, I spent 22 years searching for my community and I found it here in each of you. Postgraduate research, and the fraught months and years following, is an inexplicable experience and it has been a privilege to share this journey with you. The wisdom you have shared has instilled in me a self-compassion and self-assurance that I previously lacked. Forever and always, long live the noetics!

I owe my greatest debt to my beautiful friends and family, particularly Chezarne Cuffe, Grayson Bancroft, Joelle Price, Lachlan Morris and Timothy Merrikin. Without your unwavering support, this book would not have been possible. You have delighted in my achievements, offered quiet words of reassurance and, in the timeless words of Lachlan, remined me 'don't be so hard on yourself hun'. Foreign policy and the world of academic research can be, I will grudgingly admit, dry topics and your efforts to understand the intricacies of my research have not gone unnoticed. I offer my deepest and sincerest gratitude and can only hope to repay the unparalleled love and support you have shown.

Honae H. Cuffe
September 2021

# Introduction: A unique strategic position

> We are of European Race. Our fathers came from Europe: we have grown up to think as Europeans, and our interests have been centred in that group of nations from which our stock has come. Whilst racially we are European, geographically we are Asiatic. Our own special immediate Australian interests are more nearly concerned with what is happening in China and Japan than what is happening in ... Belgium, Holland, Poland, or other countries farther removed.[1]
>
> — Nationalist Party Senator George Pearce

Australia finds itself in a unique strategic position. Founded as a white settler outpost, the nation's identity, trade and security all flowed from the imperial connection well into the middle of the twentieth century. This connection accordingly shaped most of the frameworks through which Australia interacted with the rest of the world. This early experience of dependence naturalised a policy tradition of strategic alliance with the Anglosphere, depending on relationships with 'great and powerful friends' for the protection of the national interest.

Alongside this cultural heritage and the strategic relationships produced as a result is Australia's geography. Australia is in the Indo-Asia-Pacific region with an area of immediate strategic interest spanning the Pacific and Indian oceans and from the Pacific Islands up through South-East Asia. The divide between cultural heritage and geographic reality has contributed to a sense of isolation, from both the region and the rest of the Anglophone world. Frederic Eggleston, a public intellectual and future minister to China and the United States, captured this sense of

---

1  *Commonwealth Parliamentary Debates: Senate* [hereinafter *CPD: Senate*], 27 July 1922, No. 30 (Canberra: Australian Government Publishing Service, 1922), 822.

isolation when he observed that Australia is 'a small nation in an alien sea'.[2] This isolation, in tandem with Australia's immense and virtually defenceless coastline and fixation on maintaining racial and cultural whiteness—as embodied in the longstanding White Australia Policy—has, in the words of historian John Fitzpatrick, given way to a 'threat ethos' in settler Australia: a longstanding suspicion of its northern neighbours, which underscores the importance of powerful Anglophonic protectors.[3] Alongside these anxieties, the Asia-Pacific region offers significant trade opportunities. Managing economic opportunities and fears of a potential threat from the north has been a longstanding feature of Australia's foreign, trade and defence policies.[4]

At the time of writing, the Asia-Pacific region is experiencing a period of disruption and transition as China's economic and military growth challenges US predominance in the region. The China–US contest has been likened to Thucydides's Trap ('it was the rise of Athens and the fear that this instilled in Sparta that made war inevitable'): as each nation flexes its proverbial soft and hard power muscles in a bid to exercise influence in the region, the other party becomes increasingly defensive and conflict is more likely.[5] This contest has played out across many stages—most notably, the China–US trade war that erupted in March 2018 and the ongoing military brinkmanship in the South China Sea. The COVID-19 pandemic has accelerated this strategic trend within the region. Australia, too, has increasingly done away with diplomatic niceties during the pandemic. In an address launching the *2020 Defence Strategic Update* and an additional A$270 billion in defence spending in the coming decade, Prime Minister Scott Morrison openly acknowledged the 'fractious at best' US–China relations. He went on to predict a post-COVID-19 world 'that is poorer, that is more dangerous, and that is more disorderly'.[6]

---

2    Frederic William Eggleston, *Reflections on Australian Foreign Policy* (Melbourne: F.W. Cheshire for Australian Institute of International Affairs, 1957), 1.
3    John Fitzpatrick, 'European Settler Colonialism and National Security Ideologies in Australian History', in *Middling, Meddling, Muddling: Issues in Australian Foreign Policy*, eds Richard Leaver and David Cox (Sydney: Allen & Unwin, 1997), 116.
4    For comprehensive studies of Australia's strategic and economic perception of Asia, see Sandra Tweedie, *Trading Partners: Australia and Asia, 1790–1993* (Sydney: UNSW Press, 1994); David Walker, *Anxious Nation: Australia and the Rise of Asia 1850–1939* (Brisbane: University of Queensland Press, 1999).
5    Thucydides, *The History of the Peloponnesian War*, cited in Graham Allison, *Destined for War: Can America and China Escape Thucydides's Trap?* (New York: Houghton Mifflin Harcourt, 2017), vii.
6    Scott Morrison, 'Address: Launch of the 2020 Defence Strategic Update', Speech, Royal Military College, Duntroon, ACT, 1 July 2020, available from: www.pm.gov.au/media/address-launch-2020-defence-strategic-update.

## INTRODUCTION

With China and the US representing Australia's greatest trading partner and greatest security partner, respectively, Australia's position amid the unfolding power transition is a tenuous one. According to military and intelligence strategist Hugh White, Australia has historically 'taken for granted' that its security would be protected by a great and powerful friend. Australia's neighbours have accordingly been relatively insignificant in terms of strategic planning. The rise of China undermines 'the geopolitical foundations on which Australia's strategic outlook has been built'. Until recently, White's proposed solution for the 'new world' Australia faces was a power-sharing arrangement between China and the US in which Australia would act as a mediator.[7] In this scenario, Australia would not be forced to choose between China and the US and could continue to enjoy economic and strategic benefits.[8] White has since renounced this power-sharing thesis as unachievable because of the US decline and China's resolve to not share power.[9] White's reversal was vindicated in the latter half of 2020, as two Australian journalists fled China fearing detainment following police questioning, and China and Australia launched a series of punitive trade measures against a raft of each other's exports.[10]

As this book will reveal, the situation Australia now faces is not a novel one. Rather, it is grappling with geopolitical issues that go well back into the nation's history. The assertion that Australia has historically taken for granted that its powerful allies will provide for its military security effectively discounts the nation's distinctive geographical interests in policymaking. The strategic outlooks of Britain and the US, as global powers, have predominated, often at the expense of Australia's immediate regional and particular interests. Australia has long considered itself a Principal Power in the Asia-Pacific, with certain rights and responsibilities in regional

---

7   Hugh White, *The China Choice: Why America Should Share Power* (Melbourne: Black Inc., 2013), 12.
8   White's thesis has been developed over the past decade and a half in a series of publications. These include, Hugh White, 'The Limits to Optimism: Australia and the Rise of China', *Australian Journal of International Affairs* 59, no. 4 (2005): 469–80; Hugh White, 'Powershift: Australia's Future Between Washington and Beijing', *Quarterly Essay* 39 (2010): 1–74; White, *The China Choice*.
9   Hugh White, 'Without America: Australia in the New Asia', *Quarterly Essay* 68 (2017): 1–81.
10  Matthew Doran and Stephen Dziedzic, 'Australian Correspondents Bill Birtles and Mike Smith Pulled Out of China After Five-Day Diplomatic Standoff Over National Security Case', *ABC News*, 8 September 2020, available from: www.abc.net.au/news/2020-09-08/bill-birtles-mike-smith-evacuated-china-safety-concerns/12638786; Prianka Srinivasan, 'China's Trade War With Australia Is Affecting A Growing Number of Industries. How Did We Get Here?', *ABC News*, 10 December 2020, available from: www.abc.net.au/news/2020-12-10/chinas-trade-war-with-australia-export-industry/12967190.

decision-making. A prominent feature in Australia's foreign policy history has been navigating the strategic priorities of the great powers and compelling them to acknowledge the nation's Principal Power status.

This book assesses the interrelation between Australia's geography and great-power relations and the development of a foreign policy over the period 1921–57. This chosen period is a somewhat unusual one. This book holds the view that the years 1921–57 mark a period of transition, in terms of both the economic and strategic situation in Australia's region and the nation's relationships with Britain and the US. Moreover, the focus on years not usually prioritised in studies of the genesis and development of Australia's foreign policy—the tendency generally being to centre on World War II and the years immediately following—uncovers a much longer process of theorising and experimentation by Australian policymakers and intellectuals.

In 1921, Australia relied on the UK and its imperial machinery for diplomatic representation and economic and material security. The unprecedented changes under way in the Asia-Pacific region challenged this relationship. The US was the emerging Pacific hegemon, yet isolationism precluded the development of a complete regional policy. Japan's rise threatened to displace British commercial and military influence, exacerbating Australia's longstanding fears about aggressive regional expansion with potential designs on the Australian continent.[11] By 1957, US defensive predominance was unequivocal, the Sterling Area was very much in its twilight and Australia was conducting its foreign affairs planning in line with the US order. While 1957 was not the end of high-level Australian–British relations, with significant commercial, military and cultural links present well into the 1960s, it marked a departure from the traditional Australian–British relationship of patronage and protection and the point at which the centre of gravity in Australian foreign policy shifted decisively to the US.[12]

---

11   D.C.S. Sissons, 'Attitudes to Japan and defence, 1890–1923' (MPhil thesis, University of Melbourne, 1956); Neville Meaney, *A History of Australian Defence and Foreign Policy 1901–23. Volume 1: The Search for Security in the Pacific, 1901–1914*, 2nd edn, and *Volume 2: Australia and World Crisis, 1914–1923* (Sydney: Sydney University Press, 2009).
12   James Curran and Stuart Ward, *The Unknown Nation: Australia After Empire* (Melbourne: Melbourne University Press, 2010).

## INTRODUCTION

The central task of this book is to examine the gradual development of an assertive and pragmatic Australian foreign policy. The Australia of the interwar years is often seen as lacking instinct and confidence in international matters, preferring instead to deal 'with the world one step removed through Whitehall'.[13] This approach seemingly remained when Australia transferred its dependency to the US following the collapse of the British imperial war effort in the Pacific theatre in 1941–42.[14] As this book demonstrates, this assessment misreads Australia's approach to foreign policy and its interactions with Britain and the US in the years before and after 1941–42. There was a pragmatism—rather than uncritical loyalty to Britain or toadying to the US—that informed Australia's Asia-Pacific policy in the period covered in this book. Granted, this pragmatism at times necessarily took the form of alignment and it was not without its weaknesses. Nevertheless, this book highlights a far more engaged and assertive policymaking practice—one informed by the lessons gleaned from past failures and successes. This is a lens not previously applied in the existing literature.

The Australian governments of the interwar years recognised the shifting power distributions under way in the global and Asia-Pacific orders. The 1920s and, in particular, 1930s reveal the genesis of a distinct Australian foreign policy that developed in response to this recognition. This policy was tailored to the nation's particular geography, size and strategic capabilities and informed by the acknowledgement that, while necessary security partners, neither Britain nor the US completely served the national interest. The Australian government identified in this the need to intervene in the policies of the great powers to ensure its particular interests were incorporated. In the pages that follow, this book investigates how this interventionist approach to foreign policy that was conceived in the interwar years went on to shape the governments of John Curtin, Ben Chifley and Robert Menzies—at least until 1957, the point at which there was a shift as Australia accepted that the 'Fourth Empire' and the

---

13   Christopher Waters, *Australia and Appeasement: Imperial Foreign Policy and the Origins of World War II* (London: I.B. Tauris, 2012), 7.
14   Harry Gelber, *The Australian–American Alliance: Costs and Benefits* (Melbourne: Penguin Books, 1968), 25; Eric M. Andrews, *A History of Australian Foreign Policy: From Dependence to Independence* (Melbourne: Longman Cheshire, 1979), 70–2; T.B. Millar, *Australia in Peace and War: External Relations Since 1788* (Canberra: Australian National University Press, 1978), 21–3, 92.

maintenance of a British world system were unattainable.[15] It demonstrates a marked continuity in how Australia's political elite approached foreign policy and defined the national interest.

Both Australia's junior-partner status and the dynamics of Anglo-American competition and alliance complicated attempts to navigate great-power relations. In the period 1921–57, America's priorities were not always acceptable to Britain or Australia. Postwar plans for Japanese reconstruction as the Asian bulwark against communism, for instance, were seen to undermine the foundation of British economic power (preference and protectionism within the Sterling Area), the Commonwealth's status in the Asia-Pacific region and Australia's economic and physical security.[16] Similarly, as US military predominance was solidified during the 1950s and Australia signed the Australia, New Zealand, United States Security Treaty (ANZUS) and Southeast Asia Treaty Organization (SEATO), it remained unclear whether the US could be relied on to lead in the Asia-Pacific region in a way that was conducive to Australia's national interest. The Menzies government accordingly promoted—albeit with little success—US–British cooperation in the leadership and defence of the Asia-Pacific region. The focus on the interplay between the great powers presented in this book underscores Australia's gradual and uneven transition from the British order to that of the US, as Australian leaders made frank assessments about which relationship best served the nation's interests in the Asia-Pacific.

The secondary aim of this book is to examine the idea of an integrated policy—that is, one that balanced Australia's regional realities with great-power relationships and, in assessing those relationships, ensured Australia's economic, diplomatic and strategic interests were met. The primary focus here is the importance of trade. Among Australian historians and political scientists, there was a longstanding tendency to view strategy and diplomacy as 'high politics' and the true work of foreign

---

15  The 'Fourth Empire' refers to Britain's attempt to maintain its great-power status in the years after World War II. The British Commonwealth of Nations was central to maintaining the British world system, with the British and Australian governments hoping to engage the disparate regions of the Commonwealth to develop specialist area knowledge for regional economic, defence and diplomatic arrangements. For an overview of the Fourth Empire, see David Lee, *Search for Security: The Political Economy of Australia's Postwar Foreign and Defence Policy* (Sydney: Allen & Unwin, 1995), Chs 1 and 2.
16  The Sterling Area was a group of countries—mostly members of the British Empire—which pegged their exchange rates to the pound sterling, conducted trade in sterling and stored their currency reserves in London. Ian M. Drummond, *The Floating Pound and the Sterling Area: 1931–1939* (Cambridge, UK: Cambridge University Press, 1981), 3–7, 10.

policy, while trade and economic policy were considered 'low politics' and served only, as Coral Bell wrote, to 'illuminate … diplomatic and strategic decisions'.[17] In reality, the economic, diplomatic and strategic components of foreign policy intersect and shape one another, the policies pursued and the relationships formed. In 1987, the departmental machinery of government underwent a major restructure and the creation of the Department of Foreign Affairs and Trade (DFAT) formalised this interrelation and a much broader understanding of foreign policy.[18]

The assessment in 1987 that there was an interconnection between trade, strategy and foreign affairs and that this was somehow a new assertion overlooks what has long been a feature of the way Australian actors approach foreign policymaking. Amid the strategic and economic uncertainty of the interwar years, Australian policymakers came to appreciate the interrelation between trade, diplomacy and defence. An integrated foreign policy emerged in response to this realisation. In the 1930s, this was a policy in which trade served to expand Australia's regional presence in a bid to engage with and placate Japan, while simultaneously alleviating some of the commercial upheaval of the Great Depression. In the 1940s, trade and economic development played a central role in Australia's plans for the new postwar order in its immediate region. Australia hoped to facilitate the creation of a 'self-subsisting' regional system that would foster political and economic stability in South-East Asia and the South Pacific.[19] By the late 1940s and into the 1950s, economics and trade were central to Britain's waning capabilities in the Asia-Pacific, signalling to Australian actors the need for an extensive economic and strategic adjustment.

While parts of this story have certainly been covered elsewhere, the broad and comprehensive approach offered in this book is a new one. This book is grounded in close study of archival documents, several of which are previously unused or underexamined elsewhere. Moreover, to understand

---

17  Lee, *Search for Security*, 1–6; Coral Bell, *Dependent Ally: A Study in Australian Foreign Policy*, 2nd edn (Melbourne: Oxford University Press, 1984), 2. For works critiquing the division of trade, diplomacy and security, see Stuart Harris, 'The Separation of Economics and Politics: A Luxury We Can No Longer Afford', in *Academic Studies and International Politics: Papers of a Conference Held at The Australian National University, June 1981*, ed. Coral Bell (Canberra: ANU Department of International Relations, 1982), 75–83; Stuart Harris, 'The Linking of Politics and Economics in Foreign Policy', *Australian Outlook* 40, no. 1 (1986): 5–10.
18  Two separate departments, the Department of Foreign Affairs and the Department of Trade, became the Department of Foreign Affairs and Trade in 1987.
19  'Pacific Area Research Reports, April 1943', Papers of William Douglass Forsyth, National Library of Australia [hereinafter NLA], Canberra: MS 5700/7/16/3.

the interconnection between trade, strategy and diplomacy in foreign policy decision-making, attention has been given to discussions within and across key departments such as the Department of External Affairs (DEA), the Prime Minister's Department, the Cabinet and War Cabinet, the Department of Defence and Department of Trade and Customs (later Department of Trade).

In exploring the development of an assertive and integrated policy, this book has been split into three parts and follows a broadly chronological structure. Part 1 explores the economic and strategic uncertainty of the interwar years and the genesis of an Australian foreign policy in response. Chapter 1 sets out the strategic setting in the interwar world, adopting the view that the 1921–22 Washington Naval Conference was the point at which Britain's relative decline became undeniable and the US began to assert regional hegemony. This chapter examines how the conference and a series of other developments in British world leadership forced on Australian policymakers the need to give more serious attention to affairs in the Asia-Pacific. Against the backdrop of the Great Depression and the Manchurian Crisis, Chapter 2 explores the opportunity trade offered for regional engagement and the building of Australia's diplomatic capabilities. This chapter also considers how, as Australia reorientated towards the Asia-Pacific, the nation attempted to similarly shape the focus of empire policy. The third chapter examines the much-derided 1936 Trade Diversion Policy, when Australia launched a trade war against Japan, sacrificing the economic and diplomatic relations it had carefully constructed. Rather than a 'disastrous experiment' by a naive nation, as it has been labelled, the Trade Diversion Policy is presented in this chapter as a case study in the expectations of alliance—both Britain's expectation of loyalty and Australia's perception of the economic benefits of the imperial connection—and how they differed in application.[20] In the context of Australia's nascent foreign policy—predicated on integrating the national interest within the imperial outlook—the Trade Diversion Policy underscores the increasing inadequacy of the imperial machinery to achieve this goal.

Part 2 focuses on Australia's preparation for regional conflict and its response to British and US wartime strategy and postwar plans for the management of the Asia-Pacific region. Chapter 4 argues that Australia was acutely aware

---

20   Norman Harper, *Australia and the United States* (Melbourne: Thomas Nelson, 1971), 94.

of the limitations of imperial defence planning for the Asia-Pacific region and developed a policy over the period 1937–41 in response. In the same vein as the Allies' approach to the European aggressors, Australia coupled rearmament with appeasement. British actions threatened to derail these efforts and, in so doing, reiterated the diverging priorities of the UK and Australia. This chapter also touches on Australia's increasing initiative in relations with the US as the nation looked beyond the Empire for security assurances in the Pacific. Chapter 5, which examines the years 1942–45, explores the approaches taken by the DEA, Department of Defence and Prime Minister Curtin to finding a common goal of carving out a distinct role for Australia in the postwar Asia-Pacific. It explores the Australian–US antagonism that developed on Australia's realisation that its wartime ally could not necessarily be relied on to build a postwar order that would provide for its interests. The Australian government articulated its status as a Principal Power in the region and set out a strategy for how it would manage in the region in the postwar period. Central to this strategy was a renewed system for Commonwealth cooperation, the regionalisation of defence planning and establishing a friendly yet robust counterweight to US influence in the Asia-Pacific region. As detailed in Chapter 5, these principles were captured in the 1944 Australian–New Zealand Agreement (ANZAC Agreement) and Prime Minister Curtin's renewed framework for Commonwealth relations—which he called the Fourth Empire—both of which sought to articulate Australia's predominant role in the Asia-Pacific region and secure a Commonwealth defence machinery premised on cooperation and strategic zones of responsibility.

The final part of this book explores how Australia's postwar foreign policy drew together threads from interwar and wartime policy thinking and lessons learnt. This policy was directed towards expanding the nation's economic, diplomatic and defensive capabilities in South-East Asia and the South Pacific amid the shift from British world leadership to that of the US. Chapter 6 assesses Australia's return to the Commonwealth connection following the war, focusing on the level of reliance and cooperation that existed in the Anglo-Australian relationship and the regionalism and self-interest behind plans to rebuild the British world system. The Commonwealth was to be the basis of a cooperative regional security relationship. Central to this relationship was the preservation of the Sterling Area (these markets, of course, being essential to Britain's economic wellbeing and preserving its influence in the Asia-Pacific region), finding continuity in the Chifley government's approaches and the Colombo Plan for Cooperative Economic and Social Development in Asia and the Pacific, which was introduced in the first year of the new Menzies government. Finally, Chapter 7 provides a revised assessment of the ANZUS Treaty and Australia's realignment with the US. The Menzies government remained uncertain about the US taking on the leading role in the Asia-Pacific region and advocated for a Commonwealth–US strategic partnership. Ultimately, it was only after Britain's declining global power became apparent to the world in a series of crises and policy realignments in 1955–57 that Australia was forced to make frank assessments of the great powers, their priorities and capabilities and which relationship best served the national interest.

Each chapter in this book foregrounds Australia's search to define its national interest and cultivate a policy tailored to its geography, strategic capabilities and relationships with the great powers. In so doing, this book identifies a comprehensive and explicitly pragmatic approach in Australia's foreign policy tradition that has not previously been identified.

# PART 1

# 1

# The interwar setting and Australia's strategic outlook, 1921–31

Britain and its allies emerged victorious from World War I. In the course of this war for empire, Britain's greatest imperial rivals, Germany and wartime ally Russia, had either been defeated or collapsed, seemingly securing British power against future challenges. At first glance, this appeared unquestionable: the British Empire encompassed the largest population, territory and armed forces globally, while its access to natural resources was unmatched, positioning it for continued industrial growth. In reality, British power was in decline, both relative to the rising powers of Japan and the US and absolutely, as the nation struggled with imperial overstretch and the immense cost of global war.[1]

Leading voices in Australian foreign and defence history have argued that Australia accepted the international arrangements made following the war as an adequate system for maintaining peace and, through either arrogance or ignorance, overlooked Britain's waning capabilities. Neville Meaney, for instance, writes of a 'cold war' with Japan that came to an end with the 1921–22 Washington Naval Conference and the commencement of construction of the Singapore Naval Base in 1923—the cornerstone of imperial defence planning in the Far East. This attitude ushered in an era of relative complacency in Australia's international outlook that

---

1   Paul Kennedy, *The Rise and Fall of British Naval Mastery* (London: A. Lane, 1976), 267–8; John Darwin, *The Empire Project: The Rise and Fall of the British World System, 1830–1970* (Cambridge, UK: Cambridge University Press, 2009), 305–8, 324–5, 357–9.

remained in force until the outbreak of World War II.² Rather than Australia being the parochial nation that had 'few ideas and policies of its own' and indiscriminately followed British directives, key individuals were, in fact, hesitant to accept the postwar systems for maintaining peace.³ Granted, Australia was slow to act on these concerns and, when it did act, it tended to vocalise its fears rather than form a distinct policy. Nevertheless, the nation's policymakers were carefully considering the changing power dynamic in the Pacific and the capacity of Britain and its imperial machinery to protect Australia's distinct interests.

## The old power and the rising powers

Britain's financial and industrial situation following the war was critical in the shifting balance of world power. World War I was an immensely expensive undertaking for Britain. During the long years of total war, Britain came to rely on US markets for food, raw materials and machinery. The US required little in return, resulting in an enormous British balance-of-payments deficit as the government was forced to borrow dollars. For the financial year 1918–19, British national debt reached 127 per cent of gross domestic product (GDP).⁴ Although British debt had reached this level before, in the postwar world, the difference was that now the US was the world's largest manufacturing economy and largest creditor nation.⁵ The City of London was no longer the economic and financial centre of the world.⁶

Along with the immediate financial cost of war, there was the human cost and its economic implications. More than 700,000 British men were killed during the war—approximately 9 per cent of the British male population

---

2   Meaney, *A History of Australian Defence and Foreign Policy 1901–23*, vol. 2, 492–500, 512–14. See also David Day, *The Great Betrayal: Britain, Australia and the Onset of the Pacific War, 1939–42* (Melbourne: Oxford University Press, 1992), 1–16.
3   Eric M. Andrews, *Isolationism and Appeasement in Australia: Reactions to the European Crisis, 1935–1939* (Canberra: Australian National University Press, 1970), 25.
4   B.R. Mitchell, *British Historical Statistics* (Cambridge, UK: Cambridge University Press, 1988), 600–3. This compared with a national debt of 24 per cent of GDP in the 1913–14 financial year.
5   At the turn of the twentieth century, Britain represented 23.6 per cent of the relative share of world manufacturing output, compared with the United States' 18.5 per cent. Only two decades earlier, the US was responsible for 22.9 per cent of world manufacturing and Britain 14.7 per cent. P. Bairoch, 'International Industrialisation Levels from 1750–1980', *Journal of European Economic History* 11 (1982): 269–333, at pp. 296, 304.
6   Paul Kennedy, *The Rise and Fall of the Great Powers: Economic Change and Military Conflict from 1500 to 2000* (London: Fontana Press, 1988), 346, 353, 363; Darwin, *The Empire Project*, 323, 326–8.

under the age of 45—and many more had been wounded.⁷ The financial cost of the war combined with the loss of so many men of working age greatly reduced Britain's potential productivity. Its share of world trade declined accordingly, falling from 14.15 per cent to 10.75 per cent between 1913 and 1929.⁸ The British industrial machine, 'the very heart of British power', Correlli Barnett wrote, 'beat slow and weak'.⁹

In the face of immense debt and an economy under strain, the British government struggled to preserve its economic capacity to manage a two-power standard naval fleet. Following the 1919 peace settlement in Paris, the British government adopted the view that the nation would not be engaged in a major conflict for at least the next decade and should accordingly economise (the 10-year rule). Defence expenditure was informed by the 10-year rule, prompting the widespread cancellation of defence construction contracts and the rapid deceleration of defence expenditure.¹⁰ While it is not unexpected that a nation at peace would reduce its defence expenditure, the rate at which Britain did so was unprecedented. Within five years of the war's end, British defence expenditure as a percentage of GDP had fallen below prewar levels, and it continued to fall until 1936, when Germany's reoccupation of the Rhineland made clear the need for rearmament in earnest.¹¹

In contrast with the British experience, Japan and the US emerged from the war as significant rising powers. In addition to financial and economic developments, the United States' participation in the war and peacemaking process was symbolically significant. Having entered the war in the late and critical stages, the US was seen by many as the Allies' saviour. For instance, Australian Prime Minister William Morris Hughes described America's entrance into the war as 'an inspiration' and 'the most dramatic and important event … of the war'.¹² While the US ultimately did not join the League of Nations—the new organisation responsible for maintaining international peace—US President Woodrow Wilson's vision for the postwar world was instrumental in the league's

---

7   *Statistics of the Military Effort of the British Empire During the Great War 1914–1920* (London: His Majesty's Stationery Office, 1922), 237–9. This figure represents those killed in action, those who died of their wounds or as prisoners of war and those missing and presumed dead.
8   Kennedy, *The Rise and Fall of British Naval Mastery*, 269.
9   Correlli Barnett, *The Collapse of British Power* (London: Eyre Methuen, 1972), 269.
10  Kennedy, *The Rise and Fall of British Naval Mastery*, 323–5.
11  In 1914, British defence expenditure was 3.21 per cent of GDP; in 1924, this had fallen to 2.9 per cent. Mitchell, *British Historical Statistics*, 590–1.
12  'Australia to Have a Monroe Doctrine', *The New York Times*, 1 June 1918, 9.

conception and establishment.[13] With Germany defeated and Russia having collapsed in the wake of the November 1917 Bolshevik revolution, Japan emerged from World War I with the third-largest navy in the world and as a dominant power in the waters of the North Pacific. As had been the case for the US, the demands of global war had boosted Japan's industrialisation. The nation's shipbuilding output, for instance, increased from 85,000 tonnes to 650,000 tonnes between 1914 and 1919. Japan also emerged from the war a major creditor nation, having made loans to allies the UK, France and Russia.[14]

Australia was aware of the growing significance of Japan and the US and the importance of securing cordial relations with them; however, recent relations with the two nations were complex. Japan had entered the war in August 1914 on the consensus that the Imperial Japanese Navy (IJN) would escort Allied flotillas in the Indian and Pacific oceans and capture German territories in the East and South China seas. The IJN quickly extended operations, capturing Germany's North Pacific territories (the Marshall, Mariana and Caroline islands) by the end of 1914. Australia, due to its strategic isolation and overtly racialised suspicions, saw in Japan's territorial advances the accumulation of strategic points from which to launch a policy of aggressive southward expansion, with possible designs on Australia.[15]

Throughout the war, the nation's policymakers had been candid about their expectation that Australia would be granted direct control of New Guinea and the adjacent islands—islands described by Hughes as 'natural bastions' in the defence of advances from the north towards the Australian continent.[16] Given the US anticipated an Asia-Pacific power struggle between itself and Japan, Australia saw in this shared suspicion of Japan an opportunity for cooperation and sought support from the US in its regional endeavours. In mid-1918, Hughes visited the US and, in a series of meetings and speeches, called on the US to cooperate with Australia in ensuring postwar security in the Far East. According to Hughes, the potential for islands 'within striking distance' of Australia to be possessed by an unfriendly power 'means that our country must

---

13   For Wilson's postwar world vision, see Thomas J. Knock, *To End All Wars: Woodrow Wilson and the Quest for a New World Order* (Princeton, NJ: Princeton University Press, 1995).
14   Kennedy, *The Rise and Fall of the Great Powers*, 386.
15   Meaney, *A History of Australian Defence and Foreign Policy 1901–23*, vol. 2, 248–55.
16   'William Hughes, "Australia and the Pacific Island Memorandum", 6 February 1919', Papers of John Latham, NLA: MS 1009/19/1342.

always sleep with the sword half drawn'. If Australia's security was to be guaranteed, the nation needed local hegemony—'an Australian Monroe Doctrine in the Southern Pacific'. Hughes presented peacemaking as an opportunity for pre-emptive action against future 'predatory designs' on the region, calling on the US 'to stand by [Australia] around the peace tables', supporting the nation's claim to Germany's former South Pacific territories.[17]

Hughes was ultimately unsuccessful in gaining US support. At the Paris Peace Conference, Wilson, an idealistic anti-imperialist committed to gradual self-governance, and Hughes, a pragmatist and fierce patriot resolved to see Australia annex the South Pacific territories, clashed and the question of the Pacific territories threatened to derail the conference.[18] The solution was a compromise on Wilson's original mandate proposal. Three classes of mandates (A, B and C) were awarded. The C-class mandates in the Pacific were considered the furthest from self-government and 'best administered under the laws of the Mandatory as integral portions of its territory'.[19] Australia was granted a C-class mandate over New Guinea and a joint British Empire mandate over Nauru. Japan was granted a C-class mandate over the Marshall, Mariana and Caroline islands. While these mandated territories could not be fortified, Australia was granted a large measure of administrative oversight, including control of immigration, tariffs and navigation. The Japanese delegation's insistence on freedom of entry and residence in the C-class mandates—a position that was not abandoned until late 1920—coupled with their failed attempt to include a racial equality clause in the League of Nations' covenant, galvanised for Australia the risk of Japanese expansion in the Far East and the value of immigration restrictions afforded by the mandate system.[20]

---

17   'Australia to Have a Monroe Doctrine', *The New York Times*. The Monroe Doctrine (1823) stipulated that the Western Hemisphere was the United States' sphere of interest and attempts by European powers to colonise or extend influence in this area would not be tolerated.
18   Carl Bridge, *William Hughes: Australia* (London: Haus, 2011), 77–81.
19   'Peace Treaty of Versailles, 28 June, 1919: Articles 1–30 and Annex—The Covenant of the League of Nations', *The World War I Document Archive*, available from: net.lib.byu.edu/~rdh7/wwi/versa/versa1.html.
20   David Lee, 'Sir John Latham and the League of Nations', in *League of Nations: Histories, Legacies and Impact*, eds Joy Damousi and Patricia O'Brien (Melbourne: Melbourne University Press, 2018), 86–91; Bridge, *William Hughes*, 83–6; 'Premier Hughes Denounces Racial Equality Amendment', *The Gazette Times* [Pittsburgh], 28 March 1919, 2; 'Draft, Covenant of the League of Nations, 10 January 1919', cited in N. Shimazu, *Japan, Race and Equality: The Racial Equality Proposal of 1919* (London: Routledge, 1998), 20.

Although Australia made small victories in Paris, the nation's strategic outlook remained uncertain. Japan's postwar position was a strong one and, in the course of the peace negotiations, it had become apparent that Australia could not rely on US support in its search for regional security. Hughes resented Wilson and his idealistic '14 points' on which peace had been negotiated. On his return from Paris, he informed the House of Representatives: 'I have always held that that was an error, of judgement, if you like, for by those fourteen points adopted as the basis of peace, none of those things which Australia had fought for was guaranteed.'[21] This resentment added to Australia's doubts about the League of Nations' capacity to maintain global order.[22] The United States' unreliability as a leader and strategic ally for Australia was further underscored as the nation's foreign policy became increasingly isolationist. Despite Wilson's enthusiastic support for the league, Republican senators opposed membership and blocked the necessary legislation. These men feared league membership would draw the US into international affairs and further conflict—a sentiment captured in prominent Republican Senator William Borah's assessment that 'political pacts foment war, they do not augment peace'.[23] Britain accordingly remained Australia's sole protector and the nation's policymakers viewed the immediate region and the systems for global peace with uncertainty.

## The end of the Anglo-Japanese alliance

Australia's general sense of insecurity was heightened by changes in the arrangements for peace and alliance in the Asia-Pacific region. In 1902, Britain and Japan had signed an alliance in response to Russia's expanding power in the Asia-Pacific region. The Anglo-Japanese Alliance was renewed in 1905 and again in 1911. The future of the alliance first came under question in 1919, as it was due to expire in 1921. With the League of Nations now present to manage international peace, security alliances such as that between Britain and Japan were seen as not only

---

21 *Commonwealth Parliamentary Debates: House of Representatives* [hereinafter *CPD: Representatives*], 10 September 1919, No. 37 (Canberra: AGPS, 1919), 12167–8.
22 David Lee, *Australia and the World in the Twentieth Century: International Relations Since Federation* (Melbourne: Circa, 2006), 38–9.
23 Glenn P. Hastedt, *American Foreign Policy: Past, Present, Future* (Upper Saddle River, NJ: Pearson Education Inc., 2006), 37, 41; *Congressional Record*, 67th Congress, 2nd Session (Washington, DC: The United States Congress, 1923), 4075.

unnecessary, but also incongruent to the spirit of peace.[24] The situation was complicated by the US. As two rising powers bordering on the Pacific Ocean, Japanese–US relations had become increasingly tense in the postwar years. The US government's fear was that, as the Anglo-Japanese Alliance did not explicitly exclude conflict with the US, Japan may take this to mean that aggression towards the nation was viable, implicating Britain and its empire in such a conflict.[25] Alongside mounting Japanese–US tension, both nations' naval expenditure continued to increase.[26] Hughes remarked on this tension and militarisation in an April 1921 statement in the Australian House of Representatives:

> We read almost every day of disturbing rumours of great navies, the world longing for peace resounds with the clanging of hammers, nations fervently building more and more war ships, and there is rivalry openly expressed between those two great nations, the United States of America and Japan.[27]

If not addressed, there was the risk this rivalry would develop into an arms race at sea. From the perspective of the UK government, which was seeking to reduce its defence expenditure, there was concern this arms race would see Japan or, more probably, the US outflank the Royal Navy (RN).[28]

The first postwar Imperial Conference was held in mid-1921, and the future of the Anglo-Japanese Alliance dominated discussion in the months leading up to and during the conference. Australia, represented at the conference by Hughes, was anxious to see the alliance renewed. The alliance not only ensured that, through Britain, Australia and Japan shared an ally, but it also provided diplomatic leverage with which to constrain potential Japanese expansion.[29] Hughes, who was 'obsessed with the future threat of Japan', addressed the strategic consideration of the alliance in a statement at the Imperial Conference:[30]

---

24  Jaroslav Valkoun, 'Great Britain, the Dominions and Their Position On Japan in the 1920s and Early 1930s', *Prague Papers on the History of International Relations* 2 (2017): 32–46, at pp. 32–3.
25  Frederic Eggleston, 'Washington and After: An Australian View', *The Nineteenth Century and After* 92 (1922): 455–65, at pp. 458–9.
26  Darwin, *The Empire Project*, 366–7.
27  *CPD: Representatives*, 7 April 1921, Vol. 94, 7267.
28  Darwin, *The Empire Project*, 367.
29  Bell, *Dependent Ally*, 10.
30  James Cotton, 'William Morris Hughes, Empire and Nationalism: The Legacy of the First World War', *Australian Historical Studies* 46, no. 1 (2016): 100–18, at p. 105.

> Should we not be in a better position to exercise greater influence over the Eastern policy [of Japan] as an Ally of that great Eastern power, than as her potential enemy? Now, if Japan is excluded from the family of great Western nations—and mark, to turn our back on the Treaty is certainly to exclude Japan—she will be isolated, her national pride wounded in its most tender spot.[31]

The Australian government was also mindful of the United States' growing influence, in spite of its isolationist foreign policy, and the importance of fostering friendly relations. Hughes accordingly supported the proposition that had emerged in the lead-up to the conference of a reworded Anglo-Japanese alliance that would 'guard against even the suspicion of hostility or unfriendliness to the United States'.[32] Accommodating the US in the alliance would ensure the rising power remained content and, although not explicitly stated, strengthen the diplomatic leverage the alliance had over a potentially disruptive Japan.

While Australia, the UK and New Zealand supported renewing an amended Anglo-Japanese alliance, Canada and South Africa steadfastly opposed its renewal. With the Imperial Conference set to close with no decision made, US President Warren Harding invited the principal naval powers to Washington to discuss naval disarmament and the future of Far Eastern peace.[33]

## The Washington treaties

The Washington Naval Conference, held between November 1921 and February 1922, was the first US-led international gathering. This signalled an assertion of its influence in the Asia-Pacific region, albeit not backed by a complete regional policy. British public servants acknowledged the shifting distribution of power in the postwar world, evidenced in a memorandum compiled by an officer from the British Consul-General in New York that was circulated among the dominions in preparation for the conference. 'Great Britain must acknowledge,' according to the memorandum, 'the naval superiority of the United States in the Pacific. Australia, New Zealand

---

31 *Imperial Conference of Prime Ministers and Representatives of the United Kingdom, the Dominions and India Held in June, July and August 1921: Summary of Proceedings and Documents* (London: J.J. Keliher & Co. for His Majesty's Stationery Office, 1921), 19.
32 ibid., 19.
33 Valkoun, 'Great Britain, the Dominions and Their Position On Japan in the 1920s and Early 1930s', 37–8.

and Canada must recognise the ground of common interest with the United States and look to this country for protection rather than to Great Britain.' The US was viewed not as a challenger; rather, the nation's rise presented the opportunity for a 'great union of the English-speaking peoples of the world bound … by common language, common institutions and by common customs'.[34] Although this document presents the personal view of a mere consular officer rather than that of the British government, it remains significant as an open acknowledgement that Britain's power in the Far East was indeed abating.

Although the British government had initially supported the renewal of the Anglo-Japanese Alliance, pressure from within the Cabinet gradually forced the conclusion that closer relations with Washington would better serve the national interest than the renewal of the alliance.[35] The Anglo-Japanese Alliance was terminated and the Four-Power Treaty—comprising the British Empire, France, Japan and the US—was its replacement. The signatories agreed to maintain the status quo in the Pacific. If a conflict did emerge, the four nations were not obliged to provide military aid to another and the Four-Power Treaty framework would exist for discussion and, in theory, a resolution.[36]

The second and complementary treaty signed at the Washington conference was the Five-Power Treaty, a naval disarmament agreement between the British Empire, France, Italy, Japan and the US. The treaty stipulated new limits on the tonnage of capital ships, established a 10-year holiday on capital shipbuilding and required that no new naval bases were constructed or existing bases expanded. The new tonnage limitations restricted Britain and the US to 525,000 tonnes, Japan to 315,000 tonnes and Italy and France to 175,000 tonnes.[37]

---

34   'American Policy in the Far East, Memorandum, British Consul-General in New York to Foreign Office, 16 June 1921', in 'Governor-General: Correspondence and printed matter arranged according to subject ("Special Portfolio"), 1888–1936', National Archives of Australia [hereinafter NAA], Canberra: A6661, 1405.
35   Antony Best, 'The "Ghost" of the Anglo-Japanese Alliance: An Examination into Historical Myth-Making', *The Historical Journal* 49, no. 3 (2006): 811–31, at pp. 817–18.
36   'Doc. 15, Treaty between the US, the British Empire, France, and Japan, 13 December 1921', in Joseph V. Fuller (ed.), *Papers Relating to the Foreign Relations of the United States 1922, Volume I* (Washington, DC: US Government Printing Office, 1938).
37   'Doc. 77, Treaty between the US, the British Empire, France, Italy, and Japan, 6 February 1922', in Fuller, *Papers Relating to the Foreign Relations of the United States 1922*. The construction of new British and US bases in Singapore and the Philippines, respectively, was allowed to go ahead as they had already been planned prior to the conference. While this precluded Japan from establishing new naval bases, it also excluded the possibility of fortification in the area immediately to Australia's north.

THE GENESIS OF A POLICY

The treaties signed in Washington effectively resolved the tension between Japan and the US and removed the pressure on the British government to increase its military presence in the Asia-Pacific region.[38] For the US, the Washington System secured an Asia-Pacific order with American interests firmly at the centre. It promoted peace, mollifying isolationist factions in the US government by reducing the likelihood of future international entanglements and, through the new naval ratios, formalised the United States' position as a leading naval power.[39]

The Washington conference had immense implications for Australia's strategic outlook. Hughes acknowledged that the Washington conference had 'achieved great things' and he hoped the treaties signed there would establish a new and peaceful balance of power in the Asia-Pacific. However, he cautioned that the Four-Power Treaty offered only a vaguely worded guarantee of peace as, unlike the Anglo-Japanese Alliance, it was not backed by an obligatory call to arms should any of the members be attacked.[40] Shortly after his election as prime minister in February 1923, Stanley Melbourne Bruce echoed Hughes when he informed the House of Representatives that the Washington conference 'certainly did not solve the problem of the future safety of Australia … one wonders how much was really accomplished by the Washington Conference'.[41]

The British government, too, had its reservations. During the Washington conference, the British ambassador to the US, Auckland Geddes, had privately conceded that he was 'not so optimistic … about the value of the Quadruple Treaty to ensure peace in the Far East'. The 'validity' of the treaty, Geddes continued, rested 'largely on the power to enforce the treaty'.[42] The appraisal by the Committee of Imperial Defence (CID) of the Four-Power Treaty, received by Australia in December 1922, was even more forthright, judging that the long-term 'strategic position in the Western Pacific has been adversely affected'. While it was accepted that war with Japan was unlikely in the coming 10 years, the CID judged that, in the event of such aggression, 'the Four Power Pact … may not save

---

38  In addition to the four and five-power treaties, there were two other treaties dealing with the use of submarines, gas warfare and territorial integrity.
39  Cotton, 'William Morris Hughes, Empire and Nationalism', 106, 112–13; Eggleston, 'Washington and After', 459, 462–5.
40  *CPD: Representatives*, 26 July 1922, No. 99, 789–93.
41  *CPD: Representatives*, 24 July 1923, No. 30, 1484.
42  'Minutes of Meeting, British Empire Delegation to the Washington Conference, 9 December 1921', in Department of External Affairs: Volumes of microfilm printout of the personal papers of Sir George Pearce (compiled by Dr J.S. Cumpston), 1907–37, NAA: A4719, 14.

us from becoming involved in war'.[43] Ultimately, the Four-Power Treaty did not offer the diplomatic or military leverage necessary to exclude the possibility of aggressive expansionism. For Australia—ever suspicious of Japan—the Washington System could offer only temporary security.

The Washington Naval Conference also had implications for imperial power. In accepting the new tonnage restrictions, Britain had, for the first time since the Napoleonic Wars, accepted naval parity rather than mastery. Admittedly, there had been past occasions when the French possessed a larger navy than Britain, but Britain, as the centre of global finance and trade, still possessed the largest naval potential. This was no longer the case, with the US both the largest manufacturing and the largest creditor nation. During a meeting of the British Empire Delegation to the Washington conference, Rear Admiral E. Chatfield, Assistant Chief of the Naval Staff, and Australia's representative, Minister for Defence George Pearce, registered their concern that the new tonnage ratios and 10-year shipbuilding holiday would lead to the decay of specialist skills. Chatfield argued that this would 'leave the Empire with a fleet of unreliable strength destined to deteriorate progressively'.[44] Britain nevertheless accepted naval parity and the shipbuilding holiday. In this willingness to accept a compromised naval position, the British government tacitly acknowledged that it was struggling to afford the upkeep of a first-rate naval power.[45]

From the Australian perspective, the most pressing aspect of the new naval ratios was in relation to Japan. While Britain's upper limit was more than 200,000 tonnes greater than that of Japan, in terms of areas of interest, the ratio was in Japan's favour. Britain's interests spanned three oceans and the nation was required to monitor and defend the people, trade and territories within this vast area. The tonnage restriction established in Washington was only adequate to maintain these ongoing activities. If a new strategic threat developed, Britain, already at is limit, would be unable to respond adequately. Conversely, Japan's interests were limited

---

43 '"The Washington Conference and its Effect Upon Empire Naval Policy and Co-operation", CID Memorandum, December 1922', in Records of the Colonial Office, Commonwealth and Foreign and Commonwealth Offices, Empire Marketing Board, and related bodies, Colonies, General: Original Correspondence, The National Archives [hereinafter TNA], Kew: CO 323/888/29.
44 'Minutes of Meeting, British Empire Delegation Washington Naval Conference, 9 December 1921', NAA: A4719, 14.
45 Kennedy, *The Rise and Fall of the Great Powers*, 197–200, 254; Kennedy, *The Rise and Fall of British Naval Mastery*, 273–5.

THE GENESIS OF A POLICY

to the Pacific Ocean and it could concentrate its resources there.[46] In the event of an emergency in the Far East, Britain would be left to rely on the support of the US, as Frederic Eggleston publicly observed:

> In case of any ... trouble affecting British interests, as it might easily do, the British armaments available for the Pacific are not sufficient for the burdens that might be cast upon them; and unless the United States of America can be relied upon to pull her weight in the same direction as Britain the whole system [of Pacific security] might break down. Australia ... can only watch the play of forces upon which her fate depends.[47]

The end of the Anglo-Japanese Alliance and the Washington System that replaced it highlighted the evolving global distribution of power and, in the case of Australia, differing strategic outlooks as Britain appeared to prioritise relations with the US above the protection of its Far Eastern interests.[48]

## The Singapore Strategy

With two rising powers in the Pacific, it was essential Britain reinforced its regional presence. The proposed solution was the Singapore Naval Strategy, which planned for the construction of a major naval base in Singapore where a RN fleet would be stationed. The origins of the Singapore Strategy can be found in Australian actions during World War I. During that war, the Royal Australian Navy (RAN) and Prime Minister's Department paid close attention to Japan's naval movements and collated intelligence concerning the nation's intentions in the region.[49] In September 1917, Australia's Minister for the Navy, Joseph Cook, requested the British Admiralty reassess the maritime defence needs of Australia and the Asia-Pacific, suggesting a major imperial naval base was

---

46   Eric M. Andrews, *The Writing On the Wall: The British Commonwealth and Aggression in the East, 1931–1935* (Sydney: Allen & Unwin, 1987), 31–2.
47   Eggleston, 'Washington and After', 465.
48   Pearce, with full knowledge of the discussions of the British Empire delegation in Washington, implied as much in his report to Hughes. 'Pearce to Hughes, NAA: A221 ExRel V22, 334 ff.', cited in Cotton, 'William Morris Hughes, Empire and Nationalism', 113.
49   Meaney, *A History of Australian Defence and Foreign Policy 1901–23*, vol. 2, 407–9; 'Navies Japanese—Miscellaneous Telegrams AWM36 1914–1915', in Department of Defence: Official History, 1914–18 War—Naval records of Arthur W. Jose, 1912–30, NAA: AWM36, Bundle 32/1; 'The Importance to Australia of German New Guinea and the Islands (lately German) North of the Equator, 11 July 1918', in Department of External Affairs: Correspondence files, alphabetical series, 1927–42, NAA: A981 Mars 5.

required either in Australia or in another nearby British territory. Plans were made to send an Admiralty officer to Australia to investigate once the war had ended. In December 1918, the Australian government was informed that the Admiral of the Fleet, Lord John Jellicoe, would visit to review the situation.[50]

Cook's original request for the Admiralty review had been justified on the vague basis of 'the experience of the war'.[51] A cable sent in May 1919 to Jellicoe from Acting Prime Minister William Watt suggests these experiences were specifically Japan's naval advancements and new territorial acquisitions in the Pacific. Watt's cable outlined Australia's concerns and the questions he hoped would be addressed during the Admiralty review. Watt requested Jellicoe provide an assessment of the 'naval strategical problems affecting Australian waters and the Pacific'. This included probable routes of attack on Australia, 'with special reference to occupation by a foreign power of Islands north of the Equator' and Britain's strategy in the event of war with any of the Pacific powers.[52]

Jellicoe presented his report to the British government in February 1920 and it mirrored many of Australia's concerns. Jellicoe identified the Pacific as the most likely area for future conflict and judged Australia to be 'powerless against a strong naval and military power without the assistance of the British fleet'.[53] He advised that a Far Eastern fleet and major naval base be established in the Asia-Pacific in the next five years, with Singapore the recommended location. This strategy was expected to protect the lines of communication in the Pacific and Indian oceans and allow two zones of conflict to be operational, Europe and the Asia-Pacific.[54] This was the Singapore Strategy—the 'impregnable' cornerstone in imperial defence planning in the Asia-Pacific.[55]

---

50  'Attachment, Admiralty letter, 23 December 1918' and 'Naval Bases, n.d. on or after 3 January 1919', both in NAA: A981, Def 350 Part 1.
51  'Naval Bases, [n.d. (on or after 3 January 1919)]', NAA: A981, Def 350 Part 1.
52  'Watt to Jellicoe, 2 May 1919', NAA: A981, Def 350 Part 1.
53  'Jellicoe Report—1919', in Department of Defence: 'The Shedden Collection' [Records collected by Sir Frederick Shedden during his career with the Department of Defence and in researching the history of Australian defence policy], two number series, 1937–71, NAA: A5954, 1080/1.
54  'Admiral of the Fleet Viscount Jellicoe's Naval Mission to Colonies, 3 February 1920', in Records of the Admiralty, Naval Forces, Royal Marines, Coastguard, and related bodies, Admiralty: Record Office: Cases, TNA: ADM 116/1831.
55  'Penang Naval Conference—March 1921, 11 April 1921', in Department of Defence: Naval historical files, single number series with alphabetical suffixes, NAA: B6121, 311J; 'Report of the Conference held on board the HMS *Hawkins* at Penang, between the Commanders-in-Chief of the China, East Indies and Australian Stations, from 7 March 1921 onwards, 13 March 1921', NAA: B6121, 311J.

THE GENESIS OF A POLICY

In March 1921, a meeting of the commanders-in-chief of the Australian, Chinese and East Asian stations was held in Penang, British Malaya. The Admiralty requested they make recommendations for Far Eastern defence planning on the basis of a war between Japan and the British Empire. Although the Singapore Strategy was yet to be formally ratified, the recommendations that emerged at Penang were made on the basis of the strategy being the cornerstone of imperial defence planning in the Asia-Pacific. Recommendations included establishing Singapore as the centre of an imperial communications system in the region.[56]

The state of Britain's economy and the public demand for financing social services rather than defence industries meant these recommendations and even Jellicoe's original plan went beyond what could reasonably be afforded. Instead, when the Singapore Strategy was finally approved in June 1921, it was decided that a base would be constructed but only fully garrisoned when required and the recommended five-year construction timeline was pushed back to eight years.[57]

The early deviations from Jellicoe's initial recommendations heralded years of uncertainty and interruptions in the Singapore project. Work did not begin in Singapore until late 1923. This delay was due to a succession of political U-turns. First, there were the new naval disarmament agreements made at the Washington conference, which raised questions about whether the construction of a major naval base was conducive to peace and disarmament. It was not until February 1923, following the election of a conservative government the previous October, that Britain confirmed the Singapore Strategy would continue.[58] The election of Britain's first Labour government in December 1923 posed yet another obstacle. The new government was committed to international disarmament and opposed the Singapore idea, which Prime Minister

---

56   Meaney, *A History of Australian Defence and Foreign Policy 1901–23*, vol. 2, 470–1; 'Penang Conference Report, 13 March 1921', NAA: B6121, 311J. Initial estimates planned for a fleet of eight battleships and eight battlecruisers, four aircraft carriers, 10 cruisers, 40 destroyers and 36 submarines. 'Jellicoe's Naval Mission to Colonies, 3 February 1920', TNA: ADM 116/1834.
57   Malcolm Murfett, 'The Singapore Strategy', in *Between Empire and Nation: Australia's External Relations from Federation Until the Second World War*, eds Carl Bridge and Bernard Attard (Melbourne: Australian Scholarly Publishing, 2000), 188–204; 'Cabinet Minute, 16 June 1921', in Records of the Cabinet Office, War Cabinet and Cabinet: Minutes, TNA: CAB 23/26/5.
58   Ian Hamill, *The Strategic Illusion: The Singapore Strategy and the Defence of Australia and New Zealand, 1919–1942* (Singapore: NUS Press, 1981), 47–50; 'Cabinet Minute, 21 February 1923', TNA: CAB 23/45.

Ramsay MacDonald deemed a 'wild and wanton escapade'.[59] In March 1924, MacDonald ordered the cancellation of the Singapore project; the staff there were withdrawn and orders were given to sell all equipment present.[60] Later that same year, the Conservative Party was returned to power and the Singapore project was reinstated.[61]

The result of the delays and indecision surrounding the Singapore Strategy was that the initial eight-year timetable for construction passed in 1929 with the project far from complete. All there was to show was one floating dock and a number of other incomplete structures.[62]

The indecision surrounding the Singapore Strategy led key figures in Australian defence and political circles to question its feasibility and appropriateness. One of the earliest warnings came in 1921 from Rear Admiral Percy Grant, Commander-in-Chief of the Australian Naval Station and advisor on defence to the prime minister. He drew attention to the strategic weakness of Singapore, particularly the long lines of communication that would connect the base with Australia and Britain.[63] Grant's concern led Prime Ministers Hughes and Bruce to question the British government on the logistics of the Singapore Strategy. Both were mindful of the delays in initial construction in the years 1921–23. They each received the same bland reassurances that Singapore would be finished and the fleet would arrive.[64] This led Bruce, somewhat unconvinced, to remark: 'I am not quite clear as to how the protection of Singapore is to be assured, I am quite clear on this point, that apparently it can be done.'[65] That key figures in Australian policy and defence circles held some reservations about the Singapore Strategy—albeit small ones—adds credence to the view that the nation was not convinced by the system for Asia-Pacific security offered in the Washington System.

---

59   'Singapore Naval Base. HC Deb 05 March 1924 vol 170 c1360', in United Kingdom, *Parliamentary Debates: House of Commons*, available from: api.parliament.uk/historic-hansard/commons/1924/mar/05/singapore-naval-base.
60   'Sitting of 18 March 1924', in United Kingdom, *Parliamentary Debates: House of Commons*, available from: api.parliament.uk/historic-hansard/sittings/1924/mar/18.
61   Hamill, *The Strategic Illusion*, 86–7, 99.
62   Andrews, *The Writing on the Wall*, 33–4.
63   'Penang Conference Report, 13 March 1921', NAA: B6121, 311J.
64   'Minutes Fourteenth Meeting of the Imperial Conference, 4 July 1921', in Records of the Cabinet Office, Records of Imperial, Commonwealth and International Conferences, etc., TNA: CAB 32/2 Vol. 1A; 'Minutes Ninth Meeting of the Imperial Conference, 17 October 1923', TNA: CAB 32/9.
65   'Minutes Eleventh Meeting of the Imperial Conference, 22 October 1923', TNA: CAB 32/9.

Australia's questions surrounding the Singapore Strategy were never truly resolved. Despite this, Singapore remained the cornerstone of Australian regional security. This may suggest Australia was wilfully naive in relying wholly on Britain.[66] Here, however, it is important to recall Australia's acute sense of insecurity, the fact Britain remained the nation's sole security partner and that Singapore was the only available assurance against regional aggression.[67] While Australia had little choice beyond accepting the Singapore Strategy as the cornerstone of regional defence, this does not mean it necessarily accepted the strategy uncritically or failed to pursue its own defence initiatives.

## The imperial framework redefined

After the Federation of Australia in 1901 and the establishment of a government that was responsible for forming national policies, defence and foreign policies were made in relation to the British Empire and the sentimental loyalties, values and interests that bound its members.[68] The main opportunities for consultation concerning defence and foreign policy were the regular Imperial Conferences and through the offices of the prime minister, governor-general, high commissioners and Secretary of State for Dominion Affairs. Within this system, the status of British dominions, such as Australia, was an awkward one. They were self-governing nations, yet loyal to the Crown and subject to the sovereignty of British rule.[69] This was the case until 1925, at which point a process of restructuring the imperial framework began.

While the markets and human resources offered in the Empire were a great strength to Britain, there was also the immense cost of defending, financing and administering a cumbersome empire that sprawled across

---

66 Peter Dennis, 'Australia and the "Singapore Strategy"', in *Sixty Years On: The Fall of Singapore*, eds B. Farrell and S. Hunter (Singapore: Eastern Universities Press, 2002), 29–41; Murfett, 'The Singapore Strategy', 188–9.

67 Richard Devetak, 'An Australian Outlook on International Affairs? The Evolution of International Relations Theory in Australia', *Australian Journal of Politics and History* 55, no. 3 (2009): 335–59, at p. 337.

68 For an overview of the shared values of the Commonwealth, see Eggleston, *Reflections on Australian Foreign Policy*, 173–206.

69 Meaney, *A History of Australian Defence and Foreign Policy 1901–23*, vol. 1, 3–5; Peter Geoffrey Edwards, *Prime Ministers and Diplomats: The Making of Australian Foreign Policy, 1901–1949* (Melbourne: Oxford University Press for the Australian Institute of International Affairs, 1983), 1–2.

the globe.⁷⁰ The fragmentation that existed at the administrative level of the Empire called attention to Britain's experience of overstretch. In the 1920s, members of the Empire did not have representatives—diplomatic, trade or otherwise—outside London. With no formal means of liaising with one another, foreign policy and defence directives were passed down by Britain and, at best, discussed at Imperial Conferences or, at worst, slowly filtered throughout the Empire's chain of communication.

This system produced an imperial administration that Eric Andrews described as

> not like an organism with a brain and inter-connected nerves, which could therefore come to a decision, and act on it, but more like a brain dead octopus, with its tentacles acting independently of each other, and no vital connections being made at the centre.⁷¹

Most critically for Australia, from the perspective of a remote outpost of the Empire, this system was not particularly conducive to consultative policymaking.

The 1922 Chanak Crisis was indicative of the administrative disorganisation of the British Empire, the diverse interests of its members and the need for a more decentralised system. In September 1922, Turkish troops attacked and defeated Greek forces in a bid to restore Turkish rule in the Dardanelles' neutral zone. In so doing, Turkey violated the Treaty of Sèvres. The British government's response was almost immediate, declaring the Empire would enter into an armed conflict if need be to support Greece. Britain had failed to consult with its empire; in Australia's case, the government learnt of the empire commitment by way of a press release.⁷² This action was a regression from the Paris peace negotiations just three years earlier, when the dominions had been individually represented and directly involved in decision-making.⁷³

---

70  Darwin, *The Empire Project*, 323–6, 360–1, 375.
71  Andrews, *The Writing on the Wall*, 25. John Darwin has similarly compared the British Empire with an 'Octopus Power'. Darwin, *The Empire Project*, 83–6.
72  'Forster (Secretary of Prime Minister's Department) to Churchill (Secretary of State for the Colonies), 20 September 1922', in Governor-General: Decoded copies of telegrams exchanged between the Governor-General and the Secretary of State in connection with the 'Chanak Incident' with Turkey, 1922–24, NAA: CP78/32, 1.
73  Meaney, *A History of Australian Defence and Foreign Policy 1901–23*, vol. 2, 508–9.

Despite a public statement that Australia would commit troops if necessary, Hughes observed the slight and he was incensed. He contacted British Prime Minister Lloyd George, expressing his concerns that the decision—which he described as 'a bolt from the blue'—'gravely imperils the unity of the Empire'. He went on to argue that

> the Dominions ought to be consulted before any action is taken or irrevocable decision made by Britain, then and then only can our voices be heard and our counsels heeded. The Empire is one and indivisible or it is nothing.[74]

Other members of the Empire joined Australia, both publicly and privately, in rejecting the prospect of being dragged by Britain into a conflict involving neither their own region nor their national interests.[75]

The Chanak Crisis forced the British government to acknowledge that the status of dominions needed to be clarified. In 1925, the Dominions Office was established, along with the Cabinet-level portfolio of Secretary of State for Dominion Affairs. Later the same year, the British government signed the Locarno Treaties, which dealt with the postwar management of borders in Western Europe. Not only were the treaties signed by Britain alone, but also Article 9 stipulated the treaty 'shall impose no obligation upon any of the British Dominions, or upon India unless the government of such Dominion or India signifies its acceptance thereof'.[76] While these developments did not expressly define the status of dominions, they did make a clear distinction between the colonies and the dominions and their differing relationships to British sovereignty.[77]

The formal status of dominions was defined at the 1926 Imperial Conference, which was called in part to discuss the implications of the Locarno Treaties and the dominions' great diversity of interests.

---

74 'Forster to Churchill, 20 September 1922', NAA: CP78/32, 1.
75 R. Eccles, 'Australian Perspectives and the Balfour Declaration of 1926', in *Dependency? Essays in the History of Australian Defence and Foreign Policy*, ed. John McCarthy (Canberra: University College, University of New South Wales, Australian Defence Force Academy, 1989), 23. Among the most vocal opponents were Canada and South Africa.
76 'Treaty of Mutual Guarantee between Germany, Belgium, France, Great Britain and Italy, 16 October 1925 (Locarno Treaty)', in Arthur B. Keith (ed.), *Speeches and Documents on International Affairs, 1918–1937. Volume 1* (London: Oxford University Press, 1938), 116.
77 Andrews, *The Writing on the Wall*, 5; Eccles, 'Australian Perspectives and the Balfour Declaration of 1926', 25–6.

The Inter-Imperial Relations Committee was formed to consider the future form and substance of imperial relations within this context. The result was a declaration by Arthur Balfour, chairman of the committee:

> They [the dominions] are autonomous communities within the British Empire, equal in status, in no way subordinate one to another in any aspect of their domestic or external affairs, though united by a common allegiance to the Crown, and freely associated as members of the British Commonwealth of Nations.[78]

The wording of the 1926 Balfour Declaration had been carefully deliberated, as historian John Darwin has noted, with care given not to equate self-governance and equality of status with independence and a lapsing of empire membership. The effect of the prudent declaration was, first, to recognise and embrace the varied interests of the dominions. Second, the declaration redefined the imperial connection by appealing to the sentimental terms of shared 'positive ideals', including 'peace, security and progress'.[79]

The final step in the decentralisation of the imperial relationship came at the 1930 Imperial Conference, when it was decided that legislative independence should be extended to the dominions. This brought to an end the ability of the British Parliament to legislate for the dominions, granting full independence in areas such as foreign policymaking. The 1931 Statute of Westminster ratified this resolution and the 1926 Balfour Declaration.[80]

Far from dispelling Australia's fears of imperial disunity, the developments in 1925–31 generated greater anxiety. In light of Hughes's indignant response to the Chanak Crisis, Australia's reaction may at first appear counterintuitive. The concern of Hughes and other likeminded individuals was not with a definition of dominion status and freedoms, but an acknowledgement of the varied interests of the Empire and

---

78 'Summary of Proceedings 1926 Imperial Conference, 23 March 1927', in Department of External Affairs: Correspondence files, annual single number series [Main correspondence files series of the agency], 1890–1968, NAA: A1, 1927/14972.
79 Darwin, *The Empire Project*, 406–7; '1926 Imperial Conference, 23 March 1927', NAA: A1, 1927/14972.
80 'An Act to give effect to certain resolutions passed by Imperial Conferences held in the years 1926 and 1930, 11 December 1931', in Nicholas Mansergh (ed.), *Documents and Speeches on British Commonwealth Affairs, 1931–52* (London: Oxford University Press, 1953), 1–3.

a framework for integrating these interests into a unified imperial foreign policy.[81] Hughes voiced these concerns in a lengthy review of the 1926 Balfour Declaration delivered in the House of Representatives:

> I wish to point out that every important act by one dominion may affect other dominions ... We claim the right of an equal voice with Great Britain in moulding British foreign policy ... Britain's foreign policy conditions our very existence, and we should insist upon our right to have an effective voice in shaping it. Without some control over foreign policy, self-government is a farce, and we are living in a house built upon quicksands ... [A]s long as peace lasts all will be well; but if, and when, war comes along, we shall be blown to the heavens as by a charge of gelignite. Unless we are able to influence the foreign policy of the Empire our boast of freedom is nothing but empty words. No dominion parliament can be said to be master of its own domestic circumstances, unless it exercises the right to assist in moulding the foreign policy of the Empire. That applies no less forcibly to the right of all dominions to be consulted by other dominions before treaties with foreign countries are ratified.[82]

These concerns explain in part the Australian government's delayed adoption of the Statute of Westminster (in 1942).

Australia's diametric opposition to the 1926 Balfour Declaration and Statute of Westminster can understandably be viewed as reluctance to take steps towards greater autonomy in foreign policy. While the Australian government did rely on the imperial framework, the main concern was consultation—that is, full knowledge of and a voice in imperial affairs. On the basis of this assessment, Australia was not necessarily shying away from responsibility. Rather, it hoped to participate in a cohesive imperial foreign policy that gave equal attention to all the regions and the distinct interests encompassed by the Empire.

## The Manchurian Crisis

Despite the persistent concern surrounding Japanese intentions, Australia made little effort to engage with the nation or the wider Asia-Pacific. Richard Casey, for instance, wrote of a remote Asia-Pacific with which

---

81  Eccles, 'Australian Perspectives and the Balfour Declaration of 1926', 30–1.
82  *CPD: Representatives*, 22 March 1927, No. 12, 864.

Australia had little need to engage.[83] In 1925, when the newly appointed Japanese Consul-General in Sydney, Prince Iemasa Tokugawa, arrived in Australia, he brought with him an invitation from Japan's Prime Minister for Australia to make a reciprocal appointment. This appointment was part of Foreign Minister Kijūrō Shidehara's campaign to heighten Japan's international representation for economic and diplomatic purposes. Australia, however, made no such appointment.[84] Events in 1931 brought into sharp focus that Australia could no longer continue with its wilful isolation.

In September 1931, as the Statute of Westminster was being debated in the British Parliament, the Japanese Army attacked and proceeded to occupy the Chinese province of Manchuria, contravening the Covenant of the League of Nations and the Nine-Power Treaty—one of the treaties signed at the 1921–22 Washington Naval Conference, which required members to respect the territorial integrity of China and aid the nation in developing and maintaining effective government.[85] For Australia, the Manchurian Crisis confirmed fears that had fermented in the previous decade: neither the league nor the Washington System could adequately maintain peace in the Asia-Pacific. This realisation was the genesis of a distinct Australian policy for the Asia-Pacific. This policy was twofold, aiming to increase Australia's regional presence and to develop a more assertive voice within the Empire with a view to incorporating regionally specific interests within the imperial outlook. The next chapter considers how this approach developed.

---

83  Richard Casey, *Australia's Place in the World* (Melbourne: Robertson & Mullens, 1931), 9–15, 18, 62.
84  Shimizu Hajime, 'Japanese Economic Penetration into Southeast Asia and the Southward Expansion School of Thought', in *International Commercial Rivalry in Southeast Asia in the Interwar Period*, eds Shinya Sugiyama and Milagros C. Guerrero (Newhaven, CT: Yale University Southeast Asia Studies, 1994), 19–22; 'To Win Esteem', *The Sun*, [Sydney], 26 November 1925, 12.
85  Andrews, *The Writing on the Wall*, 35–7.

# 2

# Increasing assertiveness in foreign and economic affairs, 1931–35

> We have adopted European phrases and the ideas that correspond to them. From our childhood we have been accustomed to read, think, and speak of the 'Far East'. It is the Far East to Europe, to the old centres of civilisation, but we must realise that it is the 'Near East' to Australia.[1]
>
> — Australian Minister for External Affairs John Latham

With crisis in the Asia-Pacific region and neither Britain nor the US providing adequate security assurances, the Australian government was keenly aware of the need to reorient itself towards its immediate region. It did so with a careful interrogation of the relationships and policy approaches that would facilitate this process. Against the backdrop of the Great Depression and the limited opportunities offered in the British and US markets, trade played a key role in the genesis of a distinct Australian policy.

As Australia looked to the Asia-Pacific to meet its needs for more diverse markets, Japan emerged as the most promising opportunity. In the wake of the Manchurian Crisis, Australia's trade interests intersected with the nation's diplomatic and security ones. This undoubtedly shaped

---

1   'Speech by Latham on the Australian Eastern Mission, 6 July 1934', NAA: A981, Far 5 Part 16.

THE GENESIS OF A POLICY

Australia's response to the Manchurian Crisis and its attempts to convince Britain of the economic and diplomatic importance of cordial relations with Japan.

## The Great Depression and Australia's foreign debt

The Great Depression saw a worldwide contraction of economic output following the US stock market crash in October 1929. Australia's Great Depression experience was consistent with that internationally, with rapidly reduced export volumes, high inflation and unemployment.[2] The nation's particular challenge during the depression years was foreign debt.

Following World War I, Australia became a 'voracious borrower', relying on overseas loans to cover the costs of repatriating servicemen, interest on its war loans and postwar public building projects.[3] The majority of the Australian government's loans were issued by the City of London. In the years 1923–29, Australia was responsible for more than one-quarter of London's total oversees issues.[4] When the depression hit, Britain and the US ceased lending and called in existing loans, leaving Australia to fund its debt on export income alone. The combined forces of decreased global demand and a sharp drop in the price of Australia's principal exports led to the reduced volume and value of exports.[5] While the Australian Labor Party (ALP) government of James Scullin drastically reduced imports through increased customs duties, these measures proved woefully inadequate to cover overseas debt repayments.[6] By early 1931,

---

2    Unemployment in Australia reached its peak at 30 per cent in 1932. *Official Year Book of the Commonwealth of Australia*, No. 30 (Canberra: Commonwealth Government Printer, 1937), 589.
3    Boris Schedvin, *Australia and the Great Depression: A Study of Economic Development and Policy in the 1920s and 1930s* (Sydney: Sydney University Press, 1970), 96; Bernard Attard, 'Financial Diplomacy', in *Between Empire and Nation: Australia's External Relations from Federation Until the Second World War*, eds Carl Bridge and Bernard Attard (Melbourne: Australian Scholarly Publishing, 2000), 93–4, 96–100.
4    Attard, 'Financial Diplomacy', 100.
5    Schedvin, *Australia and the Great Depression*, 28–9, 110–14.
6    Tim Rooth, 'Ottawa and After', in *Between Empire and Nation: Australia's External Relations from Federation Until the Second World War*, eds Carl Bridge and Bernard Attard (Melbourne: Australian Scholarly Publishing, 2000), 110–11; Attard, 'Financial Diplomacy', 100–2.

with export stagnation, a near exhaustion of the country's reserves and an exchange rate already under pressure, Australia looked set to default on loan repayments to London.[7]

Australia was able to avoid default by departing from the gold standard and devaluing against the sterling in June 1931, which allowed the nation to export gold reserves to service overseas debt. The nation's position was also helped by a temporary postponement on war debt repayments owed to Britain and the US. The British government departed from the gold standard the following September and the Commonwealth Bank of Australia, Australia's central bank, set a fixed exchange rate according to the pound sterling (A£1.25 to £1 sterling).[8] The departure from the gold standard and the 1932 Ottawa Agreements, which is detailed below, formalised a pre-existing arrangement predicated on the preferential treatment of British capital, migration and trade within the Empire. This was known as the Sterling Area. Members of the Sterling Area pegged their exchange rates to the pound sterling, conducted trade in sterling and stored their currency reserves in London. The Sterling Area codified a structural reliance on Britain and its economic performance, as a contraction in the British economy and devaluation would, in turn, devalue the currency of all the Sterling Area members. In this way, a strong British economy and currency became a shared interest within the Sterling Area.[9]

---

[7] The New South Wales Premier, the ALP's Jack Lang, did default on interest repayments in 1931. This was part of Lang's policy response to the Great Depression, in which he called on the British government to temporarily suspend interest payments to British bondholders and reduce the interest rate on Australian government debt repayments. Lang argued that these measures would allow domestic expenditure to be prioritised. The federal government was forced to cover New South Wales's repayments. In January 1932, when Lang announced that he would again default on interest repayments in London, the newly elected United Australia Party passed the *Financial Agreement Enforcement Act*, which gave the federal government new powers to take control of state revenue. Lang withdrew more than £1 million in state revenue and instructed public servants not to pay state revenue into the federal Treasury, so as to deprive the federal government of New South Wales's revenue. The New South Wales Governor-General found Lang's actions illegal, and he was subsequently dismissed. The Lang case is significant not only in terms of state–federal government relations, but also in highlighting the Australian government's support for imperial fiscal policy. David Meredith and Barrie Dyster, *Australia in the Global Economy: Continuity and Change* (Melbourne: Cambridge University Press, 1999), 132–4.
[8] Schedvin, *Australia and the Great Depression*, 238–9; Attard, 'Financial Diplomacy', 101–3.
[9] Drummond, *The Floating Pound and the Sterling Area*, 3–7, 10, 258–61.

## Opportunities in the imperial and US markets

Australia's ability to continue servicing its overseas debt repayments and recovery from the depression relied on increased export margins. Britain was by far the most important market for Australian goods. In the first two years of the Great Depression, as the rest of the world adopted protectionist measures, Britain remained committed to free trade. As the economic crisis continued, however, key British industries began to struggle. For instance, from 1929 to 1932, coal and steel production fell by 20 per cent and 45 per cent, respectively.[10] As the British government faced increasing unemployment and a growing trade imbalance, it became clear that free trade was an unsustainable approach.[11]

The 1932 Imperial Economic Conference, held in Ottawa, Canada, was convened in response to the economic challenges presented by the Great Depression. The proposed solution was greater intra-empire trade through a system of reciprocal preferential tariffs, ratified in the Ottawa Agreements. Under the Ottawa Agreements, Britain abandoned three-quarters of a century of free-trade policy with the introduction of high import tariffs for foreign goods. The dominions received free entry into the British market and a margin of preference compared with similar foreign producers on certain exports. In return, the dominions extended preferential margins to British goods and granted domestic competitor status to British manufacturers, meaning tariffs would be reduced 'to give United Kingdom producers full opportunity of reasonable competition' with domestic producers.[12] The Ottawa Agreements were, as a young James Plimsoll, future secretary of the DEA, argued, an 'economic alliance by the Empire against the rest of the world'.[13]

---

10    Kennedy, *The Rise and Fall of British Naval Mastery*, 317.
11    Francine McKenzie, 'Imperial Solutions to International Crises: Alliances, Trade and the Ottawa Imperial Economic Conference of 1932', in *The Foreign Office, Commerce and British Foreign Policy 1900–2000*, eds John Fisher, Effie G.H. Pedaliu and Richard Smith (London: Palgrave Macmillan, 2016), 167, 171, 173–4.
12    Ian M. Drummond, *Imperial Economic Policy, 1917–1939: Studies in Expansion and Protection* (London: Allen & Unwin, 1974), 31; 'Report on the Imperial Economic Conference, Ottawa, 1932', in Department of Trade and Customs: International trade relations files, multiple number series [Main correspondence files series of the agency], 1925–56, NAA: A1667, 430/B/18.
13    James Plimsoll, 'Australia and Ottawa', *The Australian Quarterly* 13, no. 4 (1941): 14–21, at pp. 14–16.

The Ottawa Agreements offered a solution to the immediate challenges of the Great Depression; however, they were only a partial solution—one that Francine McKenzie describes as a 'defensive response to long-term decline'.[14] In relying on protectionist measures and the imperial markets, the Ottawa Agreements simply masked Britain's decline, rather than addressing the structural weakness in the nation's economy. Moreover, imperial preference restricted Britain's market access, irritating other nations and complicating trade relationships.[15] While imperial preference did aid Britain in its recovery from the Great Depression, it also marked the nation's waning economic capacity and three decades of reliance on the Sterling Area and imperial markets to mask this decline.

The Australian government recognised both the benefits and the limitations of the Ottawa Agreements and economic dependence on Britain. The concessions won by Australia in the negotiation of the Ottawa Agreements included free entry within the Sterling Area for a great number of Australian exports and increased import tariffs on foreign competitor beef and dairy. When Prime Minister Joseph Lyons first discussed the agreements in the House of Representatives, he predicted not only increased exports to Britain, but also the building of 'the strongest economic unit that history has ever known'.[16]

The imperial preference did promote intra-empire sales, contributing to an overall increase in the volume of Australian exports to Britain, rising from 49.79 per cent in the 1931–32 financial year to 52.23 per cent in 1934–35. However, this growth was inconsistent and relatively conservative. Moreover, the Ottawa Agreements restricted any future trade agreements with non-empire nations, stipulating that they could not interfere with the imperial preference.[17] This constrained Australia's opportunities in foreign markets, as the nation was left with little scope to offer other countries greater access to its market. Minister for Commerce F.H. Stewart was sceptical of the limited opportunities offered in the Ottawa Agreements. He argued that the depression and the need for protectionism had revealed that 'the Empire markets are not limitless in

---

14   McKenzie, 'Imperial Solutions to International Crises', 167.
15   Drummond, *Imperial Economic Policy, 1917–1939*, 280–4.
16   *CPD: Representatives*, 31 August 1932, No. 35, 26, 29.
17   'Report on Imperial Economic Conference, 1932', NAA: 1667, 430/B/18.

their capacity' and dependence on them was unsustainable. Accordingly, Stewart believed 'foreign trade must be fostered and increased if we are to regain our former standard of living'.[18]

**Table 2.1 Australian exports to Britain as a percentage of total exports, 1931–32 to 1938–39**

| Fiscal year | Percentage |
| --- | --- |
| 1931–32 | 49.79 |
| 1932–33 | 47.66 |
| 1933–34 | 47.78 |
| 1934–35 | 52.23 |
| 1935–36 | 49.54 |
| 1936–37 | 49.50 |
| 1937–38 | 55.52 |
| 1938–39 | 54.52 |

Sources: *Official Year Book of the Commonwealth of Australia*, No. 26 (Canberra: Commonwealth Government Printer, 1933), 238; *Official Year Book of the Commonwealth of Australia*, No. 28 (Canberra: Commonwealth Government Printer, 1935), 258; *Official Year Book of the Commonwealth of Australia*, No. 33 (Canberra: Commonwealth Government Printer, 1940), 775.

The US was also a significant market for Australian purchases. Where the imperial markets offered opportunities for growth, limited as they were, opportunities in the US were stagnant. Australian–US trade relations date back to the late eighteenth century when the Pacific Ocean was a prominent area for fishing and US merchant ships made port at the newly founded colonies in Australia. Historically, Australia bought far more from the US than it sold in return, the key reason being the two nations' similar exports. Both Australia and the US were primary industry exporters, with raw materials from the mining and agricultural sectors dominating overseas sales. Unlike Australia, the US also had an established secondary industry. Unable to produce its own manufactured goods, Australia developed an immense trade imbalance with the US, at a ratio of approximately 6:1.[19]

---

18   F.H. Stewart, 'Australian Commercial Representation Abroad', in *Australian Foreign Policy, 1934*, eds H. Dinning and J. Holms (Melbourne: Melbourne University Press for Australian Institute of International Affairs, 1935), 11.
19   Raymold A. Esthus, *From Enmity to Alliance: US–Australian Relations, 1931–1941* (Melbourne: Melbourne University Press, 1964), 6–8, 13; *Official Year Book of the Commonwealth of Australia*, No. 26 (1933), 235–9.

The Great Depression exacerbated Australian–US trade tensions. In June 1930, the *Smoot–Hawley Tariff Act* was signed into law in the US. The Smoot–Hawley Tariff was designed to combat the falling value of US imports and protect against foreign competition. The Act raised import duties on more than 20,000 goods, with an average increase of 40 per cent. The agricultural sector was granted particularly high tariffs in response to the sharp decline globally in the price of agricultural goods. The US tariff on Australian wool—the nation's principal export—increased from an already high 31 cents per pound to 34 cents per pound.[20] Combined with Australia's existing trade imbalance with the US, the new tariff rates sparked acrimony within Australian political and commercial circles. The *Daily Commercial News and Shipping List*, for instance, argued that the new higher tariffs would make the balancing of Australian trade with the US an impossibility. The paper pondered whether 'Hawley and Smoot, the two gentlemen responsible for the new Tariff … are altogether devoid of any sense of proportion'.[21] The Australian Association of British Manufacturers was particularly vociferous in its criticism of the Smoot–Hawley Tariff and Australia's longstanding trade deficit with the US, proposing a boycott against the nation.[22]

The protectionist measures of the Smoot–Hawley Tariff and the Ottawa Agreements contributed to a reduced volume of two-way trade between Australia and the US. However, as Australia still relied on the US for manufactured goods, the adverse ratio of 6:1 remained relatively consistent throughout the depression.

Faced with the embarrassment of an ongoing trade imbalance, the Australian government sought to better position its trade in the US market. In June 1934, with the worst of the depression having passed, Lyons presented a draft trade treaty to the US Consul-General in Australia. The treaty tabled lower overall tariff rates and fixed quotas on Australian

---

20 Esthus, *From Enmity to Alliance*, 6–8, 13; Richard N. Cooper, 'Fettered to Gold? Economic Policy in the Interwar Period', *Journal of Economic Literature* 30, no. 4 (1992): 2120–8, at pp. 2122–5.
21 'Australian Imports and American Tariffs', *Daily Commercial News and Shipping List*, [Sydney], 16 July 1929, 4.
22 Australian Association of British Manufacturers, *One-Way Traffic: Australia's Trade with the United States* (Melbourne: Australian Association of British Manufacturers, 1931), cited in Harper, *Australia and the United States*, 124.

meat, butter and wool.²³ Lyons' request was subsequently rejected. In the cable detailing this rejection, US Secretary of State Cordell Hull explained that the US was adopting a new framework for world trade premised on 'lessening generally the obstacles to trade' rather than restrictive trade treaties. The *Reciprocal Tariff Act*, passed in June 1934, was the first significant step towards US tariff reform. The Act gave the US President the power to negotiate bilaterally with foreign powers to reduce tariff duties on a reciprocal basis by up to 50 per cent without reference to Congress. Hull admitted that Australia would benefit little in the early stages of the trade liberalisation program, although he was optimistic that, as the program progressed, 'certain Australian products … will be placed in a more favourable position'.²⁴ In truth, the competing export industries of the two nations meant that, at least until Australia diversified its exports, it would be unlikely to receive any significant benefits from the US trade liberalisation program.²⁵ With Australia's traditional markets offering limited opportunities for growth, the government needed to locate new export markets.

## Opportunities in regional markets

Australia's first significant moves towards diversifying its export markets were in 1931. Herbert Gepp, a consultant on economic development to the Prime Minister's Department, was appointed to undertake an investigative mission to the Far East documenting the trade potential in the region. The University of Queensland Senate also commissioned a Far Eastern tour in 1931. A.C.V. Melbourne, Professor of History at the University of Queensland, visited Japan and China, making a comprehensive study of commercial, political and intellectual exchange opportunities.

---

23  'Doc. 677, Caldwell (US Consul-General in Australia) to Hull (US Secretary of State), 5 June 1934' and 'Doc. 679, O'Brien (Chairman US Tariff Commission) to Hull, 10 August 1934', in Rogers P. Churchill, Matilda F. Axton, Shirley L. Landau, N.O. Sappington and Kieran J. Carroll (eds), *Foreign Relations of the United States Diplomatic Papers, 1934, General, the British Commonwealth, Volume I* (Washington, DC: US Government Printing Office, 1950) [hereinafter *FRUS 1934*].
24  'Doc. 11, Hull to Caldwell, 15 January 1935', in Rogers P. Churchill and N.O. Sappington (eds), *Foreign Relations of the United States Diplomatic Papers, 1935, The British Commonwealth; Europe, Volume II* (Washington, DC: US Government Printing Office, 1952) [hereinafter *FRUS 1935*].
25  Esthus, *From Enmity to Alliance*, 13–18.

The final reports of Gepp and Melbourne were markedly similar. Both men found the Asia-Pacific region, with its cheap and large labour force and growing industrialisation, presented immense import and export opportunities for Australia.[26] Gepp concluded that, by virtue of these opportunities and Australia's proximity, the nation's future political and economic outlook would be 'influenced materially by Pacific affairs'.[27] To advance trading opportunities, both Gepp and Melbourne emphasised the importance of developing Australia's regional reputation, recommending the appointment of trade representatives and a trade delegation visit to the Far East.[28]

The Gepp and Melbourne reports added weight to the voices of those in the Australian press and political circles also calling for the expansion of regional trade linkages.[29] In February 1933, Stewart, who, it will be recalled, had questioned the limited opportunities in imperial markets, headed the Conference on Eastern Trade. In attendance were representatives from the federal and state governments, the Consuls-General of Japan, China and the Netherlands East Indies (NEI), along with academics and representatives from the chambers of commerce and of manufacturers from across Australia. The attendees agreed that both the empire link and geography must dictate Australia's trade relations.[30]

The Conference on Eastern Trade led to the establishment of the Advisory Committee on Eastern Trade, with federal and state-level divisions, to investigate and promote regional economic opportunities. Melbourne served as chair of the federal and Queensland divisions of the advisory committee (1933–35). In this role, he reiterated the importance of regional

---

26   Herbert Gepp, *Report on Trade between Australia and the Far East* (Canberra: Parliament of the Commonwealth of Australia, 1932); A.C.V. Melbourne, *Report on Australian Intercourse with Japan and China* (Brisbane: Fredrick Phillips, Government Printer, 1932).
27   Gepp, *Report on Trade between Australia and the Far East*, 63.
28   ibid., 10–11, 13–14; Melbourne, *Report on Australian Intercourse with Japan and China*, 76, 147–52.
29   For examples of media commentary on Australia's trade opportunities in the Asia-Pacific, see 'Eastern Export Trade', *The Argus*, [Melbourne], 8 May 1931, 4; 'Eastern Trade', *The Brisbane Courier*, 9 February 1933, 10.
30   Shannon L. Smith, 'Towards Diplomatic Representation', in *Facing North: A Century of Australian Engagement with Asia. Volume 1: 1901 to the 1970s*, ed. David Goldsworthy (Melbourne: Melbourne University Press and Department of Foreign Affairs and Trade, 2001), 70–2; 'Far Eastern Trade', *The Australian Worker*, [Sydney], 15 February 1933, 11.

representation and it was on this advice that the federal government passed the *Trade Commissioners Act 1933*, restoring the Australian Trade Commissioner Service.[31]

The Gepp and Melbourne missions and the Conference on Eastern Trade indicate that, even as the Ottawa Agreements were being delineated, Australia was exploring opportunities outside its traditional markets. In this, there was a tacit acknowledgement that the nation could not depend indefinitely on the Empire for its economic welfare.

## Australia's economic and security interests converge on Japan

In their individual reports, both Gepp and Melbourne paid particular attention to trade opportunities in Japan. Japan's economy remained relatively controlled throughout the Great Depression as a result of its government's decision to devalue the yen in December 1931, which stimulated exports. As exports grew, the Japanese government imposed exchange controls to keep imports from rising too quickly. These measures protected against overproduction, kept unemployment low and ensured a stable and relatively quick recovery.[32] Japan's recovery was further aided by the nation's organisation and access to a 'practically unlimited supply of cheap labour', allowing goods to be produced efficiently and at a lower cost to consumers.[33]

Japan's efficient and controlled economy provided a relatively safe market in which Australia could expect increasing export opportunities. Furthermore, Japan was chiefly a manufacturing nation, yet it lacked the raw materials required to meet production needs. This provided an unmatched opportunity for Australia as an exporter of primary goods.

Australian wool was in particularly high demand in Japan and came to dominate trade between the two nations. In the 1919–20 financial year, just 4 per cent of Australia's exportable wool was being purchased

---

31   James Cotton, *The Australian School of International Relations* (New York: Palgrave Macmillan, 2013), 75–6. The Trade Commissioner Service was established in 1918, only to be abandoned in 1927 after poor results. Following this, Britain assumed control of dominion trade representation.
32   Dick K. Nanto and Shinju Takagi, 'Korekiyo Takahashi and Japan's Recovery from the Great Depression', *The American Economic Review* 75, no. 2 (1985): 369–74, at pp. 370–2.
33   Melbourne, *Report on Australian Intercourse with Japan and China*, 11–13, 130–2.

by Japan. By 1931–32, this had ballooned to almost 25 per cent.[34] The wool trade with Japan was largely responsible for positioning the nation as Australia's second-best trading partner by 1930–31.[35] Given the depression had greatly reduced Australia's purchasing power, Japan's affordable manufactured goods, particularly textiles, were in high demand. A mutually beneficial trade relationship appeared to be emerging—one that played a significant role in stabilising Australia's economic position post depression.[36]

Australia's economic opportunities in Japan emerged against the backdrop of the Manchurian Crisis. Despite a longstanding fear of an expansionist Japan, Australia was reluctant to take action on the Manchurian Crisis, adopting a position of impartiality. Rather than a disinterest in international affairs, Australia's response can be better understood in relation to assessments about its economic and defensive interests.[37]

Following Japan's attack on and annexation of the Chinese province of Manchuria, the League of Nations appointed a commission of inquiry to determine the cause of the crisis and how best to remedy it. The commission was headed by the British Earl of Lytton and the report, known as the Lytton Report, was delivered in October 1932. Before the Lytton Report was made public, the situation in Manchuria deteriorated further, as the Japanese Army continued to extend its power and established the puppet state of Manchukuo. The Lytton Report, finding Japan in breach of the Covenant of the League of Nations and the Washington Naval Treaty, recommended the nation withdraw from Manchuria. Japan refused to comply and was condemned by the league as an international

---

34   I.M. Cumpston, 'The Australian–Japanese Dispute of the Nineteen-Thirties', *The Australian Quarterly* 29, no. 2 (1957): 45–55, at p. 50; Eric M. Andrews, 'The Australian Government and the Manchurian Crisis, 1931-3', *Australian Outlook* 35, no. 3 (1981): 307–16, at p. 310.
35   By 1930–31, Japan was purchasing 10.56 per cent of Australia's total exports, at a value of more than £9.5 million annually. *Official Year Book of the Commonwealth of Australia*, No. 26 (1933), 237–9.
36   Jack Shepherd, *Australia's Interests and Policies in the Far East* (New York: International Secretariat, Institute of Pacific Relations, 1940), 27–8; Boris Schedvin, *Emissaries of Trade: A History of the Australian Trade Commissioner Service* (Canberra: Department of Foreign Affairs and Trade, 2008), 46–8.
37   Ruth Megaw, 'The Australian Goodwill Mission to the Far East in 1934: Its Significance in the Evolution of Australian Foreign Policy', *Journal of the Royal Australian Historical Society* 59, no. 4 (1973): 247–63, at pp. 247–8.

aggressor. The league also adopted an official policy of non-recognition of Manchukuo. In March 1933, in response to this policy, Japan announced its withdrawal from the league, effective March 1935.[38]

Australia was reluctant to adopt the league's recommended response to the Manchurian Crisis. In addition to non-recognition of Manchukuo, the league had recommended economic sanctions against Japan in the hope this would discourage any further hostile actions. Japan was Australia's second-best trading partner, with exports valued at more than £11.6 million annually.[39] This trade was essential to the nation's economic survival, and Australia did not wish to see sanctions introduced that would threaten this lucrative relationship.[40] The Australian government voiced its disapproval of sanctions in a 1933 cable to Stanley Melbourne Bruce—who was serving as Resident Minister in Britain and was appointed High Commissioner later that year—concluding that 'economic sanctions should not be applied or even considered by the Commonwealth Government'. The hope was that Bruce could convince the British that sanctions would be regarded by the Japanese as an act of hostility.[41]

Situated at the centre of empire policymaking, Bruce had access to the most influential individuals and committees. The diplomatic culture of Whitehall in the 1930s was a matter not simply of opportunity, but also of prestige. Bruce embraced this culture, building private and professional relationships with key British figures in the hope of engendering influence. He coupled cordial relations with vigorous diplomacy, regularly attending and speaking at Committee of Imperial Defence (CID) meetings at which he raised issues of importance to Australia.[42] Official and private papers reveal that Bruce maintained regular correspondence with the Australian Prime Minister, Minister for External Affairs and other key ministers, offering advice on how best to respond to British policy developments.[43]

---

38   Andrews, *The Writing on the Wall*, 78–9; '"Actions of the League of Nations in the Sino-Japanese Crisis", Report by Bruce, 17 January 1933', NAA: A981, Chin 166 Part 2.
39   *Official Year Book of the Commonwealth of Australia*, No. 26 (1933), 237. Figures for 1931–32.
40   *CPD: Representatives*, 9 March 1933, No. 10, 139.
41   'Commonwealth government to Bruce, [n.d. (early 1933)]', NAA: A981, Chin 125 Part 2.
42   P.G. Edwards, 'The Rise and Fall of the High Commissioner: S.M. Bruce in London 1933–1945', in *Australia and Britain: Studies in a Changing Relationship*, eds A.F. Madden and W.H. Morris-Jones (Sydney: Sydney University Press, 1980), 39, 42–7; Edwards, *Prime Ministers and Diplomats*, 109–12.
43   Bruce's correspondence and private papers during his time as High Commissioner can be found in Australian High Commission, United Kingdom [London]—Office of the High Commissioner: Official papers and correspondence maintained by Stanley Melbourne Bruce in London, 1932–45, NAA: M2236.

In the case of the Manchurian Crisis, Bruce lobbied the British government to reject the sanctions against Japan. Fortuitously, Britain, with its own trade interests in Japan, was reluctant to adopt economic sanctions. The proposed sanctions were accordingly voted down due to a lack of support among the league.[44] Britain did not, however, have reservations about the non-recognition of Manchukuo, adopting this policy in August 1933 despite Australia expressing its apprehension.[45]

The second and more critical factor influencing Australia's response to the Manchurian Crisis was security. As tensions increased in the Asia-Pacific region, the British government was forced to acknowledge the inappropriateness of its recent defence planning. In February 1932, the annual defence review of the Chiefs of Staff Committee (COS) was released. The review criticised the 10-year rule and its impact on British armed power, particularly in the Asia-Pacific, where the position was deemed 'about as bad as it could be'.[46] On the advice of the COS, the 10-year rule was cancelled, in March 1932.[47] Despite the cancellation, the Australian government was cautioned that the unstable global economic situation would not permit greater defence commitments to the Asia-Pacific, with work at the Singapore base continuing but not intensifying.[48]

It is reasonable to conclude that the Australian government's noncommittal approach to the situation in Manchuria was shaped by national security interests. In taking no action on non-recognition of Manchukuo, neither Japan nor China would be offended and, in turn, further antagonism in the region could be avoided. The records of the Australian Parliament and private government correspondence indicate this indeed contributed to Australia's reluctance to take action. In the immediate aftermath of the Manchurian Crisis, the government was cautious when making comments on the situation, so much so that some accused the Lyons government of failing to keep the Parliament fully informed.[49] Australia's

---

44  David S. Bird, *J.A. Lyons: The 'Tame Tasmanian'—Appeasement and Rearmament in Australia, 1932–39* (Melbourne: Australian Scholarly Publishing, 2008), 37–8.
45  'Officer (External Affairs officer in London) to DEA, 10 August 1933', NAA: A981, Man 7.
46  'COS Annual Review 1932, 23 February 1932, TNA: CAB 4/2', cited in Andrews, *The Writing on the Wall*, 108.
47  'Cabinet Meeting, 23 March 1932', TNA: CAB 23/70/19.
48  'CID and Standing Defence Sub-Committee Meeting, 28 July 1932', in Records of the Cabinet Office, Committee of Imperial Defence and Standing Defence Sub-committee: Minutes, TNA: CAB 2/5.
49  For instance, see *CPD: Representatives*, 26 February 1932, No. 8, 413, and 3 March 1932, No. 9, 577.

Minister for External Affairs, John Latham, was particularly reluctant to make public statements. He simply emphasised his hope for a peaceful solution and avoided placing responsibility on any one nation, arguing that 'it is inadvisable to make any statement in this Parliament concerning the possibility of aggression by a nation which is now friendly to us'.[50]

Bruce was present at the League of Nations assembly when the Lytton Report was handed down. In his report to Lyons, he encouraged Australia to 'remain friends of both parties [Japan and China] and strictly impartial', suggesting no statement be made regarding non-recognition of Manchukuo.[51] The government agreed, emphasising that its particular security interests would be served by a noncommittal approach. A cable Bruce received from his government stressed:

> [W]e are anxious not to adopt at any stage any attitude which might commit us to any participation in military etc. action on account of a quarrel between China and Japan in respect to Manchuria. This should be the guiding principle.[52]

Australia postponed action on the league's recommendations, eventually choosing to adopt a position of non-alignment.[53] Clearly, Australia was tailoring its response to the unfolding crisis in its region that would deliver integrated economic and strategic outcomes.

## 'The whole of our interests': The 1934 Australian Eastern Mission

The 1934 Australian Eastern Mission (AEM) was Australia's first diplomatic mission outside the British Empire. What little has been written on the AEM tends to characterise it as the personal venture of Latham and the swansong of his political career, as he went on to retire in September 1934.[54] Far from an interesting yet ultimately unimportant episode that had 'no lasting impact on Australian policy', the AEM denotes

---

50   *CPD: Representatives*, 19 February 1932, No. 7, 142.
51   'Bruce to Lyons, 22 December 1932', NAA: A981, Chin 166 Part 2.
52   'Commonwealth government to Bruce, [n.d. (early 1933)]', NAA: A981, Chin 125 Part 2.
53   Andrews, *The Writing on the Wall*, 95–7.
54   Megaw, 'The Australian Goodwill Mission to the Far East in 1934', 247–63; Edwards, *Prime Ministers and Diplomats*, 90–1.

Australia's appreciation of the relationship between trade, diplomacy and geography and a determination to integrate its distinct regional interests into the imperial outlook.[55]

From March to June 1934, the mission, led by Latham, travelled through East and South-East Asia, visiting China, Hong Kong, Japan, Malaya, the NEI and the Philippines.[56] While the AEM was promoted as an exercise in goodwill, with newspaper reports couched in the language of a neighbourly 'courtesy call' and extending 'the hand of friendship'—both Lyons and Latham privately contacted the press to request that it be referred to as such—the vested security and trade interests are easily identifiable.[57] In his preparation for the mission, Latham meticulously studied the nations he would visit, including local politics, customs and how the Australian government's past policies had impacted its neighbours and shaped perceptions of Australia. Latham also cooperated with the British Foreign Office, drawing on its recommendations and knowledge—more extensive than that of Australia's own embryonic DEA—to inform the AEM's itinerary.[58] The enthusiasm with which Latham approached these activities suggests he was keenly aware of the strategic capital of the AEM.

On his return, Latham made a speech to parliament in which he centred the security imperatives of the AEM. 'The whole of our interests,' he concluded, 'therefore, lie in doing everything in our power to prevent the risk of war in the East from becoming a pulsing reality.'[59] He expanded on this theme in his detailed report on the mission, which was disseminated widely throughout the government and business sector:

> The continent of Australia is actually in the geographical area often described as 'the East'. The risks attendant upon any disturbance of the peace or actual outbreak of war in that region are of the greatest moment to our people … Accordingly, the maintenance

---

55  Allan Gyngell, *Fear of Abandonment: Australia in the World Since 1942* (Melbourne: Black Inc., 2017), 17.
56  'Eastern Mission, 1934. Arrangements and Documentation', NAA: A981, Far 2.
57  'The Hand of Friendship', *The Sun*, [Sydney], 19 March 1934, and 'Mission to East', *The Courier-Mail*, [Brisbane], 24 March 1934, cuttings, both in NAA: A981, Far 5 Part 14.
58  For a detailed analysis of Latham's cooperation with the British Foreign Office, see Michael Kilmister, 'Antipodean imperialist: Sir John Latham, a political biography, 1902 to 1934' (PhD thesis, University of Newcastle, 2018), 235–42.
59  'Speech by Latham, 6 July 1934', NAA: A981, Far 5 Part 16.

of friendly relations between Australia and our neighbours and, more generally, the maintenance of peace in the East, should be the major objective of Australian foreign policy.[60]

Although not specified, Japan and the situation in Manchuria were likely the focus of Latham's attention. This speculation is confirmed in private government correspondence and Latham's confidential reports—given only to Cabinet. While the AEM visited a number of Far Eastern nations, its true purpose can be found in its interactions with Japan. The significance of Japan was apparent from the preparatory stages of the AEM. The Foreign Office advised the Australian government that a visit to China was 'very desirable if Japan is visited'.[61] Latham supported this advice, however, he was reluctant to commit to an itinerary for China before plans in Japan were confirmed, fearing this would reduce the time spent in Japan.[62] In the end, Latham spent roughly equal time in China and Japan.

Latham's interest in Japan rested on the situation in Manchuria. Following the League of Nations' condemnation of Japan's actions, the nation was isolated in the international community. As historian Ian Nish argues, the Australian government identified in this isolation an opportunity to promote bilateral relations that were conducive to national interests—namely, convincing Japan to maintain league membership and stabilise the situation in Manchuria.[63] During his time in Japan, Latham met with Japan's Minister for Foreign Affairs, Kōki Hirota. The two men discussed Japan's league membership and the historical, political and social aspects of the situation in Manchuria, as Latham sought to understand Japan's view on the matter.[64]

Latham was unable to convince Hirota that Japan should remain in the league and, in the 'Secret Report on the International Position in the Far East', he was markedly candid about the situation in Manchuria. 'It appears to me,' he wrote, 'that the policy of non-recognition of Manchukuo is going to meet increasingly greater difficulties as time

---

60  'Australian Eastern Mission 1934: Report of Latham, [n.d. (July 1934)]', NAA: A981, Far 5 Part 16.
61  'Bruce to Lyons, 15 December 1933', NAA: A981, Far 5 Part 1.
62  'Latham to Bruce, 9 February 1934', NAA: A981, Far 5 Part 1.
63  Ian Nish, 'Relations with Japan', in *Between Empire and Nation: Australia's External Relations from Federation Until the Second World War*, eds Carl Bridge and Bernard Attard (Melbourne: Australian Scholarly Publishing, 2000), 132.
64  'Secret Report on International Position in Far East, 3 July 1934', NAA: A981, Far 5 Part 16.

passes. So far as one can judge there is not the slightest probability that Manchukuo will cease to exist.' Latham went on to offer a possible solution, recommending that

> consideration should be given to the possibility of discovering some formula which would enable both Japan and the League to 'save face' and get rid of what threatens to be a permanent source of poison in the relations between Japan and other countries. It is most improbable that any conceivable formula would satisfy any of the Chinese factions, but that could not be helped.[65]

Despite the vagueness of Latham's formula, the implications are clear: he judged Japan to be *the* priority for Australia's regional policy and it should somehow be accommodated.

Although the Australian government was seeking to tailor a policy to its distinct regional circumstance, it was not seeking to break away from Britain and the Empire. Australia sought to use the imperial framework to meet its regional needs. This goal is evidenced in Latham's emphasis on the significance of the AEM to the Empire. Latham's public report concluded that the mission had contributed to a 'friendly attitude towards Australia … This atmosphere should greatly assist in the solution of present and future problems'. Latham was conceivably referring to the significance of diplomatic ties in protecting Australia's strategic interests in the Asia-Pacific region. He went on to suggest that friendly relations with Japan were 'of value not only to Australia, but also to the British Empire as a whole'. The link between the Asia-Pacific and the role Australia could play there as a member of the Empire was echoed in a remark made by Secretary of State for Foreign Affairs John Simon, whom Latham cited in his final report: '[The AEM] has been of the greatest value to Australia and the British Commonwealth of Nations in promoting good relations with the countries of the Far East.'[66] In this emphasis on shared benefits, Australia was highlighting the significance of the Asia-Pacific region and the need to integrate it into the imperial strategic outlook.

The contributions of the AEM and Latham to Australia's foreign policy thinking and increasing assertiveness within the imperial framework have been largely overlooked in the existing literature. Gregory Pemberton,

---

65   'Secret Report, 3 July 1934', NAA: A981, Far 5 Part 16.
66   Simon was speaking in the House of Commons. 'Report of Latham, July 1934', NAA: A981, Far 5 Part 16.

THE GENESIS OF A POLICY

for instance, contends that Latham's interest in the Asia-Pacific differentiated him from his colleagues, precluding many of his proposals from gaining support and going on to shape policy.⁶⁷ Both the government's earlier interest in regional economic opportunities and Lyons' efforts at the 1935 meeting of the dominion leaders (Leaders' Meeting) discount Pemberton's thesis. The Leaders' Meeting was organised to coincide with the silver jubilee celebrations of King George V and Queen Mary and was not an imperial conference; Australia's express request for a gathering of this calibre had in fact been rejected.⁶⁸ Foreign affairs and defence were, accordingly, given little attention by the British government in preparations for the meeting. For Lyons, however, this being his first overseas trip as prime minister, the Leaders' Meeting was an opportunity for consultation in imperial policymaking. He arrived in London armed with a detailed report on foreign affairs and an agenda including British rearmament and imperial policy towards the mounting unrest in the Far East and Europe.⁶⁹ So seriously, in fact, did the Australian Prime Minister take the Leaders' Meeting that one newspaper reported the nation's delegation was almost equal in size to all the other delegations combined.⁷⁰

During the third session of the Leaders' Meeting, Lyons tabled the Far East and foreign policy as topics for discussion. He requested more information from the British government on its relations with Japan, indicating that the League of Nations' policy towards Manchukuo left him concerned about the prospects for long-term peace in Australia's immediate region. In a plea to restore Anglo-Japanese relations, Lyons offered a solution: 'some sort of pact of security for all the nation's [sic] bordering on the Pacific Ocean'.⁷¹ Here Lyons was echoing his predecessors Alfred Deakin and William Morris Hughes, who, in 1909 and 1918, respectively, had

---

67   Gregory Pemberton, 'An Imperial Imagination: Explaining the Post-1945 Foreign Policy of Robert Gordon Menzies', in *Menzies in War and Peace*, ed. Frank Cain (Sydney: Allen & Unwin, 1997), 160.
68   'Hankey (CID Secretary and Cabinet Secretary) Diary, 2 October 1934, TNA: CAB 63/66', cited in Bird, *J.A. Lyons*, 94.
69   '"Report on Foreign Affairs", Bruce to Lyons, 7 March 1935', in Prime Minister's Department: Correspondence files, annual single number series with occasional 'G' [General Representations] infix [Main correspondence files series of the agency], 1903–, NAA: A463, 1957/1060.
70   'Lyons' Jubilee Jaunt: London Surprised at Big Retinue', *Sunday Times*, [Perth], 27 January 1935, 1.
71   'Minutes Third Meeting of Leaders, 9 May 1935', NAA: A981, Imp 135.

proposed a Monroe Doctrine for the Pacific to be underpinned by US and British security guarantees.[72] Just as Latham's earlier so-called formula had recommended, Lyons' pact included the recognition of Manchukuo:

> Were the Japanese to be allowed to expand in their own area … and if not, was there not a fear that the Japanese would turn to the Southern Pacific? The question of the recognition of Manchukuo was relevant … The recognition of Manchukuo would go a long way to remove any feeling of antagonism on the part of the Japanese.[73]

Lyons saw in Japan a threat to Far Eastern security and feared the nation may turn its attention towards Australia. He looked to the Empire for a collective approach to prevent this from eventuating. Lyons' proposal was not taken seriously and was quickly set aside, with British representatives dismissing Manchukuo as 'irrelevant' to the future of Anglo-Japanese relations and other dominion leaders indicating that Manchukuo was a League of Nations matter and not a question for the Empire.[74]

Both the AEM and Lyons' efforts at the 1935 Leaders' Meeting represent an increasing pragmatism in Australian foreign policymaking, as the nation developed an approach distinct to its geographical locality. This approach was underpinned by a desire to shape the imperial framework to deliver regional security outcomes. The imperial response was indicative of Australia's continuing challenge to convince the rest of the Empire of the importance of the Asia-Pacific in strategic planning.

## Strategic integration into the Japanese market

Although the AEM was promoted as an exercise in friendship and goodwill and 'not', as Lyons explained to Bruce, 'in search of trade', trade invariably came into play.[75] Latham was a supporter of the Ottawa Agreements and the benefits they accrued for Australian exports. He was also candid in

---

72  'Deakin to Crewe (Secretary of State for the Colonies), 27 September 1909, TNA: FO 800/91/77', cited in Meaney, *A History of Australian Defence and Foreign Policy 1901–23*, vol. 1, 199; 'Australia to Have a Monroe Doctrine', *The New York Times*, 1 June 1918, 9.
73  'Minutes Third Meeting of Leaders, 9 May 1935', NAA: A981, Imp 135.
74  ibid.
75  'Lyons to Bruce, 13 December 1933', NAA: A981, Far 5 Part 1.

his belief that Ottawa need not constrain the development of foreign trade relationships. In a statement in the House of Representatives, Latham remarked that the Ottawa Agreements were 'the first step towards maintaining and extending the most important of all these markets [the imperial market] for the Australian producer'. He went on to share his hopes that agreements 'along the same line' as Ottawa would develop between Australia and foreign nations, concluding:

> Without foreign trade, there would be no chance whatever of our maintaining anything approaching our present standard of living. Australia needs her markets overseas. It is important to us that we shall develop and cultivate real and friendly relations with nations that afford markets for our producers of many commodities.[76]

While he acknowledged that intra-empire economic cooperation was valuable, he believed it was 'obvious that our economic destiny … is already largely and may be determined even more largely in the future by the volume of trade we do with the countries of the East'.[77]

Following the AEM, Latham prepared three confidential reports on Australia's trade interests in the Asia-Pacific. By virtue of Japan's large volume of trade with Australia, there was an entire report dedicated to Australian–Japanese bilateral trade. The nation also featured prominently in the other two reports, which dealt with wool sales and the appointment of Australian trade commissioners. During the AEM's visit to Japan, Arthur Moore, an information officer from the Department of Trade and Customs, met with Saburō Kurusu, the Director of the Commercial Bureau in the Japanese Department of Foreign Affairs. Although it was agreed that no definite decisions would be made, the meeting allowed both men to voice their hopes for future trade relations. Kurusu presented a litany of grievances concerning Australian trade policy and potential solutions. Chief among his requests was the negotiation of a trade treaty and establishment of a direct link with Australia, rather than, as had been the case in the past, a British official acting on the nation's behalf.[78] While

---

76 *CPD: Representatives*, 23 May 1933, No. 21, 1933, 1651.
77 'Speech by Latham, 6 July 1934', NAA: A981, Far 5 Part 16.
78 'Confidential Report on Trade between Australia and Japan, 30 July 1934', NAA: A981, Far 5 Part 16; Schedvin, *Emissaries of Trade*, 50–3.

Latham made no specific recommendations for the negotiation of a trade treaty, believing this to be beyond his jurisdiction as Minister for External Affairs, he did note that 'it would be very wise to act promptly'.[79]

The AEM reports and the increasing importance of the Japanese market influenced the Australian government's decision to commence trade treaty negotiations with Japan.[80] In December 1934, a small Japanese delegation arrived in Australia to negotiate the Treaty of Friendship, Commerce and Navigation. Negotiations opened in February the following year.[81] The Japanese government identified high tariffs and the imperial preference system as barriers to the export of Japanese goods. Early negotiations accordingly focused on remediating these barriers.[82] Although the negotiation of a trade treaty appeared to be a natural progression of Australia's expanding economic and diplomatic interests in Japan, as will be seen in Chapter 3, imperial interests complicated this process.

Latham enthusiastically supported the appointment of an Australian trade commissioner in Tokyo with visions of a dual role.[83] The first role was the more obvious, being a representative of Australian trade interests. For the financial year 1932–33, Japan's purchases from Australia totalled more than £13.9 million. Australia's purchases were £3.7 million in return.[84] At a ratio of more than 3:1, this was not a sustainable exchange for Japan and Latham reported criticism among the Japanese government and the press concerning the imbalance. He accordingly encouraged greater purchases if Australia wished to maintain, and in time increase, its share in

---

79  'Confidential Report on Trade, 30 July 1934', NAA: A981, Far 5 Part 16.
80  The Japanese government had initially proposed a trade treaty in April 1932. The Australian government, however, postponed action until after the upcoming Imperial Economic Conference. The Ottawa Agreements ultimately limited action on bilateral trade treaties with foreign nations and the treaty discussions with Japan were set aside. 'Confidential Report on Trade, 30 July 1934', NAA: A981, Far 5 Part 16.
81  *CPD: Representatives*, 12 December 1944, No. 50, 1077.
82  'Australia and Japan Seek Trade Treaty', *Far Eastern Survey* 4, no. 11 (1935): 86–7; '"Draft Treaty of Commerce and Navigation between Japan the Commonwealth of Australia", Memorandum by Abbott (Comptroller-General Department of Trade and Customs) to Prime Minister's Department, 7 February 1935', NAA: A981, Trad 68 Part 2.
83  'Confidential Report on Appointment of Trade Commissioners, 20 July 1934', in Prime Minister's Department: Papers collected in the offices of the Secretary and the Prime Minister, 1901–39, NAA: CP290/1, 10; 'Broadcast Address of Leader of Australian Eastern Mission, Rt Hon. J.G. Latham, during his visit to Japan, 15 May 1934', in D.B. Copland and C.V. Janes (eds), *Australian Trade Policy: A Book of Documents* (Sydney: Angus & Robertson, 1937), 257. Trade commissioners were also dispatched to China and the NEI.
84  *Official Year Book of the Commonwealth of Australia*, No. 28 (1935), 255, 257.

the Japanese market. The appointment of a trade commissioner in Tokyo would aid this process, as they could report to the government on bilateral trade opportunities and act as an advocate for Australian exports in the Japanese market.[85]

Latham also believed a trade commissioner could assume the role of a quasi-diplomat. The trade commissioner posting would provide a permanent link between Japan and Australia. Latham emphasised the significance of a quasi-diplomatic role in view of the 'powerful influence' of the Japanese press, which 'plays a big part in forming public opinion'.[86] A trade commissioner could build a rapport with the media, government and public in what Latham described as a 'persistent and tactful … propaganda'.[87] In this way, Australian policy pertinent to Japan could be immediately clarified, ensuring misunderstanding and potential resentment were avoided. Not only would this diplomatic activity promote Australia's trade interests, it also would improve relations with Japan, theoretically contributing to regional stability and protecting the nation against future hostility.

Latham paid great attention to the character of the man who would be appointed as trade commissioner in Tokyo, detailing the honour and respect bestowed on government officials in Japanese culture. It was, he stressed, imperative someone be appointed who would 'inspire confidence, trust and friendliness'.[88] Lieutenant-Colonel Eric Longfield Lloyd, who had served as an advisor and interpreter during the AEM and, significantly, had a background in intelligence, was appointed Australia's first trade commissioner in Tokyo with a personal recommendation from Latham. He arrived in Tokyo in October 1935.[89]

William Macmahon Ball, who worked with Longfield Lloyd in Japan following the nation's defeat in and occupation after World War II, later questioned his suitability for the posting. Macmahon Ball was critical of Longfield Lloyd's Japanese-language skills and believed his knowledge

---

85  'Report of Latham, July 1934' and 'Confidential Report on Trade, 30 July 1934', both in NAA: A981, Far 5 Part 16.
86  'Report of Latham, July 1934', NAA: A981, Far 5 Part 16.
87  'Confidential Report on Trade Commissioners, 20 July 1934', NAA: CP290/1, 10.
88  'Confidential Report Appointment of Trade Commissioners, 20 July 1934', NAA: CP290/1, 10.
89  Nish, 'Relations with Japan', 133.

of Japan to be 'exceedingly meagre and unreliable'.[90] These criticisms aside, Longfield Lloyd approached his dual role with much industry, particularly as a quasi-diplomat. Official dispatches from Tokyo reveal that he established a close working relationship with Japanese officials. As economic historian Boris Schedvin notes, he was particularly 'assiduous in digging out material and making it available to Australian authorities', providing fastidiously detailed reports about the political and economic situation in Japan as it related to Australia.[91] These reports included strategic insight. For instance, Longfield Lloyd monitored Japan's developments at the Yampi Sound mine in Western Australia, commenting on the likelihood of Japan using economic projects in Australia as a base for an offensive strategy.[92] From the perspective of Australia—in an unpredictable region and with a desperate need to expand its export markets—economic engagement with Japan could contribute to the nation's economic and physical security.

In addition to trade commissioner appointments, 1935 also saw the DEA undergo a major restructure and receive full administrative autonomy. Previously, the DEA had been presided over by the Prime Minister's Department and the two departments had shared a secretary. In April 1934, as foreign affairs took on increasing significance and required greater resources, the position of Assistant Secretary of the DEA was established and filled by Lieutenant-Colonel William Roy Hodgson. Hodgson had an extensive military background, having served as the Australian Military Forces (AMF) head of military intelligence (1925–34). In this role, he had specialised in military intelligence in the Far East, including the rise of Japan and how Australia could respond to the threat of regional aggression. In November 1935, the DEA gained full administrative autonomy and Hodgson was appointed secretary.[93]

---

90 'Report to the Prime Minister on a Mission to Japan, 1 September 1947', in W. Macmahon Ball, *Intermittent Diplomat: The Japan and Batavia Diaries of W. Macmahon Ball*, ed. Alan Rix (Melbourne: Melbourne University Press, 1988), 272–3.
91 Schedvin, *Emissaries of Trade*, 61. There are numerous dispatch files from Longfield Lloyd. Those most pertinent to his early years as trade commissioner include 'Japan–Australia Trade Relations Dispatches from Trade Commissioner', in Department of Commerce: Correspondence files, multiple number series, 1935–48, NAA: A601, 402/17/28; 'Japan—General File—Part I', NAA: A601, 402/17/15; 'Japan—General File—Part II, NAA: A601, 402/17/2.
92 'Implications of Japanese Southward Expansion Movt', NAA: A601, 402/17/30.
93 Edwards, *Prime Ministers and Diplomats*, 92–3; W.J. Hudson, *Towards a Foreign Policy, 1914–1941* (Melbourne: Cassell, 1967), 37–8.

While there is nothing to suggest the AEM or the appointment of trade commissioners influenced the restructuring of the DEA, against the backdrop of these developments, the decision is a marker of Australia's growing attention to foreign affairs and the need for its own professional, if embryonic, diplomatic service.

Australia's activities in the years 1931–35 do not constitute a complete foreign policy; however, they do demonstrate a concerted attempt by Australian policymakers to define the national interest in relation to Australia's unique regional, economic and strategic circumstances. Foresight and keen appreciation of the components of the national interest accordingly emerge. This is a pragmatism that has been largely overlooked and, when it is noted, it is gestured to, rather than unpacked and its development carefully traced, as has been done here. Though the Australian government was developing an increasing assertiveness in foreign and economic policy, there was nothing to suggest this was at the expense of the imperial link. Rather, Australia actively sought to enmesh its region-specific interests within the imperial framework, in an attempt to reshape the outlook of the Empire into one that better served Australia's unique strategic position. Yet, as the next chapter explores, balancing regional and imperial interests was not so easily achieved.

# 3

# Expectations of the empire connection and the Trade Diversion Policy, 1936–37

Hugh White, in what has become a familiar refrain in assessments of Australia's contemporary relations with China and the US, argues that today is the first time in the nation's history that 'our biggest trading partner—and our biggest potential trading partner—has not been a close ally'. This situation is complicated by the fact that China is a strategic rival of the US.[1] While White rejects the notion, many hold that Australia need not choose between China and the US and the trade and security interests they represent.[2] These assertions disregard the situation in the 1930s, when Japan was both a significant market for Australian goods—at one

---

1   Lowy Institute, 'In conversation: Hugh White on How to Defend Australia' (Lowy Institute, Sydney, 16 July 2019), available from: www.lowyinstitute.org/news-and-media/multimedia/audio/conversation-hugh-white-how-defend-australia. See also, Peter Greste, 'China Rising: The Challenges for Australia as China and the US Struggle for Supremacy in Asia', *Four Corners*, [ABC TV], 3 October 2016, available from: www.abc.net.au/4corners/four-corners-china-rising-promo/7890504.
2   For assertions and assessments of this view, see Alex Lavelle, 'Australia Doesn't Have to Choose US Over China or Vice Versa', *The Age*, [Melbourne], 1 March 2018, available from: www.theage.com.au/national/australia-doesn-t-have-to-choose-us-over-china-or-vice-versa-20180301-p4z2cd.html; Rod Lyon, 'What Happened to the "Canberra Consensus" on Australia–China Relations?', *The Strategist*, 3 July 2019 (Canberra: Australian Strategic Policy Institute), available from: www.aspistrategist.org.au/what-happened-to-the-canberra-consensus-on-australia-china-relations/. Remy Davidson judged the 2017 Foreign Policy White Paper to be a continuation of Australia's policy of hedging its bets. Remy Davidson, 'Australia is Hedging its Bets on China With the Latest Foreign Policy White Paper', *The Conversation*, 23 November 2017, available from: theconversation.com/australia-is-hedging-its-bets-on-china-with-the-latest-foreign-policy-white-paper-88009. Until recently, White was himself of the view that Australia need not choose between China and the US as the two nations could be convinced to share power.

point, Australia's second-best export market—and a challenger to British commercial interests and dominance in the Asia-Pacific region. The 1936 Trade Diversion Policy was a point at which Australia did, in fact, choose, highlighting the interplay between trade, diplomacy and defence and the nation's longstanding dilemma of constructing foreign policy within an asymmetrical relationship.

On 22 May 1936, Henry Gullett, who was responsible for the negotiation of trade treaties, announced a new protectionist policy targeting Japanese textile imports. This policy was known as trade diversion. Japan's immediate and predictable response was to boycott Australian exports, leading to a heated, albeit short-lived, trade war. Although the Australian government suggested the trade diversion measures were designed to eradicate its trade deficit, Japan was the nation's second-best trading partner with a balance of trade firmly in Australia's favour.[3]

There are two prevailing assessments of the Trade Diversion Policy. For many, the contradictory economic logic of trade diversion renders the episode a disaster that 'achieved a maximum of irritation with a minimum of benefit' as Joseph Lyons' government naively sacrificed trade relations with Japan for the sake of British textile producers.[4] Kosmas Tsokhas and others reject this 'imperial fallacy' in which Australia was a 'passive victim' of British pressure.[5] Instead, trade diversion was a calculated gamble influenced by domestic politics that was designed to better position Australian exports in the British market, and any benefits afforded to Britain were only of secondary importance.[6]

---

3    '"Considerations which led to the Adoption of the Trade Diversion Policy", Department of Trade and Customs Memorandum, [n.d. (1937)]', NAA: A1667, 430/B/52A.
4    Eggleston, *Reflections on Australian Foreign Policy*, 3. See also J.B. O'Brien, 'Empire v. National Interest in Australian–British Relations During the 1930s', *Historical Studies* 22, no. 89 (1987): 569–86; Stuart Ward, 'Sentiment and Self-Interest: The Imperial Ideal in Anglo-Australian Commercial Culture', *Australian Historical Studies* 32, no. 116 (2001): 91–108, at p. 93.
5    Kosmas Tsokhas, 'The Wool Industry and the 1936 Trade Diversion Dispute Between Australia and Japan', *Australian Historical Studies* 23, no. 93 (1989): 442–61, at p. 459.
6    ibid., 442–61; Kosmas Tsokhas, *Markets, Money and Empire: The Political Economy of the Australian Wool Industry* (Melbourne: Melbourne University Press, 1990), 12–15, 98–118. See also Drummond, *Imperial Economic Policy, 1917–1939*, 375–6, 398–406; D.C.S. Sissons, 'Manchester v. Japan: The Imperial Background of the Australian Trade Diversion Dispute With Japan, 1936', *Australian Outlook* 30, no. 3 (1976): 480–502, at pp. 495–8; D.C.S. Sissons, 'Private Diplomacy in the 1936 Trade Dispute With Japan', *Australian Journal of Politics and History* 27, no. 2 (1981): 143–59.

Despite their differences, these two assessments similarly depict trade diversion within a vacuum, overlooking the range of pressures that contributed to the policy and had been building for several years. This chapter broadens the historical understanding of the trade diversion episode and its aftermath by bringing into focus the interplay between economics, security and the expectations of empire membership, in terms of both British pressure to act on behalf of its economic interests and what Australia sought to negotiate in return. What emerges from the Trade Diversion Policy case study is an important lesson, for the Australian policymakers of the 1930s and today.

## The Trade Diversion Policy

In February 1935, in what appeared to be a very natural progression after years of increasing commercial relations, negotiations opened between Japan and Australia for the Treaty of Friendship, Commerce and Navigation. Early negotiations focused on a reciprocal most-favoured nation (MFN) status and greater liberty for cargo ships to port.

The negotiation process appeared outwardly smooth and it was generally assumed a mutually beneficial settlement would be reached.[7] It therefore came as somewhat of a surprise when negotiations reached a stalemate in March 1936. The central issue was Gullett's advice to the Japanese Consul-General, Kuaramatsu Murai, that unless Japan agreed to a voluntary quota on rayon and cotton piece goods exported to Australia, negotiations could not continue. The proposed quota was 75 million square yards (62.7 million square metres) per annum, compared with the 152 million square yards (127 million sq m) purchased by Australia in the previous financial year. In return, Gullett offered an intermediate tariff rate. This rate established a median between the tariff rates foreign nations paid and those paid by empire nations as stipulated in the 1932 Ottawa Agreements.[8] In the context of negotiating a trade treaty and Australia's significantly favourable trade balance, Japan expected reciprocal trade to be

---

7   'Revised Draft Treaty of Commerce and Navigation between Japan and the Commonwealth of Australia, 13 February 1935', NAA: A981, Trad 68 Part 2. MFN grants the best possible trade terms to a trading partner. Other MFNs would be treated equally, but not better. For Australia, this would be MFN status outside the benefits enjoyed by other members of the British Empire.
8   'Longfield Lloyd (Trade Commissioner in Japan), to Murphy (Secretary Department of Commerce), 12 March 1936' and 'Longfield Lloyd to Murphy, 16 March 1936', NAA: A601, 402/17/28.

expanded rather than restricted. Gullett's proposal was simply unacceptable and Japan's refusal to cooperate led to the breakdown of negotiations. On 22 May 1936, Gullett announced the Trade Diversion Policy.[9]

With a narrow range of primary exports and reliance on foreign markets for manufactured goods, Australia continued to struggle to maintain a balance-of-payments surplus. The Trade Diversion Policy was promoted as addressing this problem by increasing sales of primary exports, expanding the nation's developing secondary industries and, in turn, increasing employment. The Trade Diversion Policy amended the licensing system for foreign goods, prohibiting the importation of more than 90 classes of goods unless the Australian government granted special approval. Additionally, the customs duties on foreign rayon and cotton were increased to 40 per cent and between 68 and 85 per cent, respectively.[10]

These measures targeted so-called bad customers—those nations benefiting from unfair trade advantages or with whom Australia had a trade imbalance. It was hoped the threat of exclusion would force bad customer nations to pursue a more favourable position in Australia's market. Conversely, 'good customers' could easily apply for a licence, thereby exempting them from the new restrictions. Australia expected to benefit in kind with increased purchases from good customers.[11] In this way, Gullett informed the House of Representatives: '[W]e have resolved to give more room in this market to those who are our great buyers, and somewhat less room to those who are indifferent buyers.'[12]

The two countries most affected by trade diversion were the US and Japan. The US was a bad customer. In the face of a continuing trade imbalance, a series of embarrassing and ill-fated proposals for an Australian–US bilateral trade agreement and mounting pressure from commercial circles, the Australian government 'had no alternative but to seek an adjustment of the unsatisfactory trade position by unilateral action'.[13] Trade diversion sought to protect Australia's primary and fledging secondary industries

---

9    *CPD: Representatives*, 22 May 1936, No. 21, 2211–20.
10   ibid.; 'Adoption of Trade Diversion Policy, [n.d. (1937)]', NAA: A1667, 430/B/52A.
11   '"Government's Courageous Trade Policy", Press Release, Prime Minister's Department, 1 June 1936', in Prime Minister's Department: Records relating to the Imperial Conference, 1937, NAA: CP4/2, 33.
12   *CPD: Representatives*, 22 May 1936, No. 21, 2213.
13   'The Trade Diversion Policy, [n.d. (1937)]', NAA: A1667, 430/B/52A.

against the United States' developed and heavily subsidised industries.[14] The Department of Trade and Customs estimated an annual gain of more than £580,000 in increased sales from Australia's secondary industries as a result of the new measures affecting the US.[15]

While the US was undeniably a bad customer, the same could not be said of Japan. That nation's response was swift and harsh. On 25 June 1936, the Japanese government announced a boycott of Australian wool purchases. A special import duty of 50 per cent was also introduced for other Australian goods. The Australian government retaliated by placing licensing restrictions on a further 38 classes of Japanese exports.[16] The two nations were locked in a trade war.

The inconsistency of trade diversion in Australia's recent trade relations with Japan sparked a great deal of criticism among the Australian public. R.L. Curthoys, former editor of Melbourne's *The Argus* and an Australian correspondent for *The Times* of London, concluded that the policy was 'a complete repudiation' of the 1934 AEM and the appointment of a trade commissioner in Tokyo, 'the obvious implication' of which was 'that Australia intended to do more business with her Pacific neighbours'.[17]

Among the most vocal in their criticism of trade diversion were, unsurprisingly, Australian wool producers. Prior to May 1936, Australia had provided Japan with an estimated 85–95 per cent of its raw wool requirements—one-quarter of Australia's total annual wool clip.[18] Joseph P. Abbott, Vice-Chairman of the Australian Woolgrowers' Council and President of the Graziers' Association of New South Wales, described Japan's wool purchases as having sustained the Australian wool industry during the Great Depression and being 'an outstanding factor' in the nation's ongoing economic recovery.[19] The architects of trade diversion had initially assumed that Japan's dependence on Australian wool would force the nation to negotiate a quick settlement and accept a voluntary

---

14   ibid.
15   *CPD: Representatives*, 22 May 1936, No. 21, 2214. It was estimated that more than £1.7 million in trade would be diverted annually from the US. For a recent assessment of the impact of trade diversion on Australian–US commercial relations, see Shannon Tow, *Independent Ally: Australia in an Age of Power Transition* (Melbourne: Melbourne University Press, 2017), 84–113.
16   R.D. Westmore, 'Japan and the Trade Diversion Policy', *The Australian Quarterly* 9, no. 1 (1937): 93–6, at p. 95.
17   R.L. Curthoys, 'Australia in the Changing East', *Foreign Affairs* 15, no. 4 (1937): 750–6, at p. 752.
18   Cumpston, 'The Australian–Japanese Dispute of the Nineteen-Thirties', 50.
19   'Statement by Vice-Chairman of Australian Woolgrowers' Council, J.P. Abbott, at deputation to Prime Minister, J.A. Lyons, 17 July 1936', in Copland and Janes, *Australian Trade Policy*, 295.

textile quota. Although Australian wool was preferable, Japan was able to meet its needs by importing from South Africa.[20] With the boycott in place and an alternative wool supply sourced, the value of Japan's wool purchases from Australia fell by almost 50 per cent between 1935–36 and 1936–37.[21] During the 1937 annual conference of the Graziers' Association of New South Wales, an irate Abbott restated the damages of trade diversion, remarking that wool was Australia's 'lifeblood' and 'those who would cut us off from our international markets would cut the carotid artery of the nation and bleed Australia to death'.[22]

For Abbott and his contemporaries, it appeared that Australia's commercial interests had been sacrificed on the 'altar of Imperial sentiment'.[23] In addition to the higher import duties on foreign textiles introduced under trade diversion, the imperial preference tariff on British textiles was lowered.[24] In terms of fiscal returns, Britain was the largest benefactor of trade diversion. Of the estimated £2.3 million that would be diverted annually from bad customers, £1.3 million would benefit British producers. Australia expected to receive considerably less at £845,000. The remanding trade would be diverted to other good customers, predominantly within the Empire.[25] To critics of trade diversion, the government appeared to have disregarded Japan's competitive advantage in textile production, along with the benefits to Australian consumers of affordable manufactured goods, in an attempt to protect British trade interests.[26]

Following Japan's retaliatory actions, Australian Prime Minister Joseph Lyons offered his government's justification for the trade diversion measures in a nationwide radio broadcast. Lyons lay 'the entire

---

20  'Longfield Lloyd to Murphy, 16 June 1936', NAA: A1667, 194/B/4/A/2 Part 1.
21  Japan's wool purchases from Australia for 1935–36 totalled £14.6 million; for 1936–37, wool purchases totalled only £7.5 million. *Official Year Book of the Commonwealth of Australia*, No. 30 (1937), 511, and No. 31 (1938), 515.
22  'Address of the President of the Graziers' Association of NSW, J.P. Abbott, at Twentieth Annual Conference, 1 Mach 1937', in Copland and Janes, *Australian Trade Policy*, 298.
23  Edward Masey, *Is It Necessary? An Examination of the Commonwealth Government's Trade Diversion Policy* (Sydney: Stafford Printing, 1936), 11.
24  *CPD: Representatives*, 22 May 1936, No. 21, 2215–17.
25  ibid., 2214; Earl Page, *Truant Surgeon: The Inside Story of Forty Years of Australian Political Life*, ed. Ann Mozley (Sydney: Angus & Robertson, 1963), 246. These figures did not account for motor vehicle chassis—exports of which received a separate licensing system and duties to account for British Empire member Canada's proximity to the US—nor benefits to Lancashire, which were estimated at £10 million annually.
26  Masey, *Is It Necessary*, 3, 10, 14–18; 'Press Statement by the Premier of Queensland, William Forgan Smith, 28 December 1936', in Copland and Janes, *Australian Trade Policy*, 323.

responsibility' for trade diversion at the foot of Japan and its textile exporters, who had 'continuously and drastically' reduced the prices of their goods beyond reasonable competition. The Australian textile market had traditionally been reserved for British exports. As Japan's prices fell, the market in Australia for British textiles 'was doomed to extinction'.[27] In 1932, Britain had sold 167 million square yards (140 million sq m) of cotton piece goods and 8 million square yards (6.7 million sq m) of rayon piece goods to Australia. By 1935, this had fallen to 90 million square yards (75.3 million sq m) and 7.25 million square yards (6 million sq m). In 1932, foreign producers—for the most part, Japanese—accounted for 40 million square yards (33.4 million sq m) of cotton piece goods and 13 million square yards (10.9 million sq m) of rayon piece goods. By 1935, this had increased to 90 million square yards and 68.5 million square yards (57.3 million sq m), respectively.[28] Trade diversion sought to arrest this.

Lyons argued that Australia refused to 'weaken in its firm resolve to adhere to its Empire trade treaty obligations and—above and beyond all material considerations—to the Empire bond'. Britain's textile market was closely linked to Australia's overseas trade. Australia had a narrow range of primary exports and relied on British purchases.[29] In the past, textile purchases from Britain had partially offset Britain's immense purchases from Australia. However, as Australia's market for British textiles contracted—Japan having replaced Britain as Australia's largest textile supplier in 1934—the nation could not expect Britain to continue purchasing large volumes of its exports. Lyons pointed out that if sales to Britain fell Australia would 'sell very little indeed' anywhere else, leaving the nation's farmers and graziers to 'face ruin'. Valuable as trade with Japan was, for every pound it spent in Australia, Britain spent four. Moreover, Japan's purchases were centred on wool and wheat, while Britain purchased from across Australia's primary and incipient secondary sectors.[30]

---

27  '"The Truth about the Japanese Trade Position", Lyons broadcast, 25 June 1936', NAA: A981, Trad 68 Part 2.
28  *CPD: Representatives*, 22 May 1936, No. 21, 2214–15.
29  Britain was Australia's best overall customer, purchasing nearly 50 per cent of Australia's total overseas trade. *Official Year Book of the Commonwealth of Australia*, No. 30 (1937), 506.
30  '"The Truth about the Japanese Trade Position", Lyons broadcast, 25 June 1936', NAA: A981, Trad 68 Part 2.

THE GENESIS OF A POLICY

The Trade Diversion Policy overlapped with attempts by the Australian government to increase its beef exports to Britain. Tsokhas argues that trade diversion pandered to imperial sentiment and the appearance of sacrifices in the Japanese market in the interest of British textile manufacturers in exchange for a privileged position for Australian meat and other primary produce in the British market.[31] While government documents confirm that exports to Britain did shape the Australian government's approach to trade diversion, Tsokhas's assessment disregards the strategic object of the economic and diplomatic relations Australia had cultivated with Japan over the previous half-decade. These activities are rendered as little more than part of a broader political ploy designed to pressure the British government. This is a misrepresentation of the relationship between the domestic and international spheres in Australian decision-making. To understand what motivated the Australian government to adopt trade diversion and the protracted process of arriving at this decision, we must consider events unfolding prior to 22 May 1936.

## Pressure, protectionism and Australia's reluctance to act against Japan

Some have diminished the significance of the Australian–Japanese trade treaty negotiations, suggesting Australia was only making a show in the hope this would placate Japan without having to make any definite commitment. Tsokhas only gives the negotiations passing mention and Sandra Tweedie writes that 'far from contemplating a treaty', Australian officials actively sought to resist Japan, and it was only after 'insistent Japanese demands' that the nation finally yielded.[32] These assessments do not acknowledge the intersection of Australia's trade interests with diplomatic and broader strategic interests in the years preceding trade diversion, nor the nation's reluctance to act against Japan in the face of British pressure.

Japan's textile industry was highly organised, modern and, due to lower wages and longer working hours, competitively priced. The British textile industry was slow to adopt modern techniques like mass production

---

31   Tsokhas, *Markets, Money and Empire*, 12–15, 105–9; Tsokhas, 'The Wool Industry and the 1936 Trade Diversion Dispute Between Australia and Japan', 442–4.
32   Tsokhas, *Markets, Money and Empire*, 105; Tweedie, *Trading Partners*, 141–5.

and consisted of hundreds of small, independent units. This resulted in unnecessary administrative costs, a lack of cooperation and ineffective production.[33] Japan's competitive advantage saw the nation replace Britain as the world's largest cotton market in 1933.[34]

The textile producers in Lancashire, who held significant political leverage, lobbied Whitehall to limit Japan's competitive advantage.[35] There was particular embitterment surrounding Australia's textile purchases from Japan. The Australian government's slow action on implementing the Ottawa Agreements further exacerbated this situation. Australia had failed to comprehensively reduce tariffs so as to treat British producers as domestic competitors, even increasing duties to protect its emerging cotton industry despite an adverse effect on Lancashire.[36] British textile producers directly contacted Lyons and Bruce, High Commissioner in London, calling on Australia to use anti-dumping duties against Japan and act on 'the *principles* for which it accepted responsibility at Ottawa'.[37] The British Foreign Office and Tariff Board also criticised Japan, accusing the nation's producers of extensive cost-cutting. The Tariff Board accordingly recommended that members of the Empire enforce anti-dumping duties against Japan to protect the British textile market.[38] Despite this pressure, the Australian government refused to adopt prohibitive measures on the grounds that Japanese textiles, dumped or otherwise, did not directly compete with Australian exports. In ignoring the recommendations of the Tariff Board, Australia had contravened the Ottawa Agreements.[39] It is worth recalling that the Tariff Board recommendations came soon

---

33   A. Trotter, *Britain and East Asia, 1933–1937* (London: Cambridge University Press, 1975), 27–9; Masey, *Is It Necessary*, 10–15.
34   Sissons, 'Manchester v. Japan', 490.
35   Antony Best, 'Economic Appeasement or Economic Nationalism? A Political Perspective on the British Empire, Japan and the Rise of Intra-Empire Trade, 1933–37', *The Journal of Imperial and Commonwealth History* 30, no. 2 (2002): 77–101, at pp. 81–4.
36   Bernard Attard, 'The Limits of Influence: The Political Economy of Australian Commercial Policy After the Ottawa Conference', *Australian Historical Studies* 29, no. 111 (1998): 325–43, at pp. 330–2; Felicity Barnes, 'Lancashire's "War" with Australia: Rethinking Anglo-Australian Trade and the Cultural Economy of Empire, 1934–36', *The Journal of Imperial and Commonwealth History* 46, no. 4 (2018): 707–30, at pp. 707, 713–18.
37   'Manchester Chamber of Commerce to Lyons, 17 August 1932', in Australian High Commission, United Kingdom [London]: Correspondence files, multiple number series (Class 400), 1913–60, NAA: A2910, 413/5/135 Part 1; 'W.H. Milsted and Sons to Bruce, 14 February 1933', NAA: A2910, 413/5/135 [emphasis in original].
38   '"Japanese Competition", Memorandum by the Board of Trade, 11 December 1933', in Records created or inherited by the Foreign Office, Foreign Office and Foreign and Commonwealth Office: Embassy and Consulates, Egypt—General Correspondence, TNA: FO 141/755/7.
39   Cumpston, 'The Australian–Japanese Dispute of the Nineteen-Thirties', 51.

after the Manchurian Crisis and Australia's rejection of sanctions against Japan based on economic and security imperatives. Against this backdrop, Australia's response can be better understood.

As the British government and manufacturers encouraged greater protectionism, Australia continued to explore opportunities in Japan. During the AEM, Australia again quietly defied the principles of imperial economic cooperation. Saburō Kurusu, Director of the Commercial Bureau in the Japanese Department of Foreign Affairs, expressed his government's 'keen appreciation' for Australia's decision not to implement anti-dumping duties. Arthur Moore, an information officer from the Department of Trade and Customs who was part of the AEM, emphasised 'the difficult political position' in which Australia had been placed as a result of rejecting the Tariff Board's recommendations, remarking that this 'showed very clearly its regard for maintaining friendly relations with Japan' and was 'concrete evidence of the value placed on Japanese trading relations with our country'.[40]

Britain made a renewed effort to emphasise the expectations of imperial economic reciprocity in 1935. As preparations for the 1935 Leaders' Meeting began, the British government indicated that trade measures to strengthen imperial economic relations would take precedence in the forthcoming discussions. Australia's poor performance in implementing the Ottawa Agreements was singled out by Secretary of State for Dominion Affairs James Henry Thomas. He described it as 'a source of difficulty to the commercial relations between the two countries', which had given 'rise to much dissatisfaction on the part of trade organisations in the United Kingdom'.[41] Lyons responded to Thomas's criticism with his own litany of complaints about the Ottawa system. The Australian government was preparing for trade treaty negotiations with Japan and Lyons informed Thomas that the Ottawa Agreements presented 'obstacles which at present appear unsurmountable' as the ambit of imperial preferences left Australia with little scope to offer foreign countries greater access to its market. Australia's restricted access to foreign markets would make it difficult for the nation to increase export revenue and, in turn, increase purchases from the British market.[42] Lyons asked that some of the Ottawa preference margins be narrowed and requested that Bruce 'stress' in London that

---

40 'Confidential Report on Trade, 30 July 1934', NAA: A981, Far 5 Part 16.
41 'Thomas to Lyons, 2 January 1935', NAA: A1667, 430/B/22A.
42 'Lyons to Thomas, 4 January 1935', NAA: A1667, 430/B/22A.

a 'number of foreign countries have been penalising Australia because of Ottawa Margins'.[43] The British government resolved that the margins would remain unchanged.[44] This appeal indicates Australia's seriousness in its approach to trade treaty negotiations with Japan and that the nation had not, as Tweedie suggests, entered into negotiations under duress. Moreover, the reluctance to act against Japan despite British pressure suggests Australia judged the value of close economic and diplomatic relations with Japan outweighed the ideal of imperial reciprocity.

## Trade promotion in Britain

There was a marked change in Australia's position towards the Ottawa Agreements and British textiles from early 1936. The reason for this can be found in Australia's overseas trade position. In 1935, foreign markets accounted for most of Britain's beef supply. Britain's trade treaty with Argentina, a major beef exporter, was due to expire in December 1935 and the nation was looking to increase frozen and tinned beef purchases in the renewed treaty. The new treaty would result in a further reduction of British purchases from Australia and the other dominions. With meat making up a significant portion of Australian exports, the Australian government deemed Britain's plans to be 'inconsistent with the spirit and intention of the Ottawa Agreement'.[45] While in London for the Leaders' Meeting, Lyons and Gullett lobbied the British government to introduce higher import duties and quotas in the interest of improving the position of Australian beef. They were unsuccessful in this undertaking.[46]

Lyons remained in London for some weeks following the Leaders' Meeting. During this time, he met with representatives from the Tariff Board and the Lancashire Chamber of Commerce. While little detail was given about these meetings in the local press, a cable from the Dominions Office reveals the representatives urged Lyons to 'take action that will safeguard Lancashire's important trade to Australia', making clear that unless Australia upheld the principles of economic reciprocity, the nation

---

43  'Lyons to Bruce, 7 February 1935', NAA: A981, Trad 68 Part 2.
44  Drummond, *Imperial Economic Policy, 1917–1939*, 397–8.
45  'Lyons to Thomas, 4 January 1935', NAA: A1667, 430/B/22A.
46  Sissons, 'Manchester v. Japan', 495–6; Tsokhas, *Markets, Money and Empire*, 107.

could expect its share in the British market to shrink.[47] In view of Australia's narrow range of primary exports and reliance on British purchases, the British government and Lancashire had sent a clear message: Australia would not long survive without the British market for its goods. Lyons indicated that he would bring the issues discussed before his government.[48]

The months following Lyons' return home from London were marked by grim news. The US had again rejected Australia's offer of a trade agreement.[49] This was exacerbated by low wool sales in 1934–35, which greatly depleted Australia's reserves, and a rise in the prices of wool and wheat in 1935–36, triggering an escalation of imports while exports increased only marginally. It seemed likely that Australia would, for the second consecutive year, face a balance-of-payments deficit and be forced to default on loan repayments to Britain and the US.[50] Faced with this situation, Cabinet conceded on 23 January 1936 that some action should be taken to reduce the volume of Japanese textile purchases in favour of British exporters.[51]

Soon after Gullett began drafting proposed quotas for Japanese textiles, a delegation from the Manchester Chamber of Commerce arrived in Australia. The Manchester Mission was headed by H.C.N. Ellis, Special Commissioner for Trade for the Manchester Chamber of Commerce, and Ernest Thompson, the chamber's former president. The mission was designed to mobilise support for prohibitive measures against the Japanese textiles that had 'invaded' the Australian market and discuss measures to 'secure the maximum demand' for Australian exports in the British market.[52] With the Australian government having already decided to introduce quantitative restrictions, this pressure was no longer

---

47 'Thomas to Isaacs (Governor-General) 15 August 1935', in Records created or inherited by the Dominions Office, and of the Commonwealth Relations and Foreign and Commonwealth Offices, General Records of the Dominions Office, TNA: DO 35/284/1.
48 'Mr Lyons in Manchester', *Telegraph*, [Brisbane], 13 June 1935, 13.
49 Australia's offer of a trade treaty had been rejected in January 1935, yet the nation continued to inquire throughout 1935 and early 1936 whether the US had changed its position. 'Doc. 13, Memorandum by Hull (Secretary of State), 9 July 1935' and 'Doc. 14, Hull to Moffatt (Consul-General Sydney), 23 September 1935', in Churchill and Sappington, *FRUS 1935*.
50 'Adoption of Trade Diversion Policy, 1937', NAA: A1667, 430/B/52A; 'Doc. 582, Moffat to Hull, 4 March 1936', in Matilda F. Axton, Rogers P. Churchill, N.O. Sappington, John G. Reid, Francis C. Prescott and Shirley L. Phillips (eds), *Foreign Relations of the United States Diplomatic Papers, 1936, General, British Commonwealth, Volume I* (Washington, DC: US Government Printing Office, 1953).
51 'Cabinet Meeting, 23 January 1936', in Secretary to Cabinet/Cabinet Secretariat: Lyons and Page Ministries—Folders and bundles of minutes and submissions, 1932–39, NAA: A2694, 245.
52 'Plea for Trade', *Sydney Morning Herald*, 13 March 1936, 11.

necessary. Nevertheless, the Manchester Mission highlights the logic that had influenced the Australian government's decision to act against Japan: Britain could not be expected to continue its preference for Australian goods without reciprocal treatment.

The Australian government was candid in its expectation that trade diversion would afford inroads for Australian beef into the British market. In a 10 May 1936 cable to British Prime Minister Stanley Baldwin, Lyons outlined the trade diversion measures. He couched the policy in the language of imperial economic cooperation and stressed his expectation that his government's actions would 'receive full compensation in [the form of] increased British imports from Australia'.[53] Lyons restated this in a cable sent to Baldwin the following week, writing that the trade diversion measures concerning textiles had been 'made to meet the express wishes of your government' and were expected to result in 'very substantial and increasing benefits' for British textile manufacturers. Lyons, noting that these measures would likely elicit retaliatory action from Japan, stressed that his government looked 'to these restrictions to confer benefit upon Australia by increasing opportunity for our exports in the United Kingdom'.[54] There was a willingness among Australian policymakers to act in favour of imperial interests on the basis of what would be received in return. Baldwin replied that the trade diversion measures would 'be of material assistance … and we greatly appreciate them'. He also informed Lyons that 'we share your hope' that trade diversion will 'help to solve the particular problems of Australia'.[55] It appeared that Britain endorsed Australia's actions and the anticipated returns in the British market. This enthusiasm soon dissipated.

In April 1936, Page and Robert Menzies, the Attorney-General and Minister for Industry, left for London to discuss Australian beef sales. The British government offered an increased duty on foreign beef and a restriction on the volume of Argentinian chilled beef sales in favour of cheaper frozen beef. The dominions would be free to fill this newly vacant market for chilled beef. However, the actual volume of dominion and Argentinian beef sales would not change, being set at existing levels.[56]

---

53  'Lyons to Baldwin, 10 May 1936', TNA: DO 35/278/3.
54  'Lyons to Baldwin, 18 May 1936', TNA: DO 35/278/3.
55  'MacDonald (Under-Secretary of State for Dominion Affairs) to Prime Minister's Department, 20 May 1936', in Department of Trade and Customs: Correspondence files, annual single number series [Main correspondence files series of the agency], 1935–, NAA: A425, 1939/2673. MacDonald was speaking on behalf of Baldwin.
56  Sissons, 'Manchester v. Japan', 496–7.

Page described this offer as 'useless' and a betrayal of the principles of Ottawa.[57] It was only through the intervention of Lyons—who stressed that a failure to deliver on beef and legitimate the trade war with Japan would likely lead to a loss of government—that Australia was able to secure a small concession. The British Cabinet agreed to a 5 per cent increase in Australia's chilled beef exports over three years at the expense of foreign suppliers.[58] Australia's hard-fought concession suggests trade diversion was introduced with an implied rather than a clear agreement that Britain would reciprocate with preferential treatment of Australian beef.[59] The Australian government ultimately misjudged the dynamics of the imperial relationship, in which Australia was expected to make sacrifices in the name of imperial economic cooperation, while Britain would not necessarily reciprocate.

## Defence and Australia's secondary industries

The Trade Diversion Policy cannot be divorced from defence planning and Australia's strategic outlook. The year 1936 was one of turmoil in international affairs. Nazi Germany violated the Treaty of Versailles, Locarno Treaties and League of Nations Covenant when the German Army reoccupied and remilitarised the Rhineland in March 1936. The year also marked the lapse of the Washington Treaties and Japan's withdrawal from the second London Naval Conference and the Treaty for the Limitation and Reduction of Naval Armament following Britain and the United States' rejection of Japan's demand for naval parity. These developments spelt doom for collective security, drew attention to the influence of the military in the Japanese government's policymaking and, as Melbourne's *Herald* grimly concluded, left Japan with 'a free hand in the Pacific'.[60]

---

57 'Telephone call, Page, Lyons and Gullett, 24 June 1936', in Papers of J.A. Lyons, NLA: MS 4851/1/10.
58 'Minutes of Meeting, Cabinet Committee on Trade and Agriculture, 24 June 1936, TNA: CAB 27/619', cited in Sissons, 'Manchester v. Japan', 498.
59 O'Brien, 'Empire v. National Interest in Australian–British Relations During the 1930s', 582; Paul Jones, 'Trading in a "Fool's Paradise"? White Australia and the Trade Diversion Dispute of 1936', in *Relationships: Japan and Australia, 1870s – 1950s*, eds Vera Mackie and Paul Jones (Melbourne: University of Melbourne, Department of History, 2001), 137.
60 'Japan Upsets Naval Parleys', *The Herald*, [Melbourne], 15 January 1936, 1.

Australia began rearming in 1933, with a particular focus on modernising its defence equipment. Rearmament depended on a stable financial situation—achieved through consistently strong exports—and an established domestic secondary industry with access to strategic materials such as steel and iron. That defence and rearmament considerations influenced trade diversion is evidenced in Gullett's remark that the policy, in promoting the development of Australia's secondary industries, would 'make a significant indirect contribution to defence'.[61] Lyons also spoke to the relationship between trade diversion and imperial defence, invoking the maxim of 'Men, Money and Markets' in a cable to Baldwin by suggesting that the growth in Australia's secondary industries prompted by trade diversion would encourage intra-empire migration, making 'a useful and timely … contribution to Empire defence'.[62] While trade diversion was not predicated on defence considerations, it was certainly shaped by Australia's pre-existing concerns about regional stability and defence planning for the Asia-Pacific region.

## Australia's strategic outlook in the aftermath of trade diversion

The Australia–Japan trade war was short-lived, arguably because the conclusion of the semi-successful beef negotiations in June removed the imperative for a hardline position towards Japan. In August, Australia amended the duties on foreign textiles 'as a gesture of amiability' and, by December, a settlement had been made.[63] Japan removed the 50 per cent tariff on Australian goods and the boycott on Australian wool, while Australian duties on foreign textiles were again lowered. In the 18 months from 1 January 1937, Japanese cotton and rayon exports entering Australia were restricted to a total of 102.5 million square yards (85.7 million sq m)—compared with the 152 million square yards (127 million sq m) Australia had purchased the previous year. Australia also granted Japan

---

61  *CPD: Representatives*, 22 May 1936, No. 21, 2211–12.
62  'Lyons to Baldwin, 18 May 1936', NAA: A425, 1939/2673. The Bruce–Page coalition adopted 'Men, Money and Markets' as the basis for economic development. The premise was that, in obtaining labour and capital from Britain for Australia's expanding secondary industries, products would be produced for purchase in British Empire markets with the benefit of protection under preferential tariffs. Growth in population from British migration could service Australia's new industries and could be called on to defend Australia and the Empire in the event of war.
63  'Abbott (Comptroller-General of Customs) to DEA, 24 August 1936', NAA: A981, Trad 68, Part 2.

the intermediate tariff rate. Japan agreed to purchase 800,000 bales of Australian wool for the same 18-month period. This quota fell well below the 1935–36 export volume when Japan had purchased 750,000 bales for the financial year.[64]

The new restriction on textile purchases accomplished Gullett's initial aim of a textile quota system that served to reserve a place for British textiles in the Australian market. Yet in achieving this goal, the Australian–Japanese trade relationship was seriously damaged and Australia's sales to Japan steadily decreased over the coming years.

**Table 3.1 Two-way trade between Australia and Japan, 1935–36 to 1938–39, pound sterling value and as a percentage of Australia's total exports**

| Fiscal year | Australian exports to Japan | |
|---|---|---|
| | % | Value (£ million, rounded up to nearest pound) |
| 1935–36 | 14.19 | 17.1 |
| 1936–37 | 6.54 | 9.7 |
| 1937–38 | 4.16 | 5.9 |
| 1938–39 | 3.97 | 4.9 |
| | Australian imports from Japan | |
| 1935–36 | 4.9 | 6.1 |
| 1936–37 | 4.0 | 4.5 |
| 1937–38 | 5.3 | 4.9 |
| 1938–39 | 4.1 | 4.2 |

Source: *Official Year Book of the Commonwealth of Australia*, No. 32 (Canberra: Commonwealth Government Printer, 1939), 507–10.

Along with the economic implications of trade diversion, the episode created fissures in Australian–Japanese diplomatic relations. In May 1936, on learning of Australia's intentions, Baron Goh, President of the Japanese Chamber of Commerce in Sydney, contacted Minister for External Affairs George Pearce. Goh believed the Japanese government regretted trade diversion and believed it would not only harm economic relations, but also 'invariably react on friendship and goodwill existing between us'.[65]

---

64  'Abbott to DEA, 22 September 1936' and 'Statement by Gullett, 27 December 1936', both in NAA: A981, Trad 68 Part 2. It was also agreed that Australia would purchase an extra 2 million square yards (1.82 million sq m) of cotton and rayon for every additional 10,000 bales of wool Japan purchased.
65  'Baron Goh (President of the Japanese Chamber of Commerce) to Pearce, 13 May 1936', NAA: A981, Trad 68 Part 2.

Australia's trade commissioner in Tokyo reported a similar feeling in Japan, noting the hostile and 'rather reckless attitude' of Japan's highly influential press.[66] From the Australian perspective, the risk was that trade diversion, having affronted Japan, could threaten national security. In the weeks before the policy was announced, Gullett himself acknowledged this threat when he confided in the British High Commissioner, Geoffrey Whiskard. This conversation was then reported to the Dominions Secretary, with Whiskard remarking that Gullett was 'definitely apprehensive' that trade diversion would 'lead eventually to trouble between Japan and Australia'. Gullett reportedly 'expounded at some length … the indefensibility of Australia against Japanese attack'.[67]

Australia's security concerns were no doubt amplified by developments on the international stage. In addition to broken and lapsed treaties, 1936 saw the Japanese government give official standing to the policy of *Nanshin-ron* ('southern advance' or 'southern road'), which defined the area south of Japan as 'indispensable' to the nation's industrial development, defence and growing population.[68] The diplomatic implications of trade diversion were all the more pressing against this backdrop of international uneasiness.

From May to June 1937, an Imperial Conference was convened to discuss imperial policy in light of the recent developments in Europe and the Asia-Pacific. The Australian delegation's performance at the conference can be best understood in the context of the diplomatic damage of trade diversion and Japan's increasingly outspoken foreign policy. The Australian delegation used the Imperial Conference as an opportunity to revisit and clarify imperial defence planning, submitting a list of defence-related questions to the Chiefs of Staff Committee (COS). Particular attention was given to the Far East and the intended strategy in the event of a two-ocean war. Australia requested 'a clear definition of the strategic objective of the Empire forces in a war with Japan or with Japan and another first-class power'. Britain's response was discouraging, stating that, in the event of war with Japan and Germany, Europe would be the priority and 'we cannot count on being able to support anything more

---

66  'Longfield Lloyd to Murphy, 28 May 1936', NAA: A601, 402/17/28.
67  'Whiskard to MacDonald, 24 April 1936, TNA: FO 3097/119/23', cited in Sissons, 'Manchester v. Japan', 482.
68  Henry P. Frei, *Japan's Southward Advance and Australia: From the Sixteenth Century to World War II* (Melbourne: Melbourne University Press, 1991), 140–3. *Nanshin-ron* was codified in two documents, the 'Fundamentals of National Policy' and 'Guidelines of Imperial Diplomacy'.

than a defensive policy in the Far East'. The British also noted that 'a very considerable period may elapse' before the situation in Europe was settled and 'the redistribution of our forces permit[s] of a fleet arriving in the Far East'.[69] The 1937 Imperial Conference confirmed that the Singapore Naval Strategy was not the bastion of imperial defence it was purported to have been and Australia was left to face an increasingly uncertain future in its region.

Prime Minister Lyons used the Imperial Conference to promote diplomacy to offset reservations about imperial defence planning for the Asia-Pacific. Following the lapse of the Washington Treaties and Japan's withdrawal from the London Naval Conference, Yoshida Shigeru, the Japanese Ambassador in London, proposed an Anglo-Japanese agreement be negotiated as a replacement. He proposed mutual recognition of all existing Japanese territorial claims in China, an open-door policy and the settlement of trade competition 'on a basis of goodwill and mutual understanding of each other's difficulties'.[70] This proposal was 'naturally desirable' to the Australian government. Britain's response, however, was, according to a DEA memorandum, 'lukewarm'.[71] Lyons took it on himself to find a solution to Asia-Pacific peace. In his opening address to the first plenary session of the Imperial Conference, Lyons revived his 'Pacific pact'. His proposal was based on a broad vision of regional understanding and non-aggression between the British Empire, Japan and the US.[72] The proposal was received with only middling support and it faced insurmountable challenges: chiefly, the United States' and Britain's fraught relations with Japan, particularly in the wake of the London Naval Conference, and the ongoing question of Chinese–Japanese relations made negotiating a Pacific pact difficult. As had been the case at the 1935 Leaders' Meeting, Lyons' plans for Asia-Pacific peace were laid aside.[73] Despite the failure of the Pacific pact, on reflection, the episode is insightful. It underscores the shift in approaches to integrate Australia's national interest within the imperial policymaking framework at a time

---

69 '"Questions Raised by the Australian Delegation", Report of British COS, 9 June 1937', NAA: A5954, 1064/3.
70 R.G. Neale (ed.), *Documents on Australian Foreign Policy, 1937–49. Volume 1: 1937–1938* (Canberra: AGPS, 1976) [hereinafter *DAFP*, vol. 1], 36n.1.
71 'Doc. 13, "Review of Relations with Particular Countries having Special Significance vis-a-vis the United Kingdom or Particular Dominions", Memorandum prepared for Delegation to Imperial Conference, [n.d. (on or before 6 March 1937)]', in Neale, *DAFP*, vol. 1.
72 'Doc. 25, Speech by Lyons, First plenary session of Imperial Conference, 14 May 1937', in Neale, *DAFP*, vol. 1.
73 Bird, *J.A. Lyons*, 203–4; Waters, *Australia and Appeasement*, 21–5.

when many scholars suggest the nation's policymakers had neither the appetite nor the aptitude for such thinking. The Pacific pact episode also highlights the challenges the small nation faced in attempting to influence its powerful allies.

Both the diplomatic shortfalls of trade diversion and the disappointing outcome of the 1937 Imperial Conference were more pressing in the face of the outbreak of the Second Sino-Japanese War. In July, soon after the Australian delegation returned from the Imperial Conference, Japanese troops attacked and eventually invaded China. Lyons lamented the conflict, even suggesting it could have been avoided had his Pacific pact been taken up:

> I am very sorry that some action on the line of the Pact I proposed was not taken earlier. If something of this kind had been in existence before this trouble in the east, it is possible that some pressure might have been applied to prevent the tragic events that are now occurring.[74]

At the time, international affairs commentator Jack Shepherd drew a link between the Trade Diversion Policy and Japan's attack on China. Trade diversion served to exclude Japan from an important market, contributing to a sense that it was being 'deprived of the very means of her existence'. According to Shepherd, this hastened Japan's campaign for regional conquest in pursuit of raw materials.[75]

While Shepherd's theory is a striking one and Japan's need for raw resources was a motivating factor in its policy of aggressive expansion, it is difficult to substantiate the link between trade diversion and the outbreak of the Second Sino-Japanese War. It can, however, be reasonably concluded that Japan saw in trade diversion an attempt to build an exclusive imperial economic bloc, contributing to a sense of being threatened and a subsequent need to economically and territorially penetrate the Far East. This proposition is in part supported by a letter Lyons received from A.C.V. Melbourne, who liaised with the Australian government and Japanese Consul-General in Australia during the settlement of the Trade

---

74 'Fighting Speech', *Sydney Morning Herald*, 1 October 1937, 9.
75 Shepherd, *Australia's Interests and Policies in the Far East*, 190–1.

Diversion Policy. Melbourne wrote that the 'British aspect' of Australian foreign policy had been 'overemphasised' and subsequently estranged and offended Japan.[76]

At any rate, the trade diversion episode was a significant lesson for Australian policymakers, highlighting the liability of relying on the Empire for economic and physical security. Indeed, it informed experimentation by policymakers as accommodating Japan came to dominate Australia's foreign policy approach in the coming years as the Asia-Pacific region moved towards war.

---

76  'Melbourne to Lyons, 22 July 1936, Papers of A.C.V. Melbourne, NLA: Mfm G 14442–14446', cited in Cotton, *The Australian School of International Relations*, 82.

# PART 2

# 4

# 'A chronic lack of self-reliance'? Australia's response to the coming Pacific War, 1937–41

By 1937, war had reached the Asia-Pacific region and the world was once again drifting towards global conflict. This was likely to be a war in which Japan and Australia would be enemies. It is easy to believe that the Australia of the interwar years—a remote colonial outpost yet to assume full autonomy from Britain in foreign policy—could stand idly by, failing to prepare as war drifted towards its shores. This situation was seemingly the result of a 'chronic lack of self-reliance', as the Australian government could, according to David Day, 'see no alternative to historic[al] reliance on Britain'.[1] Others, such as John McCarthy and Ian Hamill, have offered a more measured appraisal, acknowledging that Australia realised its strategic needs differed from those of Britain and, at times, attempted to articulate this. They nevertheless conclude that, when Australia failed to deliver meaningful changes in imperial defence planning, the nation remained wedded to the Singapore Strategy.[2] Australia's disillusion was

---

1    David Horner, *High Command: Australia's Struggle for an Independent War Strategy, 1939–45*, 2nd edn (Sydney: Allen & Unwin, 1992), 15; David Day, '27 December 1941 Prime Minister Curtin's New Year Message: Australia "Looks to America"', in *Turning Points in Australian History*, eds Martin Crotty and David Roberts (Sydney: UNSW Press, 2008), 131.
2    John McCarthy, *Australia and Imperial Defence 1918–39: A Study in Air and Sea Power* (Brisbane: University of Queensland Press, 1976); Hamill, *The Strategic Illusion*.

duly revealed in December 1941 when two RN capital ships, HMS *Prince of Wales* and HMS *Repulse*, were sunk by the Japanese and, in February 1942, with the fall of Singapore.[3]

Instead, this chapter examines how Australian policymakers, having drawn on the lessons of the interwar years, were acutely aware of the limitations of imperial defence planning for the Asia-Pacific region and adopted a much more proactive policy in response. In the same vein as the Allies' approach to the European aggressors, Australia coupled rearmament with appeasement. Eastern appeasement centred on coercive diplomacy, aiming to deter Japanese aggression for long enough to allow for military preparation. In the absence of an adequate security assurance from Britain, the Australian government was also looking beyond the Empire to the US, using diplomatic pathways to draw the US into Asia-Pacific affairs and extract a military guarantee. By shifting the focus from Australia's material preparation for the coming Pacific War, Australia's independent diplomatic efforts become apparent—efforts that sought to shape the circumstances under which the war took place.

## Rearming for a regional conflict

The economics and strategy of Australia's rearmament process have been documented widely elsewhere, but it is useful to consider the changing nature of the nation's defence preparations in view of the outbreak of the Second Sino-Japanese War and the diverging strategic priorities of Australia and Britain that resulted.[4]

The 1937 Imperial Conference was, as Andrew May has written, an 'instrument of change' in Australian defence planning.[5] Shortly after his return from the conference, Joseph Lyons was thrown into campaign mode for the upcoming federal election. The United Australia Party was

---

3 Day, *The Great Betrayal*, 1–16, 210–13, 234–56; Richard Waterhouse, 'Empire and Nation: Australian Popular Ideology and the Outbreak of the Pacific War', *History Australia* 12, no. 3 (2015): 30–54; Murfett, 'The Singapore Strategy', 97–201.
4 For instance, A.T. Ross, *Armed and Ready: The Industrial Development and Defence of Australia, 1900–1945* (Sydney: Turton & Armstrong, 1995); Albert Palazzo, 'The Overlooked Mission: Australia and Home Defence', in *Australia 1942: In the Shadow of War*, ed. Peter J. Dean (Cambridge, UK: Cambridge University Press, 2013), 53–69; Andrew May, 'Fortress Australia', in *Between Empire and Nation: Australia's External Relations from Federation Until the Second World War*, eds Carl Bridge and Bernard Attard (Melbourne: Australian Scholarly Publishing, 2000), 168–87.
5 May, 'Fortress Australia', 173.

returned to power in October. Part of the party's campaign agenda was a strong commitment to defence, including a new three-year rearmament program announced in September.[6] The 1937–39 program was the third in a series. Australia's first rearmament program was announced in September 1933 and the second in December 1935, both of which focused on modernisation.[7] Although Australia's economy was still recovering from the depression, the 1937–39 program was more intensive than those that had preceded it, combining expansion with modernisation. The forward estimate for the three-year budget was £43 million, marking deficit spending on defence for the first time since the end of World War I. Of this, £24.8 million was provided for new expenditure.[8]

More than an increase in expenditure, the new rearmament program suggested the nature of Australia's approach to defence was shifting. The navy was traditionally the priority in Australian and broader imperial defence strategy, while the army and air force were largely employed for the defence of Australian territory. Although this hierarchy changed very little in the new program, the air force was given increasing significance in terms of budgetary spending.[9] With its vulnerable coastline and seemingly dangerous neighbourhood to the north, Australia's primary concern was coastal attack. The mobility of aircraft—essential in deterring and defending against coastal raids—created a particularly important role for the Royal Australian Air Force (RAAF). Accordingly, the RAAF received the bulk of the new expenditure, £8.8 million, while the Royal Australian Navy (RAN) and the Army received £7.75 million and £5.5 million, respectively.[10] New coastal aircraft bases and anti-aircraft defences at major ports were proposed as part of the government's 'priority of provision in local defence'.[11]

Particular attention was given to Australia's vulnerable north, including the construction of two new bases, at Darwin, in the Northern Territory, and Amberley, in Queensland.[12] The bases were to be filled with new

---

6   Bird, *J.A. Lyons*, 200–3; *CPD: Representatives*, 8 September 1937, No. 36, 737–81.
7   Ross, *Armed and Ready*, 111.
8   Bird, *J.A. Lyons*, 202; Paul Hasluck, *Australia in the War of 1939–1945. Series 4: Civil. Volume I: The Government and the People, 1939–1941* (Canberra: Australian War Memorial, 1970), 102. New expenditure refers to costs beyond the maintenance of existing services. This initial estimate was later reduced.
9   May, 'Fortress Australia', 169, 174, 178; Ross, *Armed and Ready*, 113; Horner, *High Command*, 14.
10  Hasluck, *Australia in the War of 1939–1945*, 102.
11  *CPD: Representatives*, 8 September 1937, No. 36, 739–40.
12  'Report on Progress of the Defence Development Programme (1937–38 to 1940–41) to 30th September 1938', NAA: A5954, 1039/1.

aircraft purchases. Avro Anson and Avro Cadets, general-purpose British-manufactured craft, were selected for coastal reconnaissance, training and to deter against raids, while combat ranks were filled with 180 Bristol Beaufort torpedo bombers. It was intended that the two Avro-class craft would be supplied by Britain's Air Ministry. However, by mid-1939, with ongoing delivery problems, the Australian government began local construction, forming the Department of Aircraft Production. Australia's decision to produce aircraft locally resulted in one of the more contentious issues in the nation's aeronautical history, the Commonwealth Aircraft Corporation (CAC) Wirraway. The Wirraway was a CAC (the Broken Hill Propriety Limited–led syndicate) adaptation of the American NA-16 light trainer, refitted with a simple undercarriage, bombs and a gun rack. Despite its original design as a trainer, the Wirraway was championed by Defence Minister Archdale Parkhill as a general-purpose aircraft, with diverse roles as a 'fighter, [in] army cooperation duties, reconnaissance tasks' and as a 'light bomber and advanced trainer'. The Wirraway was committed to frontline operations just once, in the Battle of Rabaul, only to be shot down by the vastly superior Japanese A6M Zero.[13]

Australia admittedly made some questionable decisions about rearmament, including the quality and suitability of some equipment. Nevertheless, policymakers were keenly aware of the nation's discrete defence requirements and sought to acquire equipment that would protect it and deter against future aggression.

## Eastern appeasement

Australia may have been coordinating a more self-reliant defence policy, yet these measures would be useless unless time was created in which to implement them. The Australian government, accordingly, pursued appeasement in tandem with rearmament. Although the two may appear contradictory, rearmament was characterised as defensive rather than offensive and a contingency if appeasement failed.[14]

---

13   Butlin, *Australia in the War of 1939–45*, 267–8; Horner, *High Command*, 13–15; '"Supply of Arms to Foreign Powers Statement of Air Craft and Aero Engines Under Construction and Release for Sale", Air Ministry, 20 June 1939', cited in McCarthy, *Australia and Imperial Defence 1918–39*, 103.
14   Bird, *J.A. Lyons*, 200–2.

The 1936 trade diversion episode had ruptured Australia's carefully curated diplomatic and economic relations with Japan and the government set out to rebuild them. The earliest expression of eastern appeasement following trade diversion can be identified in Australia's response to the Second Sino-Japanese War. In much the same manner as it had responded to the Manchurian Crisis, the Australian government attempted to remain impartial, promoting international consultation as the means to a resolution.

Australia's position varied from that of Britain, which, like much of the international community, had condemned Japan's actions.[15] Following the outbreak of war between China and Japan, the General Assembly of the League of Nations recommended a conference of the Nine-Power Treaty members with the hope of encouraging consultation and a resolution.[16] Both Australia and Britain were signatories of the Nine-Power Treaty and, prior to the conference proceedings, the British government privately indicated its belief that effective consultation between Japan and China was improbable, necessitating economic sanctions against the Japanese. In the case of sanctions, the Dominion Secretary Malcolm MacDonald anticipated 'a very real danger of Japan taking violent action to prevent their [the sanctions] success'. He recommended that all countries intending to impose sanctions provide a mutual 'assurance of military support in the event of violent Japanese retaliation'.[17] What MacDonald had suggested was a fatalistic acceptance that armed conflict with Japan was inevitable and imminent. This position would force Australia to abandon eastern appeasement and drift towards a war for which it was not yet ready.

In the interim between MacDonald's cable (19 October 1937) and Australia's reply (28 October 1937), Lyons stated publicly that 'the settlement of differences between nations should be sought, not by recourse to force, but by methods of cooperation and conciliation'.[18] It was of little surprise, then, when the Australian government rejected the proposed economic sanctions, making clear it would only 'consult on the basis of conciliation' as it had been 'on this understanding that the

---

15  ibid., 227–8.
16  'Doc. 75, Bruce to Lyons, 6 October 1937', in Neale, *DAFP*, vol. 1.
17  'Doc. 83, MacDonald to Commonwealth Government, 19 October 1937', in Neale, *DAFP*, vol. 1.
18  Museum of Australian Democracy, 'Australian Federal Election Speeches, Joseph Lyons, 23 October 1937, United Australia Party. Delivered at Deloraine, Tas., 28 September 1937', available from: electionspeeches.moadoph.gov.au/speeches/1937-joseph-lyons.

Commonwealth Government accepted the invitation' to the conference.[19] The Nine-Power Conference was inconclusive, finding no immediate solution to the situation. Although the situation in the Asia-Pacific region was not improved, any further antagonism of Japan had also been avoided.

The Nine-Power Conference episode is significant for two main reasons. First, it reflects a growing assertiveness within Australia's approach to foreign policy. Most critically, this was an assertiveness directed towards Britain when the imperial figurehead's policy did not reflect the geopolitical interests of its dominion. Second, in avoiding economic sanctions, the Australian government appeared to be returning to the strategic use of trade employed before the trade diversion upset. As detailed in Figure 4.1, Japan's southward advance was more than simply a policy of territorial expansion and included securing zones for immigration and raw materials. At the centre of this policy were a rapidly growing population and the need for natural resources for continued economic growth. This involved the 'economic penetration' of Far Eastern nations, using Japanese capital to invest in foreign nations and secure essential tradeable goods.[20] While this was concerning in terms of regional security, the policy of economic penetration presented Australia with a relatively easy means of appeasing Japan.

Among the most well-known examples of Australia's economic diplomacy in interwar relations with Japan are the nationwide 1937–38 waterside workers' strikes—most famously, the *Dalfram* strike of 1938, when workers refused to load strategic cargo such as iron and scrap metal on to Japan-bound ships because it would likely be used for war purposes.[21] This action compelled Attorney-General and Minister for Industry Robert Menzies to declare that Australia's international policy would be determined by the duly elected government, not 'by some industrial section'.[22] Rather than revisit in detail the well-documented *Dalfram* episode, let us consider an event that was unfolding simultaneously, yet has received little attention in histories of this period.

---

19   'Doc. 88, Commonwealth government to MacDonald, 28 October 1937', in Neale, *DAFP*, vol. 1.
20   Frei, *Japan's Southward Advance and Australia*, 1; 'Longfield Lloyd to Murphy, 6 October 1937', NAA: A601, 402/17/30.
21   For a detailed account of the strike movement, see R. Lockwood, *War on the Waterfront: Menzies, Japan and the Pig Iron Dispute* (Sydney: Hale & Iremonger, 1987).
22   'Menzies statement for press, 26 November 1938', in Attorney-General's Department: Correspondence files, annual single number series [Main correspondence files series of the agency], 1857–, NAA: A432, 1938/1301.

4. 'A CHRONIC LACK OF SELF-RELIANCE'?

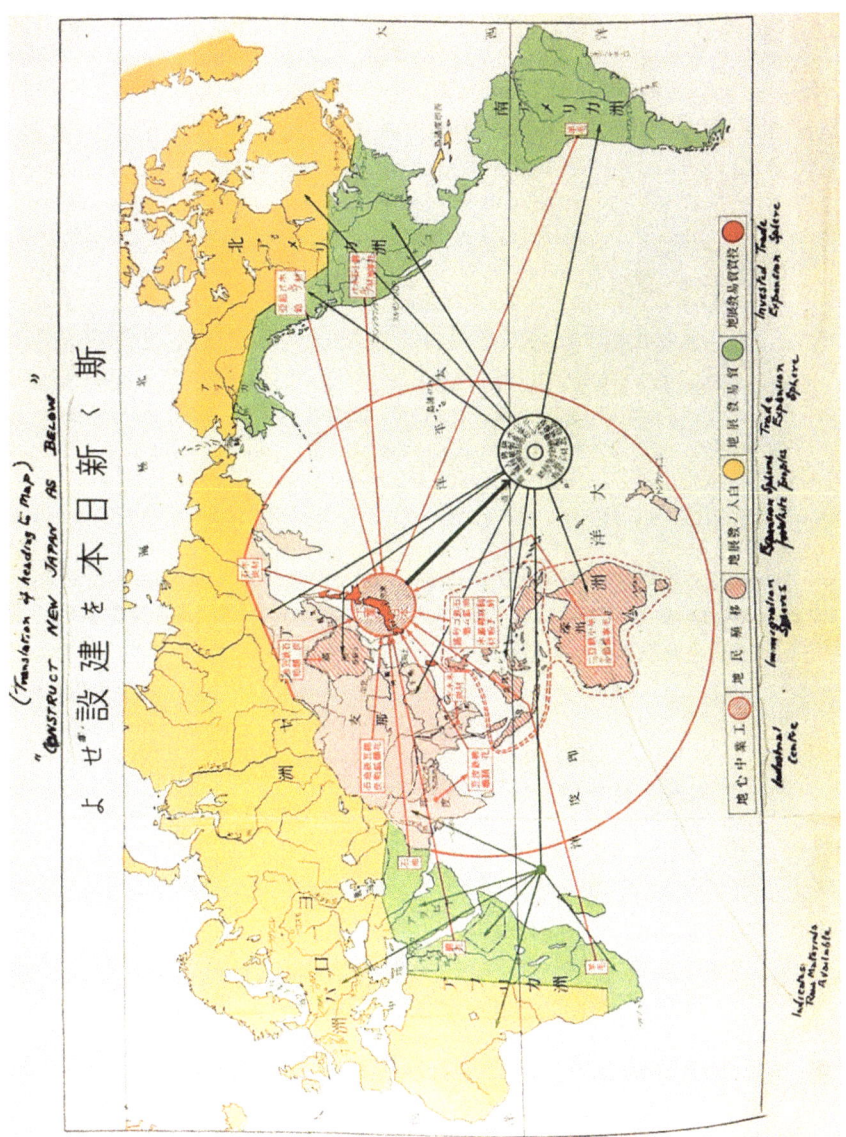

**Figure 4.1 'Construct New Japan as Below': Japan's economic penetration**

Note: Legend reads (left to right): Industrial Centre, Immigration Spheres, Expansion Spheres for White Peoples, Trade Expansion Sphere, Invested Trade Expansion Sphere.

Source: Courtesy of the National Archives of Australia, NAA: A601, 402/17/30.

In the settlement of the Trade Diversion Policy, the two nations negotiated a trade agreement. Japan committed to purchasing 800,000 bales of Australian wool (approximately 533,000 bales per annum) in the 18 months preceding 31 June 1938. As this period drew to a close and the two governments considered renewing the agreement, it was clear that Japan would fail to reach the agreed-on quota, having purchased only 503,000 bales. The Australian government understood the implications of this breach, with a March 1938 Cabinet minute noting that, unless Japanese wool imports increased or the wool-textile quota was renegotiated, Australia 'has to face a question of withdrawing the Intermediate Tariff'.[23] Despite this assessment, neither a withdrawal of the tariff nor a reduction of Australia's textile purchases was proposed. The Japanese total wool quota was reduced, with Australia guaranteed to service two-thirds of the total predicted need of 500,000 bales for the coming year. Japan would again fail to meet this revised quota.[24]

In reviewing the 1938 Australia–Japan trade negotiations, Jack Shepherd remarked that Australia made no attempt to 'drive a hard bargain', ultimately accepting an agreement that was clearly in Japan's favour.[25] This apparent complacency can be explained in terms of eastern appeasement. Cabinet recognised that retaliatory action 'would probably precipitate another tariff dispute', inciting fractured diplomatic relations. They agreed this must be avoided, and the option was not raised again. The Australian government also took into account Japan's 'abnormal political and financial conditions' when negotiating the new agreement—that is, the nation's over-reliance on foreign markets, which in turn created a trade deficit and restricted access to foreign currency.[26] In a continuation of approaches adopted in relation to the Manchurian Crisis and its reluctance to penalise Japan in the lead-up to the Trade Diversion Policy, Australia was carefully considering the strategic role of trade as it related to the deteriorating situation in the Far East.

---

23  '"Japan–Australia Trade Negotiations", Cabinet Minute, 18 March 1938', NAA: A1667, 194/B/3/A/5 Part 1A.
24  Shepherd, *Australia's Interests and Policies in the Far East*, 156–7.
25  ibid., 158.
26  '"Japan–Australia Trade Negotiations", Cabinet Minute, 18 March 1938', NAA: A1667, 194/B/3/A/5 Part 1A.

## Difficult decisions: Yampi Sound and the 1938 iron ore embargo

The iron ore embargo of 1938, in which Japan was denied access to previously contracted iron ore deposits at the Yampi Sound mines in Western Australia, is an episode incongruent with Australia's ongoing efforts to maintain cordial relations with Japan in a bid to prolong relative peace. In 1935, the Japanese operated firm H.A. Brassert and Co. Ltd secured a 50-year lease at Yampi Sound. Developments began immediately to prepare the area for extraction with a planned commencement date in 1938. In March 1937, reports emerged of an imminent world steel shortage. The Australian government concluded that it was not a lack of available resources that had created the shortage, but rather inadequate output and no move was made to restrict the exportation of iron ore.[27]

Then in May 1938, in what appeared to be a very sudden decision, the Australian government announced an embargo on the exportation of iron ore, effective 1 July 1938. This decision was justified on the basis of conservation, with the Australian government citing a recent report that indicated iron ore deposits were less than had previously been estimated.[28] During March–June 1938, a distressed Torao Wakamatsu, the Japanese Consul-General in Sydney, was in contact with Lyons on an almost fortnightly basis. He pressed Lyons to allow Japanese access to the existing Yampi project, emphasising the considerable funds that had already been invested in good faith.[29] Wakamatsu's anxiety was likely heightened by the increasingly stringent economic sanctions and restricted access to credit enforced by the US following its condemnation of Japan's actions in China.[30] Nevertheless, Australia remained firm in its resolve and the embargo was enforced.

---

27   Shepherd, *Australia's Interests and Policies in the Far East*, 87–9; 'Iron Ore: Yampi Sound', *Sydney Morning Herald*, 5 March 1937, 11; 'Doc. 15, Cabinet Minute, 9 March 1937' and 'Doc. 55, Bruce to Lyons, 4 August 1937', both in Neale, *DAFP*, vol. 1.
28   'Doc. 140, Prime Minister's Department to Longfield Lloyd, 17 March 1938' and 'Doc. 141, Lyons to Bruce, 17 March 1938', both in Neale, *DAFP*, vol. 1.
29   See Docs. 170, 178, 184, 208, 216, 249, 'Wakamatsu to Lyons', in Neale, *DAFP*, vol. 1.
30   For a summary of the United States' economic response to the Second Sino-Japanese War, see US Department of State, *Peace and War: United States Foreign Policy, 1931–1941* (Washington, DC: Government Printing Office, 1943), 32–6.

While documents since released reveal that the conservation claims were fabricated and the iron ore embargo was anti-Japanese in sentiment, it was not necessarily the end of eastern appeasement. Instead, the episode highlights Australia's pragmatic appraisal of appeasement and immediate national security requirements. While Australia supported bilateral economic relations despite the Sino-Japanese War, policymakers did not overlook the security implications of Japan's policy of economic penetration. Australia's attention to Japanese economic expansion is evidenced in the extensive strategic assessments compiled by the Australian government commissioner in Tokyo, Eric E. Longfield Lloyd. His findings were reported to various departments including the Departments of Commerce and External Affairs.

Among the activities noted by Longfield Lloyd was the Yampi Sound project. In March 1937, he reported having seen a map of the Asia-Pacific region 'upon which is shown, by the placing of a series of artificial palm trees, the extent … of Japanese so-called "Overseas Enterprise"'. One of these palm tree markers had reportedly been used to 'coolly advertise' the Yampi project as part of Japan's program of economic expansion. While Longfield Lloyd recognised the strategic implications of this expansion, he regarded it as little more than 'an impudence'.[31] By late 1937, with the outbreak of the Second Sino-Japanese War and the knowledge of inadequate imperial defence policy revealed at the 1937 Imperial Conference, Longfield Lloyd was more concerned. He described Yampi Sound as a Japanese 'foothold' within Australian territory and warned that the nation's aggressive expansion into China had been aided by a seemingly innocuous system of economic projects. He feared that allowing the Yampi Sound project to continue could 'only result in the occupation and exclusive right over a portion of Australian territory by Japanese interests and personnel'. So serious was the threat that Longfield Lloyd recommended the project be cancelled 'by any means whatsoever'. One proposed measure was an export embargo justified with a 'declaration of insufficiency'.[32] This approach, appearing the least likely to cause offence to Japan, was the one later adopted.

In this instance, Australia made the prudent judgement that its longstanding fear of invasion and still incomplete rearmament process outweighed the strategic returns of appeasement and economic diplomacy.

---

31 'Longfield Lloyd to Murphy, 20 March 1937', NAA: A601, 402/17/30.
32 'Longfield Lloyd to Murphy, 6 October 1937', NAA: A601, 402/17/30.

## Britain threatens eastern appeasement

Despite the iron ore embargo, the maintenance of stable relations with Japan and the relative peace this promoted remained a priority for Australian policymakers. Britain's relations with Japan threatened to disrupt this. In the years following the outbreak of the Sino-Japanese War, British–Japanese relations deteriorated. There was particular animosity surrounding Britain's financial assistance to the Chinese war effort and closer German–Japanese relations, with 1938 seeing Germany recognise the Japanese puppet state of Manchukuo and the announcement of a new Japanese embassy to be constructed in Berlin.[33] The most critical point in British–Japanese relations was the 1939 Tientsin incident.

The Chinese trading port of Tientsin was a concession to several nations, including Britain and Japan, the latter having partially occupied the area during the early weeks of the war with China. Co-occupation of Tientsin had been relatively peaceful until April 1939, when Chen Hsi-keng, manager of the Japanese-owned Federal Reserve Bank of North China, was assassinated by a group of anti-Japanese Chinese nationals. The British police in Tientsin aided in the arrest of four men accused of the assassination, handing them over to the Japanese police on the condition the men would not be brutalised during interrogation. On their return, the men alleged they had been tortured. When the Japanese again requested to interview the Chinese prisoners, the British police refused to cede custody and granted the men refuge in the British concession area. In the coming weeks, tension escalated between the British and Japanese governments and nationals living in Tientsin. On 14 June, Japan initiated a blockade against France and Britain at Tientsin Port, sparking concerns that unresolved tensions would result in a Japanese invasion of the British concession area.[34]

For Australia, the Tientsin incident reaffirmed fears that Britain did not appreciate the fragility of Asia-Pacific security. With neither Britain nor Australia ready for war with Japan, it was necessary that conciliation be

---

33   Bradford A. Lee, *Britain and the Sino-Japanese War, 1937–1939: A Study in the Dilemmas of British Decline* (Stanford, CA: Stanford University Press, 1973), 132–3.
34   D.C. Watt, *How War Came: The Immediate Origins of the Second World War, 1938–1939* (New York: Pantheon Books, 1989), 351–6; 'Doc. 106, Bruce to Menzies (Prime Minister), 18 June 1939', in R.G. Neale (ed.), *Documents on Australian Foreign Policy, 1937–49. Volume 2: 1939* (Canberra: AGPS, 1976) [hereinafter *DAFP*, vol. 2].

encouraged. As had been the case in the Manchurian Crisis, the individual with the greatest opportunity to advocate for Australia's interests was Australia's High Commissioner in London, Stanley Melbourne Bruce. In a meeting with Prime Minister Neville Chamberlain, Bruce stressed that war with Japan was ill-advised while the situation in Europe remained unresolved. He believed Britain had dealt with the situation in Tientsin 'on the wrong leg' and advised every possible effort be made to avoid conflict, encouraging conciliation and the handing over of the accused Chinese nationals.[35] Faced with pressure from its dominions and, more significantly, the reality that it could not successfully wage war against Japan while seeking to deal with the situation in Europe, the British government was forced to choose the path of conciliation. On 20 August 1939, the Chinese prisoners were handed over and the Japanese and British governments entered negotiations concerning the parameters for bilateral relations while Japan was at war with China.[36]

On 1 September 1939, Germany invaded Poland, prompting the outbreak of World War II in Europe. Part of Britain's war against Germany was an economic blockade. This strategy was extended to Japan, threatening to disrupt Australia's policy of economic appeasement. In February 1940, fearing Germany would gain access to strategic materials via Japan, the UK Committee for Sale of Empire Wool Abroad instructed the Australian government that the sale of any crossbred wool to certain neutral countries, Japan included, was forbidden.[37] Britain also turned its attention to Germany's access to strategic materials via the Trans-Siberian Railway. It was proposed that merchant vessels destined for the Russian port of Vladivostok would be intercepted and inspected by the RN.[38] In addition to attacking Germany's war effort, the British government was seeking to mirror the US policy of denying strategic materials to Japan in a bid to remove its war potential.[39] Britain, ill-prepared to respond to war in both Europe and the Pacific, knew the prospect of facing the

---

35  'Records of Meeting, Chamberlain and Bruce, 28 June 1939', in Records of the Cabinet Office, Cabinet Office and predecessors: Registered Files (1916 to 1965), TNA: CAB 21/893; Bruce recounts this meeting to Menzies in 'Doc. 114, Bruce to Menzies, 29 June 1939', in Neale, *DAFP*, vol. 2.
36  Watt, *How War Came*, 356, 358–9.
37  'Doc. 41, Prime Minister's Department to Bruce, 5 February 1940', in R.G. Neale (ed.), *Documents on Australian Foreign Policy, 1937–49. Volume 3: January–June 1940* (Canberra: AGPS, 1979) [hereinafter *DAFP*, vol. 3].
38  'Craigie (British Ambassador in Japan) to Dominions Office, TNA: DO 35/1034/2; 'Doc. 141, Eden to Commonwealth government, 13 April 1940', in Neale, *DAFP*, vol. 3.
39  Edward S. Miller, *Bankrupting the Enemy: The US Financial Siege of Japan Before Pearl Harbor* (Annapolis: Naval Institute Press, 2007), 1, 75–7, 84–5.

US remained the major deterrence against a Japanese declaration of war. In coordinating its economic policy towards Japan with that of the US, Britain aimed to bolster the weight of this deterrence.[40]

Australia also recognised that the US remained the main deterrent to Japanese aggression.[41] However, with no US military assurance forthcoming, the government was reluctant to act against Japan and did not meet Britain's instructions with enthusiasm. Australia's objection centred on existing wool quotas in the Australian–Japanese trade agreement (valid until 30 June 1940). The agreement stipulated that Australian wool sold to Japan could not be re-exported and the Australian government accordingly requested leniency.[42] Menzies, concerned by the effect the wool boycott would have on both regional security and postwar trade with Japan, informed the British government of

> a very strong impression here [in Australia] that our interests are being overlooked, that a course is being pursued which will gravely impair post-war trade between Australia and neutral countries, and that in particular the whole matter is creating a feeling that British authorities are indifferent to the problems of the Far East and in particular to our own vital concerns to maintain friendly relations with Japan.[43]

The Australian government also dismissed plans to intercept merchant vessels as 'provocative and ineffective', arguing that economic exclusion would make Japan more desperate and incite a force to arms.[44] In instances such as this, Australia was likely viewed in London as somewhat of a diplomatic headache. In retrospect, it reveals a prudent government that discerned in British policy not only a threat to regional security within the immediate wartime context, but also the effect that slighting Japan may have on future trade relations.

Neither of Britain's proposed measures was implemented—Bruce secured trade with Japan on a three-monthly basis and the interception of merchant vessels was deemed an impractical measure by the British

---

40  Kosmas Tsokhas, 'Anglo-Australian Relations and the Origins of the Pacific War', *History* 80, no. 260 (1995): 400–20, at p. 405; Kosmos Tsokhas, 'Dedominionization: The Anglo-Australian Experience, 1939–1945', *Historical Journal* 37, no. 4 (1994): 861–83, at pp. 866–7.
41  'Bruce to DEA, 19 June 1940' and 'Bruce to DEA, 21 June 1940', both in Australian High Commission London: Monthly War Files, 1939–45, NAA: M100, June 1940.
42  'Doc. 41, Prime Minister's Department to Bruce, 5 February 1940', in Neale, *DAFP*, vol. 3.
43  'Doc. 45, Menzies to Bruce, 6 February 1940', in Neale, *DAFP*, vol. 3.
44  'Doc. 148, Commonwealth Government to Eden, 16 April 1940', in Neale, *DAFP*, vol. 3.

government—and crisis was avoided in Tientsin. These developments did, however, reinforce the divergent priorities of Australia and Britain.[45] Moreover, as Kosmas Tsokhas has argued, in the case of the interception of merchant vessels, the limits of imperial defence were glaring.[46] The US indicated it was unwilling to provide military aid if hostilities occurred in the course of the RN intercepting and searching Japanese vessels. This would necessitate the transfer of additional RN forces to act as a deterrent or, failing this, to respond to Japanese aggression. It was at the risk of causing 'offence to the susceptibilities of the Japanese' that the British government had decided not to intercept Japanese ships.[47] In this way, Britain again acknowledged that it did not have the military resources to respond adequately to Japan if it became aggressive.

There are, of course, contemporary parallels between the 1938 iron ore embargo and recent concerns about Chinese commercial inroads in Australia and the Pacific Islands. As in 1938, these concerns hinge on questions of political influence and security implications and have led to limits on foreign property investments, the banning of foreign political donations and Australia's Foreign Relations (State and Territory Arrangements) Bill 2020, which seeks to bring state, territory and university arrangements with foreign governments in line with Australian foreign policy.[48] Directly north of Australia, China's infrastructure program, the Belt and Road Initiative, has sparked speculation that the nation is using debt-trap diplomacy to secure economic leverage for strategic gains.[49] With this in mind, the 1938 iron ore embargo serves as a warning against over-reliance and an opportunity to invest in new and comprehensive partnerships.

---

45   Tsokhas, 'Anglo-Australian Relations and the Origins of the Pacific War', 410–13.
46   ibid., 406–9.
47   'Doc. 180, Eden to Commonwealth government, 27 April 1940', in Neale, *DAFP*, vol. 3.
48   For discussion of Chinese influence in Australia, see Clive Hamilton, *Silent Invasion: China's Influence on Australia* (Melbourne: Hardie Grant Books, 2018); 'Ensuring a consistent Australian foreign policy', Joint media release, Prime Minister, Minister for Foreign Affairs, Minister for Women, Canberra, 27 August 2020, available from: www.pm.gov.au/media/ensuring-consistent-australian-foreign-policy.
49   Debt-trap diplomacy sees countries being granted unsustainable loans. If a nation were to default on a loan, the risk is China would use this economic leverage for political influence in the country and perhaps even gain access to the infrastructure project to use as it saw fit.

## An Australian diplomatic service

As the war in Europe unfolded, imperial defence continued to weigh on the minds of Australian policymakers. The first half of 1940 was near-cataclysmic for the Allies: Germany swiftly conquered Denmark, Norway and the Low Countries throughout April and May; Italy declared war on the Allies on 10 June; and a week later France sought an armistice. By the end of June, the British Empire stood virtually alone in the defence of the North Atlantic, Mediterranean, Pacific and Britain's local defence.

These developments had ramifications beyond Europe, sparking fears that Japan would capitalise on the Allies' vulnerable position in the Asia-Pacific. In May, the British government requested urgent help in the defence of the Far East, asking Australia to make available additional sloops, armed merchant cruisers and two squadrons each of Wirraway general-purpose aircraft and Hudson bombers, as well as the early dispatch of Australian Imperial Force (AIF) troops earmarked for Singapore.[50] Then, on 13 June—the same day Australia agreed to make available some of the requested equipment—Britain, pre-empting the fall of France, informed the Australian government that, for the time being, it was 'most unlikely that we could send adequate reinforcements to the Far East' in the event of Japanese aggression. Previously, Britain had been prepared to abandon the Mediterranean on Japan's entrance into the war, relying on the French to contain the situation there. This course of action was no longer practicable.[51]

In the fallout of the deteriorating Allied position in Europe, Bruce openly criticised the lack of direction in imperial defence planning, remarking at a meeting of the Joint Planning Committee of the General Staff that it was

> impossible to expect the Australian Government to feel anything other than extremely anxious in her cooperation if she had not a clear picture of what it was in the minds of those who were responsible here [in London] for the conduct of war.[52]

---

50   Horner, *High Command*, 35–8.
51   'Doc. 376, Caldecote to Whiskard, 13 June 1940', in Neale, *DAFP*, vol. 3. For Australia's decision to make equipment available, see 'Doc. 372, Menzies to Whiskard, 13 June 1940', in Neale, *DAFP*, vol. 3.
52   'Doc. 19, Bruce to Menzies, 8 July 1940', in R.G. Neale (ed.), *Documents on Australian Foreign Policy, 1937–49. Volume 4: July1940 – January 1941* (Canberra: AGPS, 1980) [hereinafter *DAFP*, vol. 4].

Britain attempted to dispel Australia's anxieties, suggesting the US might be willing to declare 'any alteration of the status quo in the Far East and the Pacific as a *casus belli*'.[53] In reality, the US government faced an unfavourable opinion of the war in the Congress and among the public, and doggedly refused to commit to actions that might lead to a force of arms.[54] British Prime Minister Winston Churchill also assured the Australian government that if Japan invaded Australia or New Zealand, Britain would 'cut our losses in the Mediterranean and sacrifice every interest' to come to their aid.[55] Privately, Churchill believed Japan would not enter the war until at least late 1941 and anticipated raids rather than a large-scale invasion of Australia. With Australia half a world away and earnestly fearing invasion and a *casus belli* highly unlikely, neither assurance was particularly comforting.

Australia's immediate response to the crisis of 1940 was to strengthen its diplomatic representation. Australia had long been content with international representation via the British diplomatic service, believing formal representation was not required due to the 'fundamental similarity' the imperial framework lent to the two nation's foreign policies.[56] By June 1940, however, this similarity was no longer so apparent and it was essential Australia establish formal diplomatic relations with Japan. On 19 June, just two days after France began suing for peace, the Australian War Cabinet agreed the nation required its own diplomatic service in Tokyo. Here it is significant to note that the War Cabinet concluded such an appointment was necessary 'before the international situation deteriorate[s] further', highlighting once again the intersection of defence and diplomacy in Australia's preparation for the Pacific War.[57]

The attempt in June 1940 was in fact not the first to try to establish an Australian diplomatic service in Japan. In March 1939, Lyons had suggested to the British government that Australia make formal diplomatic appointments in Japan and the US. These appointments would have been Australia's first outside Britain and were, Lyons argued, 'imperative' to national interests.[58] Britain endorsed the proposed legation in Washington

---

53 'Doc. 406, Caldecote to Whiskard, 19 June 1940', in Neale, *DAFP*, vol. 3.
54 Christopher Thorne, *Allies of a Kind: The United States, Britain and the War Against Japan, 1941–1945* (London: Hamish Hamilton, 1978), 39–40, 76; Horner, *High Command*, 38–40.
55 'Churchill to Menzies, 11 August 1940', cited in Horner, *High Command*, 38.
56 'Mr Lyons on Australian Proposal', *The Times*, [London], 8 June 1937, 13.
57 'Doc. 405, War Cabinet Minute, 19 June 1940', in Neale, *DAFP*, vol. 3.
58 'Doc. 63, Lyons to Caldecote, 30 March 1939', in Neale, *DAFP*, vol. 2.

but opposed the proposal for Tokyo. The Secretary of State for Dominion Affairs, Lord Caldecote, believed an appointment in Japan would 'weaken the Imperial bond' as it suggested that Australia and Britain were not coordinated in their views on the nation's aggressive actions in China. The situation was further complicated by the fact that no legation had initially been proposed for China, suggesting favourability towards Japan in the continuing Sino-Japanese War.[59] Australia did not act on its proposal for a legation in Japan, although private discussions continued. In March 1940, Menzies remarked in a cable to Bruce that 'the increasing significance of the Far East to Australia appears to outweigh other considerations'.[60] These other considerations were presumably the appearance of condoning Japanese actions and, although only implied, imperial unity.

By June 1940, Australia's concern was so acute it acted regardless of Britain's disapproval. On 22 June, the Australian government informed Caldecote of the decision to establish an Australian legation in Tokyo, requesting he immediately initiate the necessary steps.[61] John Latham was selected as Australia's first Minister to Japan on the basis of his past experience as Minister for External Affairs and in the 1934 AEM.[62] With this appointment, Australia diverted from what had formally been a united foreign policy with Britain.

In the months between the decision to appoint a minister in Japan and Latham's arrival in December, Japan became further entangled in European and Far Eastern aggression. On 16 July, the relatively moderate Japanese Prime Minister Mitsumasa Yonai and his Cabinet were forced to resign due to pressure from the Imperial Japanese Army and the War Minister.[63] The incoming government included Prime Minister Prince Fumimaro Konoe, an aggressive nationalist who had been prime minister during Japan's invasion of China in 1937, and, as Foreign Minister, Yosuke Matsuoka, who had led the Japanese delegation during its withdrawal from the League of Nations.[64] Once in office, the Konoe

---

59  'Doc. 75, Caldecote to Whiskard, 29 April 1939', in Neale, *DAFP*, vol. 2.
60  'Doc. 89, Menzies to Bruce, 4 March 1940', in Neale, *DAFP*, vol. 3.
61  'Doc. 418, Commonwealth government to Caldecote, 22 June 1940', in Neale, *DAFP*, vol. 3.
62  'Doc. 182, Advisory War Council Minute, 29 October 1940', in Neale, *DAFP*, vol. 4.
63  'Doc. 1079, Grew (Ambassador in Japan) to Hull (Secretary of State), 17 July 1940', in John G. Reid, Ralph R. Goodwin and Louis E. Gates (eds), *Foreign Relations of the United States Diplomatic Papers, 1940, The Far East, Volume IV* (Washington, DC: US Government Printing Office, 1955) [hereinafter *FRUS 1940*].
64  Lionel Wigmore, *Australia in the War of 1939–1945: The Japanese Thrust. Series 1: Army. Volume 4* (Canberra: Australian War Memorial, 1957), 22.

Cabinet announced its intentions to form foreign policy in the 'strictest of relations with the Axis powers' and with 'vigorous prosecution of the plan for the establishment of a new order in East Asia'.[65] Konoe's new government was quick to act on this declaration: in August, Japan sought to align itself with the pro-Axis Vichy government in German-occupied France; on 22 September, the Japanese Army invaded northern Indochina; and, on 27 September, the nation signed the Tripartite Pact with Germany and Italy, in which each signatory recognised the other's vision and sovereignty within their respective regions and committed to mutual assistance in the event of war.[66]

Australia remained firm in its commitment to establish a diplomatic representative in Japan, even as Britain requested the appointment be postponed and the British Ambassador in Japan contemplated evacuation.[67] The rationale underpinning Australia's position can be gleaned through an Advisory War Council minute of late October 1940 that outlined Latham's role in Japan. The Advisory War Council hoped an appointment in Japan would grant Australia 'prestige'. Although Latham's appointment was 'not an act of separation' between the British and Australian governments, he was cautioned that he 'should not be or even appear to be in the pocket of the Ambassador of the United Kingdom Government'. The government did not believe that war with Japan could be avoided; however, if Latham could soften perceptions of Australia and the Empire as a whole, this would perhaps delay Japan's entry into the war. Australia would, in turn, 'gain time to allow for the development and the growing strength of [its] defences'.[68] The value of this approach was no doubt amplified as Longfield Lloyd reported mounting hostility in Japan towards the British—for instance, the menacing words of Sankichi Takahashi, outspoken former commander of the Combined Japanese Fleet, that Britain 'is standing in our way and is doing her best to defeat our national task'. He cautioned the Japanese people not to take immediate action against Britain, for defeat was presently the likely outcome, but to wait and 'listen to the commands of the captain'.[69]

---

65 'Doc. 1082, Grew to Hull, 13 July 1940', in Reid et al., *FRUS 1940*.
66 Frei, *Japan's Southward Advance and Australia*, 143, 147–9.
67 'Menzies to Bruce, 9 July 1940', in Prime Minister's Department: Master sheets (used stencils) of outwards cables, annual single number series, 1939–49, NAA: A3196, 1940/15; 'Craigie to Commonwealth government, 3 October 1940', NAA: A981, Far 14 Part 1.
68 'Doc. 182, Advisory War Council Minute, 29 October 1940', in Neale, *DAFP*, vol. 4.
69 '"Latest Situation in the South Seas and Japan's Position—Japanese People Must be Prepared for What May Happen"', 19 October 1940', cutting, in NAA: A601, 402/17/30.

As noted, Australia proposed the establishment of a legation in Washington in March 1939. One of Australia's principal aims in the two years preceding the outbreak of the Pacific War was to draw the US into Pacific affairs and extract from it a military guarantee. The legation in Washington was central to this aim, as evidenced in a cable Menzies received from Bruce, who was briefly considered for the appointment:

> In Washington my activities would be directed towards ensuring maximum cooperation of the United States while she is out of the war; her military help should war go unfavourably to Allies, her diplomatic collaboration in resolving Far Eastern problems, and her armed intervention should Japan become actively hostile.[70]

The man eventually charged with the task as Australia's first Minister to Washington was Richard Casey.

Casey arrived in Washington in February 1940 and his approach as minister mirrored Bruce's earlier assessment. Casey pursued a twofold strategy of public and private diplomacy, seeking to draw attention to Australia's plight in the war in Europe and overlapping Australian and US interests in the Pacific.[71] Casey's diaries from his time in Washington recount dozens of public addresses, press releases and invitations to dine with the US political elite.[72] Casey judged the result of his publicity campaign to be that a great many Americans who had previously little to no knowledge of the far-flung Commonwealth country were now at least aware of the nation, its culture and concerns.[73]

Casey's second task of formal diplomacy was a more difficult one as he had to contend with US isolationism and opposition to war, which were, as Casey's biographer W.J. Hudson has noted, amplified by the

---

70   'Bruce to Menzies, 18 October 1939', in Prime Minister's Department: Miscellaneous cables, 1937–43, NAA: CP290/6, Bundle 1/1.
71   Carl Bridge, '"The Other Blade of the Scissors": Richard Gardiner Casey, Australia's First Minister to the United States, 1940–1942', in *Diplomats at War: British and Commonwealth Diplomacy in Wartime*, eds Christopher Baxter and Andrew Stewart (Leiden: Martinus Nijhoff, 2008), 127–48; Carl Bridge, 'R.G. Casey, Australia's First Washington Legation, and the Origins of the Pacific War, 1940–42', *Australian Journal of Politics and History* 28, no. 2 (1982): 181–89.
72   For Casey's Washington diaries, see Carl Bridge (ed.), *A Delicate Mission: The Washington Diaries of R.G. Casey, 1940–1942* (Canberra: National Library of Australia, 2008).
73   'Doc. 149, Casey to McEwan (Minister for External Affairs), 16 April 1940', in Neale, *DAFP*, vol. 3.

THE GENESIS OF A POLICY

1940 presidential election.[74] The crisis in Europe in the first half of 1940 prompted the DEA, Menzies and Bruce to request Casey seek some measure of support from the US, be it material assistance or a declaration of war.[75] With firsthand experience of US isolationism, Casey placed little confidence in the likelihood of the nation taking such a course of action.[76] Nevertheless, he called on President Franklin D. Roosevelt and other key officials, expressing his government's desire to see the US make a declaration of war.

One such meeting was with the US Undersecretary of State Sumner Welles, with whom Casey had formed a friendship and whom he described as 'receptive' and someone to whom he could 'talk freely and easily'. He painted a grim picture for Welles in which Germany, following the imminent collapse of France, 'would be free and in a good position to concentrate all efforts by sea and air on Britain'. In this scenario, the landing of German troops on British soil was 'perfectly possible'. Casey believed the RN 'would not give up itself under any circumstance', leading to heavy losses and possible immolation. Welles judged this to be 'an extremely unwise and illogical' course of action for, while 'the British Fleet remained in existence it was possible to retrieve the situation at some later date'.[77] Welles doubtless appreciated Casey's implied message that the RN was vital to the protection of US interests in Europe, for it alone prevented Germany turning its gaze across the Atlantic Ocean to the US. Although Welles promised to report Casey's message to Roosevelt, he was soon informed that a US declaration of war remained 'unthinkable'.[78]

As the presidential campaign progressed and it appeared likely that Roosevelt would be re-elected, there was a private shift in the US position on the war. In October, the US and British governments agreed to share decoded information from Japanese and German communications. In December, Roosevelt approved Secretary of State Cordell Hull's

---

74   W.J. Hudson, *Casey* (Oxford, UK: Oxford University Press, 1986), 117. See also, James Prior, *America Looks to Australia: The Hidden Role of Richard Casey in the Creation of the Australia–America Alliance, 1940–1942* (Melbourne: Australian Scholarly Publishing, 2017), 53–63.
75   'Doc. 239, DEA to Casey, 15 May 1940', 'Doc. 280, Menzies to Casey, 26 May 1940' and 'Doc. 287, Bruce to Casey, 27 May 1940', all in Neale, *DAFP*, vol. 3.
76   'Doc. 257, Casey to DEA, 20 May 1940', in Neale, *DAFP*, vol. 3.
77   'Doc. 319, Casey to Menzies, 30 May 1940', in Neale, *DAFP*, vol. 3.
78   'Doc. 9, Memorandum by Hull, 6 June 1940', in Rogers P. Churchill, N.O. Sappington, Kieran J. Carroll, Morrison B. Giffen and Francis C. Prescott (eds), *Foreign Relations of the United States Diplomatic Papers, 1940, The British Commonwealth, The Soviet Union, The Near East and Africa, Volume III* (Washington, DC: US Government Printing Office, 1958).

suggestion that Anglo-American joint discussions be held, specifically focusing on the general military resources and strategies to be adopted on US entry into the war. These meetings would take place in Washington in early 1941.[79]

Casey was able to report a small victory for Australia. Roosevelt had agreed to host an Australian naval office to 'investigate and expedite Australian orders in the United States in respect of Australian naval requirements'. Commander Henry Burrell was duly appointed, arriving in Washington in November 1940. Admittedly, Roosevelt requested the naval appointment and subsequent discussions not be publicised in the US or Australian press, lest he and his government be seen as warmongers.[80] Nevertheless, this appointment indicated the US was aware of its shared security interests with Australia—even if it would not yet act on them—and was assessing the logistics of coordinated US–Australian operations.

As the US position on the war shifted, Casey frantically made a case for Singapore. In meetings with State Department staff and high-ranking military planners throughout November and December, Casey encouraged the transfer of US warships to Singapore, contending that 'with a sufficiently strong demonstration the Japanese might be deterred from carrying things very much farther'.[81] Casey judged Hull to be receptive, appreciating that the war was entering 'a new and dangerous phase'.[82] Hull's own retelling of this meeting was far less encouraging, noting that the US wished to see the effect of economic embargoes before it committed to deploying naval vessels. Hull, accordingly, 'could not undertake to go into [Casey's] inquiry'.[83] No decision was made regarding Singapore and 1940 closed without a military guarantee from the US.

From January to March 1941, the British–US discussions were under way in Washington. During these months, it became even more urgent to convince the US of Singapore's significance. Throughout February, reports

---

79  Bridge, 'R.G. Casey, Australia's First Washington Legation, and the Origins of the Pacific War', 184; 'Doc. 213, Casey to DEA, 2 December 1940', in Neale, *DAFP*, vol. 4.
80  'Doc. 177, Casey to Menzies and McEwen, 17 October 1940', in Neale, *DAFP*, vol. 4.
81  'Doc. 257, Memorandum of Conversation by Berle (Assistant Secretary of State), 15 November 1940', in Reid et al., *FRUS 1940*. See also 'Doc. 252, Memorandum of Conversation by Hull, 12 November 1940', in Reid et al., *FRUS 1940*; 'Casey to DEA, 15 November 1940', in Australian Legation United States of America: Correspondence files, annual alphabetical series (Washington), 1939–87, NAA: A3300, 11, in which Casey recounts a meeting with Secretary of the Navy Frank Knox.
82  'Doc. 216, Casey to DEA, 4 December 1940', in Neale, *DAFP*, vol. 4.
83  'Memorandum of Conversation by Hull, 3 December 1940', in Reid et al., *FRUS 1940*.

arrived that the Japanese Army, already occupying northern Indochina, was making moves towards Cam Rahn Bay in the south-east. It was also reported that the nation was looking towards the proposal for the Kra Isthmus canal, which would afford Japan a strong position from which to attack Malaya, Thailand and, most critically for Australia, Singapore.[84] Despite these developments and Casey's reasoning, US policymakers remained unconvinced that Singapore was vital to their own interests. Instead, they believed their forces needed to be reserved for the United States' Pacific and Atlantic bases—expressly for the defence of the nation's territory.[85]

While the British–US discussions offered welcome news for war in Europe, this did not extend to Australia's region of strategic concern. The Australian legation staff and Burrell, who was present at the joint talks, reported that only an attack on US possessions would induce the nation to declare war on Japan. In this scenario, both the British and the US delegates agreed that Europe would be the priority, necessitating a holding war in the Pacific until Germany and Italy had been defeated.[86] This decision was, as historians have established, the earliest suggestion of what would come to be known as the 'Beat Hitler First' policy.[87] The US delegates recognised the strategic importance of Singapore in a war against Japan, admitting its loss would be 'unfortunate', but they were not convinced it would 'have a decisive effect on the issue of the war'.[88] The Atlantic and Mediterranean theatres were the primary concerns. If necessary, the US would 'contemplate … abandoning the Far East in order to ensure maximum concentration in [the] Atlantic and Mediterranean'.[89] The US delegates made clear in the strongest possible terms that 'it would be a serious mistake for the United Kingdom [and its empire] in making their

---

84   'Doc. 277, Caldecote to Whiskard, 7 February 1941' and 'Doc. 304, Caldecote to Whiskard, 17 February 1941', both in Neale, *DAFP*, vol. 4.
85   'Casey to DEA, 24 February 1941', NAA: A981, Far 25 Part 1. This report was compiled by Burrell and sent through the Washington Legation.
86   'Watt to DEA, 7 February 1941' and 'Watt to DEA, 13 February 1941', both in NAA: Far 25 Part 1. For a report on the final Anglo-American arrangements, see 'Casey to DEA, 14 March 1941', in NAA: A981, Far 25 Part 1. These reports were compiled by Burrell and sent through the Washington Legation.
87   Bridge, 'R.G. Casey, Australia's First Washington Legation, and the Origins of the Pacific War', 184–5; John Robertson, 'Australia and the "Beat Hitler First Strategy", 1941–1942: A Problem in Wartime Consultation', *Journal of Imperial and Commonwealth History* 11, no. 3 (1983): 300–21, at pp. 301–5.
88   'Casey to DEA, 24 February 1941', NAA: A981, Far 25 Part 1. This report was compiled by Burrell and sent through the Washington Legation.
89   'Watt to DEA, 13 February 1941', NAA: A981, Far 25 Part 1.

strategic dispositions to withstand a Japanese attack against Singapore to count on prompt military support by [the] United States'.[90] Quite simply, Britain and the US were fully occupied with affairs in Europe, leaving the Japanese threat on the periphery of their grand strategy for a global war.

At this point, formal diplomacy had proved fruitless in convincing the US that it shared security interests with Australia. Australia sought a new diplomatic strategy to tether its interests to those of the US and, in July 1941, it was presented with an opportunity.

## From appeasement to deterrence

Japan faced restricted access to strategic materials as a result of British and US sanctions in response to its activities in northern Indochina. The Japanese government and army placed increasing pressure on the NEI for greater market access throughout the first half of 1941. Failing this, invasion was the likely recourse. The British government, judging continued economic pressure to be the most effective means of deterring aggression, proposed decisive action: a total economic embargo against Japan and the renunciation of the 1911 Anglo-Japanese Treaty of Commerce and Navigation. For the full weight of these measures to be felt, dominion cooperation was necessary.[91]

The Australian government understood it was now time to make a decisive shift from appeasement to deterrence, agreeing that a full economic embargo would effectively hinder Japan's capacity to carry out regional expansion. However, the nation would not accept deterrence without certain parameters and wanted to ensure more perilous measures against Japan included a safeguard against retaliatory hostility. With the knowledge that, in the case of Japanese aggression, Britain could not, and the US would not, respond with an adequate counterforce, the Australian government postponed making a final decision.[92]

---

90  'Casey to DEA, 24 February 1941', NAA: A981, Far 25 Part 1.
91  'Doc. 386, Cranborne (Secretary of State for Dominion Affairs) to Commonwealth government, 5 April 1941', in Neale, *DAFP*, vol. 4.
92  Tsokhas, 'Anglo-Australian Relations and the Origins of the Pacific War', 402, 414–17; 'Commonwealth government to Dominions Office, 14 May 1941', TNA: DO 35/1035/1.

On 9 July, Casey's friendship with Welles provided vital information in Australia's campaign to draw the US into Pacific affairs. Welles confided in Casey that the interception and decoding of Japanese diplomatic cables had revealed its army was poised to move south through Indochina, Thailand and the NEI. The US planned to respond with a full and immediate economic embargo. Although Welles admitted this course of action would 'likely provoke Japan to war with them [the US] before long', he believed it useless to continue issuing warnings to Japan without acting on them.[93] Here was an opportunity for the Australian government to coordinate its policy with the US.

Casey immediately informed his Prime Minister and Minister for External Affairs of this conversation. The following day, Menzies made known his government's decision on the British government's proposed economic embargo against Japan. He informed Britain that Australia would cooperate on the condition that such action was 'part of a carefully weighed plan with adequate safeguards for us'. These safeguards were a coordinated Australian–British–US economic embargo against Japan and, critically, a commitment from the US to support Allied merchant ships in the event of Japanese aggression, even if no attack had been made against US ships.[94] Britain agreed to Menzies' conditions, informing the government that it expected the US would mirror British policy; unbeknown to Australia, the US was holding off on announcing an embargo so it could coordinate action with Britain.

On 26 July, some 140,000 Japanese troops positioned themselves to invade southern Indochina. Britain renounced the Anglo-Japanese trade treaty and the US announced the seizure of Japanese assets, a total trade embargo and the policy of protecting merchant ships.[95] Within a fortnight, Australia renounced its own commercial treaty with Japan and imposed a full embargo. With this, Australia shifted from appeasing Japan to deterring it.[96]

---

93   'Doc. 2, Casey to Menzies and Stewart (Minister for External Affairs), 9 July 1941', in W.J. Hudson and H.J.W. Stokes (eds), *Documents on Australian Foreign Policy, 1937–49. Volume 5: July 1941 – June 1942* (Canberra: AGPS, 1982) [hereinafter *DAFP*, vol. 5].
94   'Doc. 4, Menzies to Bruce, 10 July 1941', in Hudson and Stokes, *DAFP*, vol. 5.
95   'Doc. 15, Cranborne to Commonwealth government, 25 July 1941', in Hudson and Stokes, *DAFP*, vol. 5.
96   Tsokhas, 'Anglo-Australian Relations and the Origins of the Pacific War', 418–19.

In the days before Australia announced the economic embargo, the government assessed how best to implement sanctions. In a 29 July meeting of the Advisory War Council, it was acknowledged that economic sanctions came with the risk of inciting a Japanese declaration of war or further aggressive action in other parts of the Far East. Valuable as the July embargo was in presenting a united response, the fact remained that the US had made no commitment to the defence of Australia and only an attack on US possessions would lead to a declaration of war. Menzies noted that when Australia notified the US of the economic measures being taken 'it should be intimated that the possible consequences of such action … [were] realised and we assume that the United States Government also realized them'. He hoped to force on the US an acknowledgement that a hardening policy towards Japan came with certain risks and responsibilities.[97]

Throughout 1941, Japan and the US had been in the process of bilateral negotiations, which aimed to persuade the Japanese Army to withdraw from China and Indochina in exchange for diplomatic and economic assistance. Both these negotiations and the US policy of protecting merchant vessels provided further time in which the Allies could prepare, allowing a battleship and two destroyers to be transferred to Singapore.[98] By late 1941, the US–Japanese negotiations were reaching the final stages and it was clear that Japan, facing a steady decline in the reserves vital to its expansion policy in the Asia-Pacific region, would have to either submit to US demands or resort to war. The latter was the most likely outcome.[99]

On 26 November, Hull presented the Japanese negotiators, ambassadors Kichisaburō Nomura and Saburō Kurusu, with a list of general US demands.[100] The next day, Casey reported on meeting with a 'depressed' Hull, who saw little hope for the negotiations. He showed Casey several recent cables from consular officers in Indochina detailing 'considerable military activity' by the Japanese, predicting correctly that the nation was readying itself to invade Thailand.[101] The Australian government did

---

97 'Doc. 21, Advisory War Council Minute, 29 July 1941', in Hudson and Stokes, *DAFP*, vol. 5.
98 Bridge, 'R.G. Casey, Australia's First Washington Legation, and the Origins of the Pacific War', 186.
99 Miller, *Bankrupting the Enemy*, 189–90, 236–40.
100 'Doc. 129, Casey to Curtin (Prime Minister) and Evatt (Minister for External Affairs), 26 November 1941', in Hudson and Stokes, *DAFP*, vol. 5.
101 'Doc. 133, Casey to Curtin and Evatt, 27 November 1941', in Hudson and Stokes, *DAFP*, vol. 5.

not resign itself to accept this grim reality. In a 28 November meeting of the Advisory War Council, it was agreed that the Japanese–US negotiations were 'of great value, and they should continue, in view of the importance of gaining time'. In prolonging the US–Japanese negotiations, Australia would be provided time in which to 'bring home' the shared security concerns of Australia and the US, the Australian government's commitment to a coordinated strategy and, in turn, a hoped-for US military guarantee.[102] The council accordingly agreed that Australia's approach would be to maintain 'contact as to what is happening [in the negotiations] and expressing opinions where asked for or where it is deemed prudent to suggest a word of advice'.[103] On the basis of this directive and Minister for External Affairs H.V. Evatt's express request, Casey sought to insert himself in US–Japanese diplomacy.[104]

In a 29 November meeting with Hull, Casey proposed he act as a third party in the US–Japanese discussions. He believed relations between the two countries 'had become such that neither side could initiate further approach to the other'. As Australia was 'in a rather different position', he wanted to meet with the Japanese ambassadors as an 'intermediary' between the two nations. Hull was reportedly 'appreciative' of Casey's offer and gave his support for the meeting, although he showed little enthusiasm for the prospect of a positive outcome.[105] Casey met with Nomura and Kurusu the following day and left the meeting with no new points for Hull to consider, for the Japanese had nothing to offer. It was clear Japan had no intention of negotiating further.[106] Nevertheless, Casey identified a small victory in the episode, informing Curtin and Evatt that Hull had 'used the term "we" in the sense of the United States and British countries' when discussing how to respond to Japanese aggression.[107] At the very least, this suggested a coordinated response was the United States' chosen strategy.

---

102 Bridge, 'R.G. Casey, Australia's First Washington Legation, and the Origins of the Pacific War', 187. See also, Hudson, *Casey*, 126–7.
103 'Doc. 132, Advisory War Council Minute, 28 November 1941', in Hudson and Stokes, *DAFP*, vol. 5.
104 'Doc. 137, Evatt to Casey, 29 November 1941', in Hudson and Stokes, *DAFP*, vol. 5.
105 'Doc. 140, Casey to Curtin and Evatt, 29 November 1941', in Hudson and Stokes, *DAFP*, vol. 5.
106 'Doc. 144, Casey to Curtin and Evatt, 30 November 1941', in Hudson and Stokes, *DAFP*, vol. 5.
107 'Doc. 140, Casey to Curtin and Evatt, 29 November 1941', in Hudson and Stokes, *DAFP*, vol. 5.

As Casey was urgently seeking to secure a US military guarantee, intelligence confirmed that Japan was set to attack Thailand, moving into Burma and Malaya and further into China.[108] On 1 December, Roosevelt met with the British Ambassador in Washington, Lord Halifax, to discuss strategies in response to this situation. Halifax reported 'the whole tenor' of the conversation had been 'that we should both recognise any of these hypothetical actions to be [a] clear prelude to some further action and threat to our common interests against which we ought to react together at once'. Roosevelt made clear that, in the event of an attack on Thailand, Britain could 'count on their support'.[109] On the same day, Casey reported a comment made off the record by Welles, who believed

> the line beyond which we cannot allow the Japanese to pass has been reached for three reasons (a) we cannot allow ourselves to be cut off from essential defence needs (b) we cannot be out in [the] position of asking Japanese permission to trade in the Pacific and (c) we cannot allow Burma Road, our last remaining means of sending supplies to be China, to be cut.[110]

On the basis of this scenario, Welles declared 'the British will fight and we will move in behind them'.[111] On learning of this, Evatt cabled Casey, Bruce and Frederic Eggleston, Minister to China, commending their efforts to encourage US armed resistance on behalf of the Allies and to prevent the breakdown of bilateral talks. He made careful note of these measures being pursued during the period before the RN ships' arrival in Singapore and of the time that had been created for the final preparations for war in the Pacific.[112]

After years of uncertainty and repeated appeals by Britain and Australia, the Roosevelt government was finally willing to commit armed forces in the Far East beyond its own territories. Based on this assurance, Britain and Australia negotiated contingency plans for their response to Japan's entrance into the war. In the event of an attack or increased pressure on Thailand or China, they would 'follow the lead' of the US, withholding from a declaration of war until a joint response could be

---

108 'Evatt to Casey, 1 December 1941', NAA: A3300, 100.
109 'Doc. 152, Casey to DEA, 1 December 1941', in Hudson and Stokes, *DAFP*, vol. 5, in which Casey forwarded Halifax's report.
110 'Casey to DEA, 1 December 1941', NAA: A3300, 100.
111 ibid.
112 'Doc. 155, Evatt to Bruce, Casey and Eggleston, 3 December 1941', in Hudson and Stokes, *DAFP*, vol. 5.

coordinated. Attacks on Russia, the NEI or Portuguese Timor would result in a declaration of war irrespective of US entry.[113] In the end, these contingencies were unnecessary as, in the early hours of 7 December 1941, Japan attacked the US Naval Station Pearl Harbor in Hawai`i. Within hours, Guam and the Philippines—both US possessions—had also been attacked.

The years leading up to the Pacific War were marked by immense uncertainty for Australia as Japan expanded its regional dominance and Britain—overstretched, underprepared and preoccupied with European affairs—pushed Asia-Pacific concerns to the periphery. It was also this uncertainty in tandem with the lessons learnt in previous years that motivated the Australian government to seek out a policy that created time in which to prepare for war and, from 1940, drew the US into Asia-Pacific affairs. Granted, Australia's efforts alone did not secure a US military commitment, nor did they prevent the fall of Singapore and the assessment that the Pacific theatre was of secondary importance. Nevertheless, Australia's response to the coming regional conflict remains a significant and overlooked development in the emergence of a lucid and opportunistic foreign policy in which policymakers carefully assessed international developments, the strategies of the great powers and the opportunities available to project the national interest. Australia now sought to integrate its national interest within British and US wartime strategies and visions for the postwar world. As has been a consistent theme throughout the previous chapters, this was a challenging task in which Australia's junior status and the often-divergent visions of the British and US were significant barriers.

---

113 'Prime Minister's Department to Casey, 2 December 1941', NAA: A3300, 100; 'Doc. 153, Commonwealth government to Cranborne, 2 December 1941', in Hudson and Stokes, *DAFP*, vol. 5.

# 5

# 'An undoubted right to speak': Projecting Australia's influence in the postwar Asia-Pacific, 1942–45

On 27 December 1941, Prime Minister John Curtin advised that Australia 'looks to America, free of any pangs to our traditional links or kinship with the United Kingdom'.[1] These words have been popularly heralded as the turning point in Australian–US relations and the basis of a smooth and natural progression to a postwar relationship and the eventual ANZUS alliance.[2] Certainly, Curtin's message was a public acknowledgement that Australia faced an imminent crisis in the Asia-Pacific to which Britain was unable to respond and the nation now depended on the US for its security. His message, however, was not indicative of Australia's shift from strategic dependence on Britain to the US, or even a particularly pronounced Australian–US affinity.

---

1   'John Curtin, "The Task Ahead",' in F.K. Crowley (ed.), *Modern Australia in Documents. Volume 2: 1939–1970* (Melbourne: Wren Publishing, 1973), 51.
2   For examples of works emphasising Curtin's 'look to America' aphorism as a turning point, see Gareth Evans, 'The Labor Tradition: A View From the 1990s', in *From Evatt to Evans: The Labor Tradition in Australian Foreign Policy*, eds David Lee and Christopher Waters (Canberra: Allen & Unwin with the Department of International Relations, Research School of Pacific and Asian Studies, The Australian National University, 1997), 12; Malcolm Fraser with Cain Roberts, *Dangerous Allies* (Melbourne: Melbourne University Press, 2014), 73–80; Bruce Grant, *Crisis of Loyalty: A Study in Australian Foreign Policy* (Sydney: Angus & Robertson for Australian Institute of International Affairs, 1972), 15–16.

With Australia's wartime experiences the focal point for much of the existing literature concerning the nation's foreign policy, much of this story has been chronicled elsewhere. This is particularly so in the case of the wartime origins of External Affairs Minister H.V. Evatt's particular brand of assertive regionalism.[3] This chapter builds on this work through a focus on developments after the crisis years of the Pacific War, as Australian policymakers realised the US could not necessarily be relied on to build a postwar order conducive to its national interest. It holds that Australian assertiveness was not limited to Evatt's initiatives, placing him alongside other key thinkers. Their shared goal was articulating Australia's status in the Asia-Pacific and setting out a strategy for managing in the region in the postwar period. The result was an Australian-led plan for renewed Commonwealth cooperation, which aimed to regionalise defence planning and establish a friendly yet robust counterweight to US influence in the Asia-Pacific region.

## The great powers' grand strategy

The early months of the Pacific War were ones of crisis for Australia. The initial foundation of Allied strategy in the war against Japan was the American–British–Dutch–Australian Command (ABDACOM), hastily established at the Arcadia Conference (22 December 1941 – 14 January 1942).[4] ABDACOM was formed without prior consultation with either the Dutch or the Australians, and directives came only from Britain and the US. This led Evatt to label it an 'AB organisation' rather than 'a true ABDA organisation'.[5] More critically, the initial ABDACOM boundaries excluded the continent of Australia, yet expected the nation's forces to be made available for the defence of the area. It was only because of strong representations by the Australian government that Britain agreed to expand the ABDACOM boundaries. This expanded boundary included part of the northern Australian mainland, while the ANZAC Area (Australia and New Zealand) was established as an associated support

---

3 Examples of the many works dedicated to Evatt's life and his foreign policy legacy include Alan Renouf, *Let Justice Be Done: The Foreign Policy of Dr H.V. Evatt* (Brisbane: University of Queensland Press, 1983); Ken Buckley, Barbara Dale and Wayne Reynolds, *Doc Evatt: Patriot, Internationalist, Fighter and Scholar* (Melbourne: Longman Cheshire, 1994); David Day (ed.), *Brave New World: Dr H.V. Evatt and Australian Foreign Policy, 1941–1949* (Brisbane: University of Queensland Press, 1996).
4 Wigmore, *Australia in the War of 1939–1945*, 646–9.
5 'Evatt to Casey, 7 January 1942', NAA: A981, WAR 54.

area.⁶ The expansion of ABDACOM was significant not only in terms of providing for local defence, but also because it linked to the Australian government's hopes to insert itself into the grand strategy of the great powers. Australia was anxious to institute an ANZAC Area with itself as a main base in the Pacific theatre, rather than it being at the periphery of Allied activities.⁷

The loss of Malaya and Singapore and the rapidly deteriorating situation in the NEI highlighted the strategic neglect of the Asia-Pacific region and frustrated Australian–British relations. Tensions famously came to a head in February 1942. In January, the British government requested the 6th and 7th divisions of the AIF be transferred from the Middle East to the NEI to join British troops in creating a defensive line against Japan's southward advance.⁸ The Australian government initially supported this request, seeing in the concentration of the AIF in the Pacific theatre an opportunity, as Secretary for Defence Frederick Shedden informed Curtin, to strengthen 'our claim to a voice in the higher direction of operations in this region'.⁹ In mid-February, with the 7th Division in transit, the Supreme Commander of ABDACOM, General Archibald Wavell, informed Australia that the NEI could not be held and the 7th Division should be diverted to Burma. Senior Australian military officials—cognisant of Australia's insecurity in the wake of Singapore's recent collapse—advised the 6th and 7th divisions should be returned home for local defence. On 19 February, Curtin informed the British government of his decision to return the two divisions to Australia.¹⁰ Remarkably, Churchill ignored this directive, instructing the British Admiralty, which was overseeing the transport of the Australian division, to deliver the troops to Burma. This incensed Curtin, who accused Churchill of threatening the security of Australia and the men on board

---

6   For Curtin's initial response to the ABDACOM machinery and boundaries, see 'Doc. 185, Memorandum of Conversation by Stewart (Division of European Affairs), 12 January 1942', in Frederick Aandahl, William M. Franklin and William Slany (eds), *Foreign Relations of the United States: The Conferences at Washington, 1941–1942, and Casablanca, 1943* (Washington, DC: US Government Printing Office, 1958) [hereinafter *FRUS: The Conferences*].
7   Buckley et al., *Doc Evatt*, 228–30; Horner, *High Command*, 147–9.
8   Joan Beaumont, 'Australia's War: Asia and the Pacific', in *Australia's War, 1939–45*, ed. Joan Beaumont (Sydney: Allen & Unwin, 1996), 33–4.
9   'Shedden to Curtin, 9 January 1942, NAA: MP1217, 573', cited in Horner, *High Command*, 149. Curtin repeated this assessment to Earl Page, the Australian representative to the London Pacific War Council and British War Cabinet. 'Doc. 334, Curtin to Page, 15 February 1942', in Hudson and Stokes, *DAFP*, vol. 5.
10   'Doc. 345, Curtin to Page, 19 February 1942', in Hudson and Stokes, *DAFP*, vol. 5.

the convoy of ships. He insisted the troops be returned home.[11] While the British government quickly complied, the episode had made clear that Australia's views on strategic planning in the Pacific theatre were of little account to Britain.

As British power in the Asia-Pacific region collapsed and Australia was left exposed, the Curtin government pursued greater cooperation with the US. In early 1942, Evatt spent six weeks in the US, where he successfully petitioned for increased war supplies (mainly aircraft) and the creation of the Pacific War Council (PWC) in Washington—a body established for intergovernmental consultation and decision-making concerning Allied strategy in the Pacific theatre—in which Australia was directly represented.[12] The PWC did not play an effective role in strategic decision-making, as it remained largely advisory in function.[13] Owen Dixon, who served as the Australian representative on the PWC, later described the body as neither effective nor well informed, with no agenda or minutes kept and discussions 'always' avoiding the 'critical issues' of the war in the Pacific.[14]

Australia was presented with a new opportunity for direct representation in Allied strategic decision-making when the Pacific theatre was named an area of US strategic responsibility in March 1942. ABDACOM was replaced with the South West Pacific Area (SWPA), which encompassed Australia, New Guinea, Papua, the Philippines, the western part of the Solomon Islands and most of the NEI. With Malaya, Singapore and the NEI having already fallen and Japan on the verge of capturing the Philippines, the US needed a new base from which to launch actions against the Japanese. Australia was the only viable option. General Douglas MacArthur was ordered to leave the Philippines and travel to Australia, where he took up the role of Supreme Commander of the SWPA, with authority over Allied naval, land and air forces in the area.[15] Newspapers across Australia documented the enthusiastic crowds who welcomed

---

11 'Doc. 366, Curtin to Attlee (Secretary of State for Dominion Affairs), 23 February 1942', in Hudson and Stokes, *DAFP*, vol. 5.
12 'Doc. 446, Evatt to Curtin, 29 March 1942' and 'Doc. 649, Evatt to Curtin, 18 April 1942', in Hudson and Stokes, *DAFP*, vol. 5. There was already a London PWC on which Australia was represented by Earl Page.
13 Buckley et al., *Doc Evatt*, 157.
14 'Doc. 187, War Cabinet Minute, 12 May 1943', in R.G. Neale (ed.), *Documents on Australian Foreign Policy 1937–1949. Volume 6: July 1942 – December 1943* (Canberra: AGPS, 1983) [hereinafter *DAFP*, vol. 6].
15 Beaumont, 'Australia's War', 35; Horner, *High Command*, 181.

MacArthur, who looked to be the nation's salvation. The arrival of US troops and equipment in the coming months appeared to confirm this.[16] Privately, senior Australian military officials and MacArthur agreed that an attack on Australia or its supply lines was highly possible in the near future. MacArthur advised the 'first step' in organising Australia as an effective base was 'to make Australia secure'.[17] The defence of Australia finally appeared to be a strategic priority, and Curtin, MacArthur and Shedden worked closely to develop a comprehensive plan to achieve this goal.[18]

Despite the initial promise of a voice in strategic decision-making, Australia's new status in the SWPA came with limitations. The Allies' grand strategy—the so-called Beat Hitler First policy—named Germany 'the prime enemy' and prioritised the Atlantic and European theatres. Until Germany was defeated, the Pacific War would be a holding war with 'the minimum force necessary' provided for defensive operations.[19] Joint US–Australian operations in the SWPA resulted in significant victories at Midway and in the Coral Sea; however, the US continued to refuse MacArthur's and the Australian government's requests for the increased reinforcements necessary to launch a counteroffensive against Japan.[20] Evidently, Australia's immediate security concerns were only to be accommodated when they did not jeopardise the great powers' grand strategy. Australia's place in this grand strategy foreshadowed the challenges the nation would face in seeking to influence the management of the postwar Asia-Pacific region.

---

16   'American Troops Here: USA Announces', *The Courier-Mail*, [Brisbane], 18 March 1942, 1; 'Enthusiastic Thousands Give Welcome to MacArthur', *The Sun*, [Sydney], 22 March 1942, 1; 'General MacArthur: City's Rousing Welcome', *The Age*, [Melbourne], 23 March 1942, 3.
17   'Advisory War Council Meeting, 26 March 1942, NAA: A2684, 967', cited in Horner, *High Command*, 183.
18   For the cooperation between Curtin, MacArthur and Shedden and the machinery for strategic decision-making in Australia, see Horner, *High Command*, 189–91.
19   'Doc. 115, Memorandum by the US and British COS, 31 December 1941', in Aandahl et al., *FRUS: The Conferences*.
20   For a full account of MacArthur's and Australia's representations to the US and Britain, see Horner, *High Command*, 186–203; Buckley et al., *Doc Evatt*, 152–65.

THE GENESIS OF A POLICY

# Securing Australia in an American lake

By the second half of 1942, as the immediate threat of Allied defeat passed, Australia's attention turned to postwar planning. A significant marker of this turn was the Department of Post-War Reconstruction, established in December 1942, which was responsible for coordinating Australia's transition to a peacetime economy.[21] The rapid success of Japan's Pacific campaign had exposed the political and strategic weaknesses of the arc of islands to Australia's north, while British and US neglect of the area in strategic planning forced on the Australian government the realisation that it would have to take on greater responsibility for regional defence in the postwar world. Australia's future defence would rely on the preservation of strategic isolation, as the Commander-in-Chief of the AMF explained on behalf of the Defence Committee:

> It follows that the preservation of this isolation should be our strategic aim. While this is our chief aim, we cannot separate our safety from that of the island groups that lay in proximity on the North and East, since the seizure of these by any hostile power would facilitate the approach to our shores and remove this isolation.

This could be achieved through the control of the islands to Australia's north and establishment of a system of bases as 'forward defence localities'.[22]

Evatt incorporated strategic isolation into his wartime diplomacy. In particular, he had designs on the Indonesian Archipelago. Following Japan's invasion of the NEI in February 1942, the Australian government hosted the NEI administration in exile. Evatt viewed the management of the NEI as a particularly weak link in the arc of islands to its north, arguing that, having been left virtually defenceless by the Dutch, they were a 'liability of dire consequence to Australia'.[23] As Margaret George established, Evatt hoped wartime cooperation with the NEI administration would translate into a role in the postwar reconstruction of the colony. The goal was the establishment of a military base in the NEI, which would be added to Australia's own South Pacific mandates

---

21 Stuart Macintyre, *Australia's Boldest Experiment: War and Reconstruction in the 1940s* (Sydney: NewSouth, 2015), 5–15, 122–58.
22 'Blamey to Shedden, 15 January 1944', NAA: A5954, 652/1.
23 'Doc. 330, Evatt to Bruce, 20 November 1943', in Neale, *DAFP*, vol. 6.

and bases in northern Australia to form a defensive shield.[24] Evatt pressed the NEI administration to grant Australia shared control of the colony following the war or, failing this, a long-term lease of Timor and Dutch New Guinea. The Dutch consistently refused any such arrangement and would not accept that Australia had any special role in the future management of the NEI.[25]

As Evatt pursued Australian security interests in the NEI, the future management of colonies and dependent territories faced immense changes. The US promoted a liberal international system as the future basis for global peace. This vision was, in effect, a stipulation of the US entrance into World War II. The Atlantic Charter called for a future world order founded on greater economic, territorial and strategic integrity. At the insistence of President Roosevelt and to the supreme annoyance of Churchill, the Atlantic Charter included the right for all people to choose their government. In including this detail, the US had forced an acknowledgment that the age of European imperialism was drawing to a close.[26] The US instead promoted a trusteeship system, whereby colonial territories and mandates—including those stripped from the defeated Axis powers—would gradually transition to self-governance under the patronage of trustee nations.[27]

Australia was generally supportive of trusteeship for the management of the postwar Asia-Pacific and improving the living standards of those in the region. Certainly, it was not solely altruism and a commitment to liberal internationalism that underpinned this support. Realpolitik was also at play. The DEA believed the process of self-governance would be a slow one, unfolding over decades. This time and the nature of the trusteeship system would offer an opportunity to cultivate long-lasting diplomatic, economic and security relationships, including the provision

---

24  Margaret George, *Australia and the Indonesian Revolution* (Melbourne: Melbourne University Press, 1980), 14–29.
25  These exchanges can be found in 'Netherlands East Indies—Proposed establishment of Government in Australia', in Department of External Affairs: Correspondence files, multiple number series with year prefix [Main correspondence files series of the agency], 1927–45, NAA: A989, 1943/600/5/1/5.
26  Stuart Macintyre, 'Reading Post-War Reconstruction Through National and Transnational Lenses', in *Transnationalism, Nationalism and Australian History*, eds Anna Clark, Anne Rees and Alecia Simmonds (Singapore: Palgrave Macmillan, 2017), 136, 139–41; P.G.A. Orders, *Britain, Australia, New Zealand and the Challenge of the United States, 1939–46* (New York: Palgrave Macmillan, 2003), 97–100.
27  William Roger Louis, *Imperialism at Bay 1941–1945: The United States and the Decolonization of the British Empire* (Oxford, UK: The Clarendon Press, 1977), 3–4, 18, 223–4.

of military bases in Australia's trust territories.[28] Australia's strategic vision for trusteeship is captured in Evatt's private remark that trusteeship and the postwar development of the Asia-Pacific would 'allow [the] opportunity for collaboration between Australia and her Asiatic neighbours for mutual benefit while at the same time reducing the challenge that backward countries present to the living standards of white Australia'.[29] This assessment was steeped in the paternalistic and, frankly, racist ideas of 1940s international development, whereby weak and vulnerable states were seen to present a threat to themselves and their immediate region.[30]

The US, too, was forming its own plans for the management of the Asia-Pacific. From mid-1942, Secretary of the Navy Frank Knox promoted the view that, as the US had invested significant capital into the development of wartime bases and dominated the Pacific War effort, it should receive certain entitlements in the peace settlement. These entitlements included sovereignty over all the bases the US had financed during the war and many of the former Japanese territories and recaptured Allied territories. Knox believed the future security of the US relied on its capacity to project its military presence.[31] The Pacific Ocean had to become, as the popular maxim of the time stated, an 'American lake', with a comprehensive system of bases that would provide for US security and commercial interests in the region. Knox's proposal was initially met with opposition, resting on concern that the pointedly anti-imperialist US should not be seen to make territorial gains in the war.[32] By mid-1943, however, the Australian legation in Washington reported that the president, Congress

---

28 'Australian Legation in Washington to DEA, 23 December 1942', NAA: A989, 1943/735/321.
29 'Evatt to Eggleston (Australian Minister to China), 12 October 1942', NAA: A989, 1943/735/321.
30 This thinking is exemplified in P.N. Rosenstein-Rodan, 'The International Development of Economically Backward Areas', *International Affairs* 20, no. 2 (1944): 157–65.
31 Knox, quoted in *Daily News* [Chicago], December 1942 and February 1943, in 'Doc. 71, The Chargé D'Affaires, New Zealand Legation, Washington, to the Secretary of External Affairs (McIntosh), 9 February 1944', in Robin Kay (ed.), *Documents of New Zealand External Relations. Volume 1: The Australian–New Zealand Agreement, 1944* (Wellington: A.R. Shearer, Government Printer, 1972); 'Australian Department of Information, extract from letter, 28 February 1943', in Department of External Affairs: Correspondence files, multiple number system with SPTS [South Pacific Top Secret] prefix, 1943–54, NAA: A6494, SPTS 1/2.
32 Louis, *Imperialism at Bay 1941–1945*, 373; Orders, *Britain, Australia, New Zealand and the Challenge of the United States*, 112–13.

and the Departments of State and the Navy had all added their support to Knox's proposal. Significantly, the Pacific territories on which the US had designs included Australia's mandate territory of Manus Island.[33]

The US extended its brand of liberal internationalism to the postwar global economy. The US favoured a multilateral global trading system in which nations would trade on the basis of commercial competitiveness and liberal trade reform, rather than as self-serving protectionist blocs. The true production capacity of the US economy had been revealed during the war. Once prewar trade restrictions were reinstated, however, the US would again face exclusion, with a likely outcome of overproduction, falling export prices and rampant unemployment. Liberal trade reform would ensure the US no longer faced the exclusionary Sterling Area and could continue with a high volume of exports and, in turn, low unemployment.[34] The pathway to liberal trade reform was codified in Article 7 of the Mutual Aid Agreement. The Mutual Aid Agreement had been made to outline the parameters of the reciprocal aid system and how mutual aid would be settled once war ended. Article 7 called for the elimination of 'all forms of discriminatory treatment in international commerce, and to the reduction of tariffs and other trade barriers'.[35]

Along with fears that liberal trade reform and commercial competitiveness would threaten the Sterling Area and Australia's overseas markets, the United States' economic plans challenged Australia's plans for postwar regional security. World War II was fought around the deployment of air power and it was generally accepted that aviation would transform international communications, transport and defence in the postwar world.[36] The US was positioned to excel in the civil aviation market, with established trunk routes in both the Western and the Southern hemispheres and by far the most competitive commercial aircraft manufacturing industry. The nation accordingly favoured a system of 'open skies', in which liberal commercial practices would be applied to civil aviation, allowing commercial airlines

---

33  '"View of President Roosevelt on the Future of Pacific Islands", Extracts from Australian Legation Reports, 1942–43', NAA: A6494, SPTS 1/2.
34  Roger J. Bell, *Unequal Allies: Australian–American Relations and the Pacific War* (Melbourne: Melbourne University Press, 1977), 107–10; Lee, *Australia and the World in the Twentieth Century*, 83–4.
35  S.J. Butlin and C.B. Schedvin, *Australia in the War of 1939–1945. Series 4: Civil. Volume IV: War Economy, 1942–1945* (Canberra: Australian War Memorial, 1977), 612.
36  Orders, *Britain, Australia, New Zealand and the Challenge of the United States*, 19–20, 102–5; Macintyre, *Australia's Boldest Experiment*, 218–20.

to fly and land at airports anywhere in the world.[37] The US government also pushed for access to the military airfields it had financed and helped build during the war as a 'tangible return' for the labour and money it had expended.[38] Couple competitive advantage with US designs on certain Pacific bases and the nation looked set to dominate the whole system of transpacific air transport and the associated lines of communication.

Britain and the Pacific dominions opposed the open skies system. Curtin believed the South and South-West Pacific were the 'zone of security for which Australia must be specially responsible' in the postwar world. Australia required its own air industry, airfields and jurisdiction 'in order to discharge this responsibility'.[39] Britain, Australia and New Zealand cooperated to prevent the open skies system. In October 1943, informal Commonwealth discussions were hosted in London, where it was agreed that international aviation transport should be controlled by an international authority that would regulate prices, services and jurisdictions. It was also agreed the US be informed that 'any facilities created by them will carry with them no post-war rights of ownership or user[ship]'.[40] The settlement of civil aviation is a complex subject well beyond the scope of these pages, but it is indicative of Australia's suspicion that the US could not be relied on to build a regional order that supported Australia's interests and a pertinent example of the Commonwealth's role as a mediating force in the face of the domineering US.[41]

Australia was determined to be directly involved in the Pacific peace settlement. With the US having dominated the war effort and planning to control a large swathe of the region—'by force if necessary', as one

---

37  '"Post-War Freedom of Air is US Aim", 18 January 1943, *Melbourne Herald*' and 'The text of an article by the United States Vice-President, Henry A. Wallace, March issue of the "American Magazine", 10 February 1943', cuttings, both in NAA: A989, 1943/735/835/1.
38  'Attachment, "US Surveys its Post-War Aviation Role", 16 January 1943, *New York Herald Tribune*, cutting, Australian Legation Washington to DEA, 18 January 1943' and '"Report on Post-War Civil Aviation, 27 July 1943", Halifax (British Ambassador to the US) to Eden (Secretary of State for Dominion Affairs), forwarded to DEA, 11 August 1943', both in NAA: A989, 1943/735/835/1; 'Senate Speech, Senator Russell, 28 October 1943', NAA: A6494, SPTS 1/2.
39  'Doc. 292, Curtin to Bruce, 8 October 1943', in Neale, *DAFP*, vol. 6.
40  Erik Benson, 'Suspicious Allies: Wartime Aviation Developments and the Anglo-American International Airline Rivalry, 1939–45', *History and Technology* 17 (2000): 21–42, at pp. 25, 34–5; 'Attachment, UK Air Ministry Memorandum to RAF Commanders Overseas, September 1943, UK High Commissioners Office to Prime Minister's Department, 16 September 1943', NAA: A6494, SPTS 1/2.
41  For an overview of the civil aviation dispute and its eventual settlement, see Alan P. Dobson, 'The Other Air Battle: The American Pursuit of Post-War Civil Aviation Rights', *Historical Journal* 22, no. 2 (1985): 429–39.

Democratic congressman remarked pithily—Australia could not dismiss the possibility of being sidelined.[42] In late 1942, US Secretary of State Cordell Hull proposed a joint declaration of the Allies' trusteeship policy, along with a draft of this declaration for the Allies to consider. Hull's draft declaration included plans for the creation of regional councils, made up of local trustee nations, which would answer to an international trusteeship administration.[43] The Australian government—cognisant of America's designs on the Pacific—treated Hull's proposal with a great deal of caution.

William D. Forsyth of the DEA Pacific Division was charged with advising on the 'Pacific Question'.[44] His reports went on to inform the government's response to Hull's proposal. Before joining the DEA in 1942, Forsyth had served briefly in the Department of Information and had an emerging academic career with a particular interest in economics and Pacific affairs.[45] His regional knowledge and economics training were apparent in the final reports considering trusteeship. He criticised the existing system for managing colonies and dependent territories in the Asia-Pacific region, in terms of both Australia's national interest and the wellbeing of local inhabitants. According to Forsyth, the existing system 'was dependent on European rather than local and Pacific considerations' and it failed to provide for Australia's 'needs' or the 'progress and welfare' of the trustee inhabitants. In Forsyth's view, it had partly been the failings of the existing system for colonial management that had generated political and economic instability and driven the region towards war.[46] Australia's long-term security, therefore, depended on 'the conversion' of its immediate region 'from discord, backwardness, strategic weakness and international rivalry to economic strength, prosperity and political stability'.[47] To achieve this, Forsyth called for a 'self-subsisting' Asia-Pacific system, helped along by a regional commission that would guide trustee

---

42   'Australian Department of Information, extract from letter, 28 February 1943', NAA: A6494, SPTS 1/2.
43   'Attlee to Curtin, 11 December 1942' and 'Commonwealth government to Attlee, 2 January 1943', both in NAA: A989, 1943/735/1021.
44   'Attachment, Curriculum Vitae, Forsyth to Burton (DEA Secretary), 8 July 1948', NLA: MS 5700/7/16/3.
45   'Forsyth to Burton, 8 July 1948', NLA: MS 5700/7/16/3.
46   '"Departmental view on Australian Interests in the Colonial Question", 15 April 1943', NAA: A989, 1943/735/1021; 'Pacific Area Research Reports, General conclusions, [n.d. (April 1943)]', NLA: MS 5700/7/22/44. The so-called needs listed by Forsyth included regional economic interests and the development of Australian airfields and bases for national security purposes.
47   'Draft memorandum by Forsyth, 2 April 1943', NAA: A989, 1943/735/1021.

nations towards the development of good governance and economic stability.⁴⁸ He insisted Australia participate fully in the creation and management of the new regional system, encouraging the government to take on greater responsibility in the area and take 'a practical lead towards the kind of post-war settlement it wishes to see in Southeast Asia and the Western Pacific'.⁴⁹

According to Forsyth, Evatt was 'extremely pleased' with the proposal for an Asia-Pacific system with an expanded role for Australia and 'immediately took up the idea'.⁵⁰ The Australian government finally responded to Hull's trusteeship proposal in March 1943. The nation called for greater cooperation and accountability in the management of trust territories through the expanded role of regional councils, making internal supervision one of their functions. So important was the issue of accountability that Evatt argued it should be negotiated before any declaration of colonial policy was made. Much to Evatt's satisfaction, the negotiation of the international trusteeship administration and regional councils was postponed until the drafting of the UN Charter in 1945.⁵¹ Conceivably, the emphasis on accountable regional councils and Forsyth's previous recommendation that Australia take the initiative in the future management of the Asia-Pacific region came as a result of fears the US would be unwilling to share power in the region. Forsyth stated as much in a departmental report, noting that if Britain were to lose interest or influence in the region, Australia may 'have use' for a 'counter-weight to American ... influence'.⁵² In calling for the expanded role of regional councils, Australia hoped to institutionalise its significance, making clear the US alone could not determine future management of the postwar Asia-Pacific region.

The future management of the Asia-Pacific continued to weigh on the minds of Australian policymakers. In April 1943, Evatt departed on a four-month trip to Washington and London, where he was tasked with

---

48   'Pacific Area Research Reports, [n.d. (April 1943)]', NLA: MS5700/7/22/44.
49   'Memorandum by Forsyth, 29 March 1943', NAA: A989, 1943/735/1021.
50   'William Douglass Forsyth interviewed by Mel Pratt, January–February 1972, Corrected Transcript', NLA: TRC 121/27, Folder 1/1/76.
51   'Dixon to DEA, 25 March 1943' and 'Evatt to Dixon, 31 March 1943', both in NAA: A989, 1943/735/1021. For the UN trusteeship system and Australia's role in its formation, see Matthew Jordan, 'Decolonisation', in *Australia and the United Nations*, eds James Cotton and David Lee (Canberra: Longueville Books with the Department of Foreign Affairs and Trade, 2012), 107–12.
52   '"The Colonial Question", 15 April 1943', NAA: A989, 1943/735/1021.

securing additional aircraft for the RAAF.⁵³ During this visit, he witnessed at first hand the United States' increasing interest in the Asia-Pacific, including surveys of the supply position of certain Pacific islands and the construction of air and naval works that appeared to be permanent and conceivably for future occupation and use.⁵⁴ He also learnt of plans for the US to assume military and administrative control of Japan following its defeat and the Big Four—Britain, China, the Soviet Union and the US— to take control of peace negotiations on behalf of smaller powers.⁵⁵ Evatt used an address at the Overseas Press Club in New York as an opportunity to push back against the big powers dominating peacemaking. He insisted Australia was a 'key Pacific nation', naturally 'concerned as to who shall live in, develop and control' this region. Accordingly, Australia was 'anxious to … play its part in the general and regional organization' for regional security.⁵⁶

In August, as Roosevelt and Churchill met in Quebec to discuss, among other things, the organisation of the postwar world, the DEA reiterated Evatt's opposition to a 'Big-Four peace' in a cable sent to Dominion Secretary Clement Attlee. Decisions were not to be made without reference to other interested governments, the DEA insisted. Concerns were also raised about America's interest in certain Pacific islands and plans to control the occupation of Japan once it was defeated. While Australia accepted the US would go on to play a prominent role in the Pacific, it was anxious to ensure future arrangements were cooperative ones that 'take into account the interests of all powers concerned'.⁵⁷

What Evatt learnt during his 1943 visit to Britain and America had a profound impact on his attitude towards the Asia-Pacific region. He became more outspoken and increasingly drew on the language of Australia as a Principal Power in an attempt to carve out a regional identity for the nation. On 14 October, Evatt presented to the House of

---

53  'Note, Suggestions to Evatt on information to be ascertained in the course of his discussions abroad, 31 March 1943', NAA: A5954, 474/10.
54  This activity is detailed in '"Future of Pacific Islands", Extracts from Australian Legation Reports, 1942–43', NAA: A6494, SPTS 1/2; 'DEA to Attlee, 24 August 1943', NAA: A989, 1943/735/321.
55  Neville Meaney, 'Dr H.V. Evatt and the United Nations: The Problems of Collective Security and the Liberal International Order', in *Australia and the United Nations*, eds James Cotton and David Lee (Canberra: Longueville Books with the Department of Foreign Affairs and Trade, 2012), 37–8.
56  'Address at the Overseas Press Club, New York, 28 April 1943', in H.V. Evatt, *Foreign Policy of Australia: Speeches* (Sydney: Angus & Robinson, 1945), 114, 116.
57  'DEA to Attlee, 24 August 1943', NAA: A989, 1943/735/321. The sender is unclear, but is likely William Hodgson, DEA Secretary.

Representatives a report on his overseas visit. On the basis of Australia's geography, contribution to the Pacific War and economic, defensive and transport interests, he described South-East Asia and the South Pacific as 'coming within an extended Australian zone'. Accordingly, Australia 'should make a very special contribution towards the establishment and maintenance of the peace settlement in South-east Asia and the Pacific'.[58] Later that day, in a meeting with John Minter, First Secretary of the US Legation in Australia, Evatt reiterated the concept of an extended Australian zone. He reportedly drew two lines across the map of the South and South-West Pacific that the two men had been consulting. The first line started at Timor, extending through to New Ireland, then down to include Solomon Islands, New Hebrides, New Caledonia and New Zealand. The second line started at the Philippines and extended to the Marshall Islands, where it then ran up to include American Samoa, Hawai`i and the Aleutian Islands. 'This', Evatt gestured to the first line, 'I think should be Australia's and this', gesturing to the second, 'should be yours ... Ours is all south of the Equator and constitutes a natural line of defence'.[59] Evatt had defined Australia's regional sphere of interest and had made expressly clear that it should not be discounted by the US in future negotiations and security arrangements.

## The 1944 Australia–New Zealand Agreement and the case for closer Commonwealth defence cooperation

With Australian actors having consistently and openly conveyed the nation's particular interests in the Asia-Pacific region and the expectation it would be directly involved in peace discussions, the developments at the Cairo Conference were 'shattering'.[60] In August 1943, Evatt requested Australia be represented at the Cairo Conference that was to

---

58 'Ministerial Statement made by Dr Evatt in the House of Representatives, 14 October 1943', in Evatt, *Foreign Policy of Australia*, 141–2.
59 'Memorandum of Conversation between Evatt and Minter, 14 October 1943, attached Johnson (US Minister to Australia) to Hull, 29 October 1943, National Archives and Records Administration [hereinafter NARA]: 47.20/164', cited in J. Reed, 'American diplomatic relations with Australia during the Second World War' (PhD thesis, University of Southern California, Los Angeles, 1969), 259.
60 Buckley et al., *Doc Evatt*, 232.

be held in November.⁶¹ Churchill, however, assured Evatt that Australia's presence would not be necessary as the main discussions would be between himself and Roosevelt and inconsequential to Australia and its military operations.⁶² Despite assurances, the decisions made at Cairo had a material impact on the overall strategy in the Pacific and the peace settlement. In addition to plans for the defeat of Japan and conditions of surrender, the US, British and Chinese leaders had agreed that, following its defeat, Japan would be stripped of all territory in the Pacific that it had seized or occupied since World War I. Formosa (Taiwan), Manchuria and the Pescadores Islands would be restored to China, while the future sovereignty of other former Japanese territories was not disclosed. Much to the Australian government's indignation, the first news it received of the decisions made at Cairo was in a press communiqué.⁶³

In being excluded from what local newspapers reported as 'the most important conference on the Pacific since the outbreak of the war', Australia's influence in the Pacific had been publicly dismissed.⁶⁴ Evatt saw in this the seemingly unrestrained influence of the great power and was convinced Australia needed to act immediately or risk facing an 'untenable' position in the Pacific peace settlement.⁶⁵ He looked across the Tasman to New Zealand for support in this endeavour.

The Australian-New Zealand Agreement (ANZAC Agreement) was a treaty of cooperation signed between the governments of Australia and New Zealand on 21 January 1944 following a conference in Canberra. The earliest plans for a conference of Australian and New Zealand leaders was proposed by Evatt on his return home from Britain and the US.⁶⁶ In Evatt's preliminary correspondence with Carl Berendsen, New Zealand High Commissioner to Australia, topics for discussion included security arrangements for South-East Asia and the South Pacific, peace

---

61  'Doc. 260, Evatt to Glasgow (High Commissioner in Canada), 24 August 1943', in Neale, *DAFP*, vol. 6.
62  'Doc. 261, Glasgow to Evatt, 24 August 1943', in Neale, *DAFP*, vol. 6.
63  'Doc. 340, Cranborne (Secretary of State for Dominion Affairs) to Curtin, 1 December 1943' and 'Doc. 341, Bruce to Curtin, 1 December 1943', both in Neale, *DAFP*, vol. 6.
64  'Curtin Should Have Been at Cairo Conference', *Tweed Daily*, [Murwillumbah, NSW], 4 December 1943, 3.
65  'Doc. 40, Berendsen (New Zealand High Commissioner in Australia) to Fraser (Minister for External Affairs and Prime Minister), 4 December 1943', in Kay, *Documents of New Zealand External Relations*.
66  *CPD: Representatives*, 19 October 1943, No. 41, 577–6.

negotiations and the future of certain bases and dependent territories.[67] While the conference and subsequent agreement were certainly driven by Evatt, New Zealand was not, as Roger Bell has proposed, simply being carried along by the force of his enthusiasm.[68] New Zealand government documents reveal the nation's own suspicions about US encroachment in the Asia-Pacific, as well as extensive and thoughtful discussion by both parties in the drafting of the ANZAC Agreement and an emphasis on presenting a united front.[69]

The most significant clauses of the ANZAC Agreement are the three dealing with security and defence, territories and dependencies, and civil aviation. In the clause addressing security and defence, Australia and New Zealand formally defined their regional zone of strategic interest as 'stretching through the arc of islands North and North East of Australia, to Western Samoa and the Cook Islands'.[70] The two Pacific dominions declared their Principal-Power status and their 'right to speak' in decision-making pertinent to this region.[71] In a pointed reference to US plans, the agreement also stated the construction of military bases and facilities in 'any territory under the sovereignty or control of another Power' during the course of the war did not 'afford any basis for territorial claims or rights of sovereignty or control after the conclusion of hostilities'.[72]

In the clause concerning dependent territories, Australia and New Zealand disavowed changes to the sovereignty or systems of control of any dependent territories within their regional zone of influence 'except as a result of an agreement to which they are parties or in the terms of which they have both concurred'.[73] The proposed South Seas Regional Commission was a testament to this consultative theme. The commission, which would facilitate cooperation between trustee administrators in the region, took up Forsyth's earlier recommendation that Australia should take the lead in developing a postwar regional system that embodied its interests and institutionalised a voice in decision-making. Indeed, Evatt and Forsyth worked closely in the preparations for the ANZAC

---

67   'Doc. 305, Evatt to Berendsen, 21 October 1943', in Neale, *DAFP*, vol. 6.
68   Bell, *Unequal Allies*, 146–57.
69   See file 'PWR, New Zealand Australia–New Zealand Relations, Conference, 1944', NAA: A989, 1943/735/168; 'Doc. 41, Nash to Fraser, 12 January 1944', in Kay, *Documents of New Zealand External Relations*.
70   'ANZAC Agreement, 21 January 1944', NAA: A5954, 652/1.
71   *CPD: Representatives*, 10 February 1944, No. 6, 156.
72   'ANZAC Agreement, 21 January 1944', NAA: A5954, 652/1.
73   ibid.

Conference; Forsyth produced an immense document—by his recount, some 500–600 pages—which considered all aspects of Australia's regional interests.[74]

Finally, the Pacific dominions declared their support for an international regulatory authority to preside over trunk routes while upholding 'the right of each country to conduct all air transport services within its own national jurisdiction, including its own contiguous territories'.[75] Along with adding weight to the ongoing Commonwealth–US civil aviation negotiations, this clause tacitly extended Australia and New Zealand's regional zone of influence to include both the seas and the air of the South Pacific and much of South-East Asia.

Christopher Waters asserts that news of the ANZAC Agreement was 'greeted with dismay in London', going on to contribute to the growing rift in Australian–British relations.[76] While this was certainly the case in Washington, and there were initial misgivings in London—primarily that the agreement had been signed without any prior consultation with Britain—the British government, in fact, came to appreciate the value of the agreement.[77]

Both the Australian and the New Zealand governments were irritated by the Cairo Conference and Britain's failure to consult with its dominions. However, with the ANZAC Agreement's references to international trunk routes and military facilities constructed during the war, the US was clearly the prime target of their protest. Evatt did little to mask this, informing the British High Commissioner to Australia that his motivation was to offer 'a warning to the Americans whose methods of infiltration were alarming'.[78] It was not surprising, then, that the ANZAC Agreement attracted criticism in the US. The US Minister to Australia, Nelson T. Johnson, complained to Hull of the 'utmost secrecy' with which the ANZAC Conference and agenda had been organised, while

---

74  'Forsyth Interview', NLA: TRC 121/27, Folder 1/1/73.
75  'ANZAC Agreement, 21 January 1944', NAA: A5954, 652/1.
76  Christopher Waters, *The Empire Fractures: Anglo-Australian Conflict in the 1940s* (Melbourne: Australian Scholarly Publishing, 1996), 25.
77  For the British government's irritation at having not been consulted, see 'Conclusions of War Cabinet Meeting, 9 February 1944', TNA: DO 35/1989.
78  'Dominions Office to Cranborne, 27 January 1944', TNA: DO 35/1989.

one Democratic congressman reportedly complained that the agreement threatened America's 'legitimate post-war aims', including 'its security and its share in air and sea trade routes in the Pacific area'.[79]

The official US response came in a letter from Hull handed to Curtin on 3 February. The Secretary of State was 'frankly disturbed' by some of the aspects of the agreement. He flagged, in particular, the proposal for a conference of all powers with territorial interests in the South and South-West Pacific, the aim of which was to provide a forum for the 'frank exchange of view on the problems of security, postwar development and native welfare'.[80] The US government believed it premature to begin negotiating postwar regional security systems, believing such a conference would encourage regional separatism, which, if left unchecked, could threaten postwar peace.[81]

An irate Evatt responded to Hull on 24 February. The general tone of his response was defensive and, among other things, he listed instances in which the US had been deceptive in its own plans for the Asia-Pacific. This included several remarks made by the president during PWC meetings (during March 1943 – January 1944) regarding the future of some territories and bases in the region. Evatt implied the US had acted against the goals of the nascent United Nations and 1943 Moscow Declarations, 'prejudice[ing] a harmonious Pacific settlement'.[82] This date stamping suggests Australia, or at least Evatt and the DEA, had been monitoring US territorial interests with a careful eye. Curtin was later informed the US government 'frankly' did 'not appreciate the attitude of Dr Evatt' or his conduct, particularly his recording of private conversations held during the PWC.[83]

---

79 'Doc. 115, Johnson to Hull, 22 January 1944', in E. Ralph Perkins, S. Everett Gleason, John G. Reid, John P. Glennon, N.O. Sappington, William Slany, Velma Hastings Cassidy and Warren H. Reynolds (eds), *Foreign Relations of the United States: Diplomatic Papers, 1944, The British Commonwealth and Europe, Volume III* (Washington, DC: US Government Printing Office, 1965) [hereinafter *FRUS 1944*]; 'Australian Legation in Washington to Prime Minister's Department, 10 March 1944', NAA: A5954, 652/1.
80 'ANZAC Agreement, 21 January 1944', NAA: A5954, 652/1.
81 'Doc. 40, Attachment, Johnson to Curtin, 3 February 1944', in W.J. Hudson (ed.), *Documents on Australian Foreign Policy, 1937–49. Volume 7: 1944* (Canberra: AGPS, 1988) [hereinafter *DAFP*, vol. 7].
82 'Doc. 56, Evatt to Johnson, 24 February 1944', in Hudson, *DAFP*, vol. 7.
83 'Doc. 128, Memorandum of Conversation, by Hull, 24 April 1944', in Perkins et al., *FRUS 1944*.

In the months that followed, the wording of the ANZAC Agreement was softened, including a modification accepting US occupation of Japan once defeated and usage rights of the nation's former territories and military bases.[84] These developments did not, however, signal Australia's rescission of its regional rights and responsibilities. The Australian government was still determined to be directly involved in the Japanese surrender and peace negotiations, with Evatt going on to publicly denounce a big-power peace as 'intolerable'.[85] During the drafting of the UN Charter at the 1945 San Francisco Conference, Evatt championed the role of small powers in the new international organisation and secured amendments to the domestic jurisdiction clause to protect against UN intervention in matters relating to immigration and economic policies and the right to extend these policies to dependent territories.[86]

Like the US, Britain expressed some initial reservations about the ANZAC Agreement. For the most part, however, the government appreciated its merits. At the time of the ANZAC Agreement's signing, British–dominion relations remained strained following the collapse of the imperial effort in the Pacific theatre. Couple this with the United States' dominance of the overall war effort and preliminary postwar planning and the future status of the Commonwealth and British power remained uncertain.[87] Robert Stewart of the Division of British Commonwealth Affairs in the US State Department judged the ANZAC Agreement to have partially resolved this uncertainty. He believed it 'all too likely' that Britain 'warmly welcomes' the agreement, 'indicating as it does that these two members of the Commonwealth do not intend to be subservient to the United States'.[88] Johnson similarly judged the agreement to represent renewed support for the Commonwealth. In this, there was a potential challenge to America's postwar plans, as Australia and New Zealand would buttress British influence, potentially outweighing the US in decision-making.[89]

---

84  'Memorandum, Department of State, 12 September 1944, NARA: 847.00/9-1244', cited in Bell, *Unequal Allies*, 158.
85  H.V. Evatt, 'Risks of a Big-Power Peace', *Foreign Affairs* 24, no. 2 (1946): 195–209, at p. 200.
86  Meaney, 'Dr H.V. Evatt and the United Nations', 40–7; Buckley et al., *Doc Evatt*, 302–6.
87  Francine McKenzie, *Redefining the Bonds of Commonwealth, 1939–1948: The Politics of Preference* (London: Palgrave Macmillan, 2002), 116–17.
88  'Doc. 117, Memorandum by Stewart, 1 February 1944', in Perkins et al., *FRUS 1944*.
89  'Johnson to Stewart, 23 March 1943, Private Papers of Nelson T. Johnson', cited in Reed, 'American diplomatic relations with Australia during the Second World War', 318.

As Stewart and Johnson suspected, neither Australia nor Britain overlooked the role of the Commonwealth in the ANZAC Agreement and the regional system it sought to institute. While the two Pacific dominions were willing to assume a greater role in regional affairs, they recognised they were not yet able to shoulder the entire responsibility for regional defence. Cooperation with Britain, therefore, remained 'essential'.[90] Indeed, in the lead-up to the ANZAC Conference, Evatt informed Berendsen that he hoped to see a new era in dominion cooperation that would form 'the foundation of the British sphere of influence in the South-West and South Pacific'.[91] After the ANZAC Agreement was signed, the Australian and New Zealand governments proposed to Britain a cooperative Commonwealth defence bloc in South-East Asia and the South Pacific. In this defence arrangement—which was based on assessments made by the Australian Defence Committee and included the recommendation that an island defence perimeter be established to protect against long-range attacks on the Australian continent—Britain, Australia and New Zealand would have primary responsibility for defending the area south of the equator, while America would take responsibility for the area north of the equator. Australia and New Zealand made clear this arrangement 'should be made as part of a general scheme' for Pacific security and 'not [be] piecemeal'.[92] In effect, the Pacific dominions were seeking to create a cooperative Commonwealth defence arrangement that was informed by their particular regional circumstances and institutionalised their relevance as Principal Powers.

On the back of the ANZAC Agreement and the proposed Commonwealth defence bloc, Secretary of State for Dominion Affairs Lord Cranborne assessed that closer dominion cooperation was 'all to the good'. In terms of defence, he believed it was

---

90 '"The Defence of the Southwest Pacific", Statement by Curtin, 18 January 1944', NAA: A5954, 652/1. See also David Day, 'Pearl Harbour to Nagasaki', in *Munich to Vietnam: Australia's Relations with Britain and the United States Since the 1930s*, ed. Carl Bridge (Melbourne: Melbourne University Press, 1991), 63–4.

91 'Doc. 35, Berendsen to Fraser, 21 October 1943', in Kay, *Documents of New Zealand External Relations*.

92 'Copy, Australian and New Zealand governments to Dominions Office, 25 January 1944, Dominions Office to Canada and South Africa High Commission, 14 February 1944', TNA: DO 35/1989. For the recommendations of the Defence Committee, see 'Doc. 6, Attachment, "Future of Southwest Pacific Region—Conference Between Australian and New Zealand Ministers", Shedden to Hodgson (DEA Secretary), 7 January 1944', in Hudson, *DAFP*, vol. 7; 'Blamey to Shedden, 15 January 1944', NAA: A5954, 652/1.

clearly to the good that Australia and New Zealand should have stated publicly that they have a primary interest in the defence of the Pacific. This declaration may be extremely valuable when we come to arrange for the post-war period. Moreover, in advocating the principle of regional collaboration in the Pacific between all the Governments concerned they have in effect adopted the ideas which we had been considering here.[93]

Cranborne's final point was in reference to recent British attention to the future of inter-imperial relationships, the role of the Commonwealth in maintaining British world power in the face of the US and USSR and the regionalisation of imperial defence planning, in which each dominion would assume greater responsibility for local defence. Like Australia and New Zealand, Britain was wary of US encroachment in the Asia-Pacific region and was not convinced it could be relied on to share power in the postwar world. The Commonwealth could serve as a friendly yet robust counterweight to the US.[94]

## Curtin's fourth empire

Both the demeanour—'overbearing' and 'brusque to the point of being rude'—and the portfolio of Evatt have seen him dominate material dealing with this period.[95] Indeed, Australia's assertive wartime diplomacy and geopolitical consciousness in foreign policymaking have largely been characterised as Evatt's personal project.[96] Certainly, he led the way in building a geopolitically informed foreign policy that instituted Australia's role in the management of the postwar Asia-Pacific region. However, this agenda was by no means his alone. Curtin, too, was considering the future role of the Commonwealth and Australia in the changing world order and implementing his own initiatives.

Beginning in mid-1943, Curtin built a case for closer cooperation in the postwar imperial system. World War II and the fall of Singapore, in particular, revealed the weakness of the existing systems for imperial

---

93  "'Australian–New Zealand Agreement of 21 January 1944", Memorandum by Cranborne, War Cabinet Meeting, 2 February 1944', TNA: DO 35/198.
94  Waters, *The Empire Fractures*, 14–17; Orders, *Britain, Australia, New Zealand and the Challenge of the United States*, 98.
95  Buckley et al., *Doc Evatt*, 183.
96  See for instance, Meg Gurry, 'Identifying Australia's "Region": From Evatt to Evans', *Australian Journal of International Affairs* 49, no. 1 (1995): 17–31, at pp. 18–21.

communication and policymaking. Curtin championed a renewed commitment to British world leadership and the final chapter of empire evolution—what he called the 'Fourth Empire'—which would unite the disparate members of the Commonwealth under a more unified foreign and defence policy.[97] He argued directives could no longer come from Britain alone, proposing more frequent meetings of Commonwealth prime ministers, and not just in London. In theory, this would offer regular opportunities for the specific needs of the disparate parts of the Commonwealth to be voiced and incorporated into policymaking.[98] The showpiece of Curtin's Fourth Empire was a permanent imperial secretariat—a consultative body that would meet regularly to oversee the implementation of a united Commonwealth response to world affairs.[99]

From the leader who defiantly brought home the 6th and 7th divisions of the AIF, Curtin's Fourth Empire appeared to be a naive return to dependence on Britain. Moreover, as Paul Hasluck and Peter Edwards have argued, it underscored the disunity in Curtin's and Evatt's appreciation of the future thrust of Australian foreign policy.[100] James Curran identifies more merit in Curtin's proposal, yet he couches it in the language of a sentimental attachment to Britishness, rather than a pragmatic appraisal of Australia's national interest and the systems through which this could be protected.[101] A closer examination of public statements and private government documents, however, reveals a surprising pragmatism in the Fourth Empire and a level of similarity in the strategic visions of Curtin and Evatt.

Like the ANZAC Agreement, Curtin's Fourth Empire was an astute appreciation of Britain's diminishing relative influence. He believed the Commonwealth was 'the most effective structure for regional security the world has known', judging it to be 'in every country's interest and in the interest of any general security scheme that the structure should be maintained and, if possible, strengthened'.[102]

---

97  James Curran, *Curtin's Empire* (Melbourne: Cambridge University Press, 2011), 99–101; James Curran, '"An Organic Part of the Whole Structure": John Curtin's Empire', *The Journal of Imperial and Commonwealth History* 37, no. 1 (2009): 51–75, at pp. 60–6; 'Doc. 272, Press Statement by Curtin, 6 September 1943', in Neale, *DAFP*, vol. 6.
98  'Imperial Team Work', *The Age*, [Melbourne], 16 August 1943, 3.
99  'PM's Postwar Empire Council Plan', *The Argus*, [Melbourne], 7 September 1943, 5; 'Doc. 272, Press Statement, 6 September 1943', in Neale, *DAFP*, vol. 6.
100  Paul Hasluck, *Diplomatic Witness: Australian Foreign Affairs, 1941–1947* (Melbourne: Melbourne University Press, 1980), 137; Edwards, *Prime Ministers and Diplomats*, 154, 156–60.
101  Curran, '"An Organic Part of the Whole Structure"', 51–75.
102  '"Curtin Opens Fight for Empire Bureau", *The New York Times*, 5 May 1944', cutting, in NAA: A5954, 661/8.

Curtin reiterated the importance of maintaining British world leadership during the 1944 Commonwealth Prime Ministers' Conference. On 15 May, he called for greater Commonwealth cooperation in new international organisations, stressing his belief that 'the British Commonwealth and Empire would have much greater influence … than would the United Kingdom divorced from the Dominions'.[103] Although not explicitly stated, Curtin had implied that America alone could not be allowed to dominate the postwar global order. Cranborne appreciated Curtin's implications, having previously judged the Fourth Empire proposal to be indicative of Australia's growing impatience with 'the autocratic attitude of the United States' and seeing in this the opportunity 'to attach them closer to us'.[104] At the Commonwealth Prime Ministers' Conference, Cranborne accordingly agreed that more effective systems for collaboration and consultation were required if Commonwealth influence in global affairs was to be sustained.[105]

The proposed Fourth Empire was premised on 'full and continued consultation'.[106] In this way, as Curran notes, Curtin attempted to address longstanding concerns about the imperial relationship, creating a framework in which dominion voices would be present from the outset.[107] Direct representation within the Commonwealth was intrinsically linked to Australia's Principal-Power status and postwar security plans. A September 1943 newspaper article quoted Curtin as saying his Fourth Empire proposal was 'an attempt to enhance Australia's position' and, if adopted, would 'ensure Australia's development as a world Power with a dominating influence in the Pacific'.[108] This influence was to be cultivated through the creation of regional security zones and the increasing responsibility of the dominions. Curtin saw Australia as a trustee for British civilisation—'a power to stand for Democracy' in the

---

103 'Minutes, Fourteenth Meeting of Prime Ministers, 15 May 1944', in Records of the Cabinet Office, War Cabinet and Cabinet: Commonwealth and International Conferences: Minutes and Papers, TNA: CAB 99/28.
104 'Annotations by Cranborne on a note to Machtig, Record of conversation between British officials in Washington and Dixon, 5 November 1943', TNA: DO 35/1478.
105 'Minutes, Fourteenth Meeting of Prime Ministers, 15 May 1944', TNA: CAB 99/28. The Foreign Office went on to echo the assessment that, without Commonwealth collaboration, Britain would likely be overshadowed by the US. 'Foreign Office Memorandum, Stocktaking after VE Day, 11 July 1945', in Records created or inherited by the Foreign Office, Foreign Office: Political Departments—General Correspondence from 1906–66, TNA: FO 371/50912.
106 'Doc. 272, Press Statement, 6 September 1943', in Neale, *DAFP*, vol. 6.
107 Curran, '"An Organic Part of the Whole Structure"', 53.
108 'Empire Council Explained', *Army News*, [Darwin], 13 September 1943, 4.

South and South-West Pacific—and he was eager to see the nation take on a greater role in its region.[109] The Commonwealth regional defence bloc would have the threefold outcome of demonstrating Australia's status in its immediate region, ensuring region-specific interests were integrated within imperial defence planning and the removal of some of the strain on Britain to police its global empire.[110]

The Fourth Empire, at least in the form proposed by Curtin, failed to gain momentum. For the most part, this was because the other dominions—principally, Canada—did not wish to form a common foreign policy. Curtin left London with a compromise. In addition to daily meetings with the Dominion Affairs Secretary, the high commissioners would have monthly meetings with the prime minister, although these soon fell by the wayside.[111]

Despite the lack of substantive outcomes, Curtin's Fourth Empire represents a significant moment in the history of Australian foreign policy. It was an acknowledgement that a postwar alliance with the US was neither likely nor beneficial to Australia's material interests. Curtin's proposal signalled a pragmatic return to Britain and the imperial diplomatic and strategic framework, challenging the 'look to America' narrative that had become synonymous with his leadership. Significantly, although Australia was returning to the imperial connection, it was not willing to return to the prewar relationship that had so often seen its interests overlooked. In the ANZAC Agreement, Australia made clear that it expected to play a major role in decision-making in its region. Curtin's proposal, with its emphasis on direct representation and the regionalisation of defence planning, was the framework through which to implement the ANZAC Agreement's agenda. As the next chapter details, elements of these two initiatives informed the blueprint for Australia's attempts to develop strategic, economic and diplomatic capabilities in the new world order.

---

109 Curran, '"An Organic Part of the Whole Structure"', 59; 'Press Statement, 6 September 1943', in Neale, *DAFP*, vol. 6.
110 'Statement by Curtin, 18 January 1944', NAA: A5954, 652/1; 'Memorandum, "Improvements in the Machinery for Empire Co-operation desired by the Australian Government", Fourteenth Meeting of Prime Ministers, 15 May 1944', TNA: CAB 99/28.
111 Curran, '"An Organic Part of the Whole Structure"', 67–70.

# PART 3

# 6

# The new order: Australia's perspective on Commonwealth engagement with South-East Asia and the South Pacific, 1946–50

> By study of Pacific affairs, and through expansion of direct diplomatic and consular representation, Australia is setting out to make its own assessments of the problems of the Pacific. By so doing we may speak with a fresh, direct and independent voice in the councils of Pacific nations. It is our wish and intention to play a dynamic part in achieving, as a member of the British Commonwealth, a world comity. It is our destiny and duty to play that part in the Pacific.[1]
>
> — Australian Minister for External Affairs, H.V. Evatt

The experiences of World War II, coupled with sweeping changes to the colonial order, reaffirmed the perception of Australia as an outpost of white Western civilisation situated in a dangerous neighbourhood and demonstrated the nation could not rely on the resident order to adequately manage the arc of islands to its north. Australia's postwar foreign policy was accordingly directed towards establishing a regional system in which the area to its north would become a 'self-reliant and

---

1  *CPD: Representatives*, 13 March 1946, No. 186, 200.

co-operative [group of] Western Pacific states'.[2] The roots of this system, it will be recalled, dated back to reports in 1943 compiled by William D. Forsyth of the Pacific Division of the DEA. As this chapter will detail, this system was an integrated one designed to expand Australia's economic, diplomatic and defensive capabilities.

While Canberra sought to implement policies focused on region-specific goals, it continued to require strategic allies. The Chifley government accordingly pursued a cooperative security arrangement with the British Commonwealth and, to the extent possible, the US. This arrangement would be based on the principle of reciprocity, with shared access to strategic bases, intelligence and defence technology. Australia's visions for a cooperative Commonwealth–US security arrangement were complicated by emerging Cold War tensions. Britain and the US believed the Union of Soviet Socialist Republics (USSR) was the most immediate threat and accordingly gave strategic priority to Europe and the Middle East. Australia, conversely, prioritised South-East Asia and the South Pacific and remained reluctant to be coopted into a bipolar view of international affairs. Of particular concern to Australia was the management of the Allied occupation of Japan. The US planned to use the nation as a tool in the Cold War, which stoked Australian insecurity. The Asian nationalist movement—particularly the independence of India in 1947—also complicated Australian defence planning and raised questions about the future role of the Commonwealth.

Faced with this reality, the Chifley government had to find new ways to promote a regional system that was conducive to its national interest. The primary method adopted was a commitment to regional leadership. Contemporary political opponents of the Chifley government and historians since have suggested the government's foreign policy weakened the Commonwealth link in favour of liberal internationalism and assertive regionalism.[3] There were serious differences between the Australian and British governments—most notably, Australia's support for Indonesian independence and the outright refusal to support the anti-communist

---

2   '"Regional Arrangements with Special Reference to Pacific Policy", DEA Report for 1944 Commonwealth Prime Ministers' Conference, 27 March 1944', in Department of External Affairs: Correspondence files, multiple number series with year prefix [Main correspondence files series of the agency], 1914–93, NAA: A1838, 277/2 Part 1.
3   There are many works on the Chifley government's foreign policy and its legacies. A recent example is Adam Hughes Henry, *The Gatekeepers of Australian Foreign Policy* (Melbourne: Australian Scholarly Publishing, 2015), 1–7.

Western Union Defence Organisation.[4] However, the tendency to focus on points of Anglo-Australian conflict during the Chifley years downplays the degree of similarity and cooperation that still existed in the Anglo-Australian relationship.

This chapter argues that the Commonwealth became the primary vehicle for Australia's regional policy in the years 1946 to 1950. Australia prioritised the Commonwealth's presence in the Asia-Pacific region. Along with a defensive presence, Australia encouraged a Commonwealth economic and diplomatic presence by way of investment in the economic development of the South Pacific and, in particular, South-East Asia. While some like David Lee and David Lowe have briefly noted the link between the Colombo Plan and the British commercial crisis throughout 1940, there has been no dedicated study of South-East Asian economic development in relation to the Commonwealth. This chapter explores regional engagement as informed by a broader strategy directed towards strengthening the British world system and developing Australia's long-term diplomatic, economic and strategic capabilities.[5]

Robert Menzies' Coalition government, elected in December 1949, is often presented as the antithesis of the Chifley government. It was seemingly left up to Menzies to steer Australia back towards more balanced relations with Britain and the US, forgoing, for better or worse, internationalism, independence and regional relations.[6] Conversely, this chapter considers how ideas established by the Chifley government went on to inform the Menzies government's concept of the Commonwealth and Australia's immediate region. An examination of the Colombo Plan for Cooperative Economic Development in South and South-East Asia reveals that the spread of the Cold War into Asia created an opportunity for Commonwealth–US cooperation that was conducive to Australia's plans for regional engagement.

---

4   Neville Meaney, 'Australia, the Great Powers and the Coming of the Cold War', *Australian Journal of Politics and History* 38, no. 6 (1992): 316–33, at pp. 316–18, 322–6; Peter Edwards and Gregory Pemberton, *Crises and Commitments: The Politics and Diplomacy of Australia's Involvement in Southeast Asian Conflicts 1948–1965* (Sydney: Allen & Unwin, 1992), 4, 9–11, 17–18, 29.
5   David Lee and David Lowe both briefly note the link between the Colombo Plan and the British commercial crisis throughout the 1940s. David Lowe, 'Percy Spender and the Colombo Plan 1950', *Australian Journal of Politics and History* 40, no. 2 (1990): 162–76, at p. 164; David Lee, 'Protecting the Sterling Area: The Chifley Government's Response to Multilateralism 1945–9', *Australian Journal of Politics* 25 (1990): 178–95, at p. 185.
6   For an overview of works pitching the Chifley and Menzies governments' foreign policies against one another, see David McLean, 'Australia in the Cold War: A Historiographical Review', *The International History Review* 23, no. 2 (2001): 299–321, at pp. 229–301, 304–11.

THE GENESIS OF A POLICY

## The South Pacific Commission: Australia's commitment to regional leadership

In the 1944 ANZAC Agreement, Evatt made clear that Australia was a Principal Power. When World War II ended, the Chifley government set out to build an institutional framework within which to engage with its region, the centrepiece of which was the South Seas Regional Commission (later renamed the South Pacific Commission, SPC), helped along with enabling institutions like The Australian National University's School of Pacific Studies and an increasing interest in Asian languages in the Australian Public Service.[7] While the SPC was Australia's first significant foray into regional institution building—it is, in fact, still in force today under the new name of the Pacific Community—and despite the sizeable collection relating to the SPC housed at the National Library of Australia, very little has been written on its historical significance.[8] This is an unfortunate omission from the historical record, for the SPC was developed at a critical juncture in Australia's conceptualisation of the Pacific and its role there.

Originally proposed in the ANZAC Agreement and formalised in February 1947, the SPC was a cooperative regional body formed to study and guide administrative, economic and social development in the South Pacific trust territories. The SPC was in line with the development objectives of the UN Trusteeship Council, which was established in 1945 as one of the foundational bodies of the UN and oversaw trusteeship administration and the gradual move towards self-determination. While the SPC was promoted as strictly separate from political matters, there were, of course, political implications, not the least of which included regional security.[9] The SPC rested on the idea that economic and social discord in the 'backward' trust territories posed a threat to regional security. For the sake of peace, living standards had to be improved according to Western

---

7   Wayne Reynolds, 'Beyond White Australia: Australian Education and the Engagement of Asia After the Second World War', *International Journal of Learning* 13, no. 3 (2006): 7–14, at pp. 8–9.
8   Details of this collection can be found in National Library of Australia, 'South Pacific Commission' (Canberra: NLA, 2008 [revised 2019]), available from: www.nla.gov.au/selected-library-collections/south-pacific-commission.
9   Gregory E. Fry, 'The Politics of South Pacific Regional Cooperation', in *The South Pacific: Problems, Issues and Prospects*, ed. Ramesh Thakur (London: Palgrave Macmillan, 1991), 171–3; '"A New World in the South Pacific", DEA Report, South Seas Commission Conference, 13 February 1947', in Australian Mission, Political Representative to Allied Forces, Netherlands East Indies [Batavia], Correspondence files, multiple number series [first system, Djakarta/Jakarta] [Main correspondence files series of the agency], 1946–50, NAA: A4355, 17/1.

values. Paternalism and practical limitations aside—namely, uncertainty surrounding future projects being, as it was, an advisory body—the SPC was significant in terms of breaking down Australia's isolation from its region and it went on to shape the nation's involvement with more authoritative bodies such as the UN Educational, Scientific and Cultural Organization (UNESCO) and the UN Economic and Social Commission for Asia (ECOSOC).[10]

The SPC was also an important instrument in Australia's attempt to revive the Commonwealth's presence in the Pacific.[11] Britain's material and symbolic power was seriously depleted in the course of the war, yet it still had significant colonial responsibilities and commercial and military interests in the Asia-Pacific region. If Britain wished to have an enduring and legitimate role in the region, it was important it acted quickly to stake its claim there. As detailed in the previous chapter, John Curtin's Fourth Empire proposal sought to redefine the role of the Commonwealth, with a focus on engaging with its disparate parts and developing specialist area knowledge as the basis of policymaking. Although Curtin's proposal was not adopted, it can be seen that the Chifley government continued promoting his ideas through the SPC. This argument is supported by discussions during the 1946 Commonwealth Prime Ministers' Conference. British Secretary of State for Foreign Affairs Ernest Bevin described Commonwealth influence in the Pacific as 'somewhat strung out'. He went on to describe his hopes that Britain, India and the Pacific dominions would cooperate in developing a new regional organisation 'built up to provide a binding link between the different parts of the Empire'. Bevin was particularly interested in economic development—a theme on which Evatt quickly capitalised. Evatt noted the Australian–New Zealand idea for the SPC and requested it be included in future plans for a Commonwealth regional organisation, to which Bevin agreed.[12] This request by Evatt ultimately led to the 1947 South Seas Conference in Canberra at which the SPC was formalised.

---

10  For discussion of these agencies, see Peter Carroll, 'Australia, ECOSOC and the UN Specialised Agencies', in *Australia and the United Nations*, eds James Cotton and David Lee (Canberra: Longueville Books with the Department of Foreign Affairs and Trade, 2012), 147–83.
11  Gregory E. Fry, 'International Cooperation in the South Pacific: From Regional Integration to Collective Diplomacy', in *The Political Economy of Regional Cooperation: Comparative Case Studies*, ed. W. Andrew Axline (London: Pinter Publishers, 1994), 136, 141; Fry, 'The Politics of South Pacific Regional Cooperation', 172–3.
12  'Doc. 206, Minutes First Meeting of Prime Ministers, 23 April 1946', in W.J. Hudson and Wendy Way (eds), *Documents on Australian Foreign Policy 1937–49. Volume 9: January–June 1946* (Canberra: AGPS, 1991) [hereinafter *DAFP*, vol. 9].

The SPC was not strictly a Commonwealth organisation, as the US, France and the Netherlands all had interests in the area and joined the commission. Importantly, however, it was an Australian–New Zealand and, by association, Commonwealth initiative. Journalists and policymakers alike accordingly gave emphasis to the link between the SPC and the Commonwealth's enduring presence in the region. Sydney's *The Sun* newspaper, for instance, described the SPC as an 'Empire scheme', reporting that the 'approval of this scheme means that all the major portions of the Canberra Pact [ANZAC Agreement] have now been adopted as Empire policy in the South Pacific'.[13] This emphasis on a coordinated Commonwealth policy reflects the weight Australian commentators and the government gave to both the Commonwealth foreign policy framework and Britain's continued presence in this part of the world. Interestingly, the Commonwealth countries had the largest territorial interests and dependent populations in the area covered by the SPC. As a result, Britain, Australia and New Zealand agreed to finance 60 per cent of the commission's budget—the largest contribution.[14] Conceivably, there was a certain level of prestige attached to this sizeable contribution, signalling the Commonwealth's enduring investment and influence in the region.

Here, it is interesting to briefly note a parallel between the contemporary 'Pacific Step-up' and the SPC. The flagship initiative of the Pacific Step-up is the Australian Infrastructure Financing Facility for the Pacific (AIFFP), a $2 billion infrastructure development fund that 'upholds robust standards, avoids unsustainable debt burdens and targets the needs of nations in the region—as identified by them—and unlocks the potential of private sector investment in the region'.[15] This is expressly in response to the inroads made by China in its vast infrastructure program, the Belt and Road Initiative. Not only will the AIFFP theoretically contribute to sustained growth in the Pacific, increasing the likelihood of economic partnerships, but also it aims to maintain the resident rules-based order that has served Australia's interests. This is alluded to in the joint statement made by then Minister for Trade, Tourism and

13 '"New Empire Scheme Will Develop Pacific Islands", *The Sun*, [Sydney], 4 May 1946', cutting in Prime Minister's Department: Correspondence files, multiple number series with alphabetical prefix, 1899–1983, NAA: A518, AM815/1/1/A Part 1.
14 '"A New World in the South Pacific", 13 February 1947', NAA: A4355, 17/1.
15 'Realising the Pacific's vision for stability, security and prosperity', Speech, Ewen McDonald, Head of the Office of the Pacific, Canberra, 7 June 2019, available from: www.dfat.gov.au/news/speeches/Pages/realising-the-pacifics-vision-for-stability-security-and-prosperity.

Investment Simon Birmingham and Minister for Foreign Affairs Marise Payne: 'We want to remain an enabler of economic opportunity for our neighbours and work with them to build a Pacific region that is secure strategically, stable economically and sovereign politically.'[16] Where the SPC sought to institutionalise a distinct postwar role for Australia as an engaged and committed neighbour who could be looked to for support in regional development, today, the Pacific Step-up seeks to reaffirm Australia's status as the partner of choice. As we reflect on these parallels, it is important to interrogate the harmful and paternalistic ideas that underpinned Australia's engagement with the Pacific in the 1940s. It is promising, then, to observe the Pacific Step-up's claim to prioritise resilience, sovereignty and sustained partnerships.

## Defending Australia

Prominent voices have dismissed the enduring influence of the ANZAC Agreement and the Fourth Empire, with Joanne Wallis, for instance, writing of the agreement that, after the war, 'Australia began stepping away from the … plan that Australia and New Zealand would establish a regional zone of defence'.[17] In reality, as Lee argues, the Chifley government's defence policy 'took up where Curtin left off'.[18] The Chifley government's commitment to greater regional responsibility and encouraging economic, political and social stability in the South Pacific was in concert with defence plans. Australia's postwar regional defence planning was premised on the control of the arc of islands to its north to defend against long and mid-range attacks. The Australian government was eager to see this island defence perimeter incorporated into a broader cooperative regional defence arrangement. During the war, the US had indicated its intention to retain access rights to all the Pacific bases it had built during the war—including Australia's trust territory of

---

16 'Enhancing Australia's role in Pacific infrastructure projects', Joint media release, Senator the Hon. Marise Payne, Minister for Foreign Affairs, Canberra, 4 April 2019, available from: www.foreign minister.gov.au/minister/marise-payne/media-release/enhancing-australias-role-pacific-infrastructure-projects.
17 Joanne Wallis, *Pacific Power? Australia's Strategy in the Pacific Islands* (Melbourne: Melbourne University Press, 2017), 35.
18 David Lee, 'Britain and Australia's Defence Policy, 1945–49', *War and Society* 13, no. 1 (1995): 61–80, at p. 61.

THE GENESIS OF A POLICY

Manus Island.[19] On 13 March 1946, Minister for External Affairs H.V. Evatt announced to the House of Representatives that, while Australia welcomed the US using the Manus Island base, it would do so only on the basis of reciprocity and a Commonwealth–US 'overall defence arrangement'.[20] The British shared a similar vision, with Prime Minister Winston Churchill calling for a 'fraternal association' of the British Commonwealth and the US built on an 'intimate relationship between our military advisers, leading to common study of potential dangers, the similarity of weapons and manuals of instructions'.[21]

The foundation of the proposed joint Commonwealth–US arrangement was laid out at the 1946 Prime Ministers' Conference. The attendees agreed there was a need for a revised machinery for Commonwealth defence. This included greater inter-Commonwealth consultation in high-level strategic planning, the regionalisation of defence and each dominion taking on greater responsibility for local defence within its individual region.[22] It was also acknowledged that, in the future, the Commonwealth would have to work more closely with the US on issues of defence and foreign affairs. The Australian representatives pressed for the necessary next steps to be taken in formalising defence arrangements. Evatt and Chifley tabled the United States' recent request for access to Commonwealth bases in the Pacific, suggesting such access be granted in exchange for a Commonwealth–US 'common defence policy', which included reciprocal base use and certain 'defence obligations'.[23] The representatives agreed to a united Commonwealth (in this case, Australian, British and New Zealand) response to the US request that would be directed towards the establishment of a cooperative regional security arrangement 'for the maintenance ... of international peace and security in the South Pacific and South-West Pacific areas'.[24] In the coming

---

19   Norman Harper, *A Great and Powerful Friend: Australia and the United States, 1900–1975* (Brisbane: University of Queensland Press, 1986), 151.
20   *CPD: Representatives*, 13 March 1946, vol. 186, 200–1.
21   Winston Churchill, 'Sinews of peace', Speech, Westminster College, Fulton, Missouri, 5 March 1946 (Fulton, MO: National Churchill Museum, 2021), available from: www.nationalchurchill museum.org/sinews-of-peace-iron-curtain-speech.html.
22   'Doc. 208, Minutes Third Meeting of Prime Ministers, 24 April 1946' and 'Doc. 210, Minutes Fourth Meeting of Prime Ministers, 25 April 1946', both in Hudson and Way, *DAFP*, vol. 9.
23   'Doc. 206, Minutes First Meeting of Prime Ministers, 23 April 1946' and 'Doc. 208, Minutes Third Meeting of Prime Ministers, 24 April 1946', both in Hudson and Way, *DAFP*, vol. 9.
24   'Doc. 213, Minutes Fifth Meeting of Prime Ministers, 26 April 1946', in Hudson and Way, *DAFP*, vol. 9.

months, both Evatt and Chifley made repeated attempts to negotiate with the US State Department for reciprocal base use and a cooperative regional security arrangement.

Despite initially promising prospects for a Commonwealth–US security arrangement, these hopes were soon dashed. The US made paltry offers for reciprocal access to distant and strategically insignificant bases and doggedly refused to make specific defence commitments in the Pacific.[25] By mid-1947, the US government informed Australia that its 'strategic interests had already moved north'.[26] The declining strategic significance of South-East Asia and the South Pacific was largely the result of increasing US–USSR tensions and new plans for the occupation of Japan. Any opportunity for cooperation in nuclear developments was also blocked, with the administration of Harry S. Truman determining the US alone would control and manage the nuclear technology developed by the Manhattan Project.[27]

## Regional concepts and the future of Japan

The foundations of Australia's machinery for regional defence and engagement were being established as US plans for the management of Japan began evolving. The occupation of Japan was managed by two key bodies. The first was the Far Eastern Commission in Washington, which determined the broad policies guiding the occupation of Japan. The second body was the Allied Council for Japan (ACJ) in Tokyo, which advised on the implementation of Far Eastern Commission policies and worked towards peace negotiations. The Supreme Commander of the Allied Council for Japan (SCAP) was US General Douglas MacArthur, with whom the interim administrative directives rested. This system afforded MacArthur a fair amount of flexibility in decision-making and the Australian government had initially hoped it could appeal to him

---

25   'Doc. 1, Evatt to Chifley', 'Doc. 30, Evatt to Chifley, 19 July 1946' and 'Doc. 316, United States Embassy in Canberra to DEA, 12 December 1946', all in W.J. Hudson and Wendy Way (eds), *Documents on Australian Foreign Policy 1937–49. Volume 10: July–December 1946* (Canberra: AGPS, 1993) [hereinafter *DAFP*, vol. 10]; 'Acheson (Under Secretary of State) to US Embassy in Canberra, 9 December 1946' and 'Memorandum by US Admiral Denfeld, [n.d. (June 1947)]', both in NAA: A6494, SPTS 1/1.
26   'Forsyth Interview', NLA: TRC 121/27, Folder 2/2/151.
27   This decision was formalised in the *Atomic Energy Act* of 1946. Wayne Reynolds, 'Imperial Defence After 1945', in *Australia and the End of Empires: The Impact of Decolonisation on Australia's Near North, 1945–65*, ed. David Lowe (Geelong, Vic.: Deakin University Press, 1996), 121–4.

to ensure Australia played a leading role in the management of Japan.[28] Australia's William Macmahon Ball was appointed the Commonwealth representative on the ACJ, and the joint British Commonwealth Occupation Force in Japan was commanded by an Australian lieutenant general. These appointments, Macmahon Ball reflected, 'showed a new and interesting development in British Commonwealth relations'.[29]

The occupation of Japan initially operated on the basis of gradual economic reform, with strict controls to limit the nation's war potential.[30] Generally, this met Australia's desire for an occupation and peace treaty that would provide for the 'complete elimination of Japanese imperialistic militarism'.[31] From mid-1947, however, the US government began to 'Reverse Course': the promotion of economic rehabilitation through the revival and expansion of capitalism to encourage the economic and social conditions in which democracy could take hold.[32] The Reverse Course reflected the recent announcement by the USSR and China that they would no longer cooperate with the ACJ, granting the US near free rein in the management of the Japanese occupation and the opportunity to implement the burgeoning Truman Doctrine, which aimed to contain communism by helping certain vulnerable nations maintain their political and economic integrity. Occupied Japan was conducting very little regional trade, with many Asia-Pacific nations still resentful of Japan's recent belligerence. Japan accordingly relied on exports from the US, contributing to a growing dollar deficit and, in turn, susceptibility to economic and political collapse. In supporting Japan's economic development, the US hoped to establish the nation as an industrial hub for East Asia and an economic and strategic bulwark against communism.[33]

Important signifiers of Washington's evolving ideas for Japan and the foundation of US power in Asia include two visits made by US Under Secretary of the Army William Draper—the first in September 1947 and

---

28  Ai Kobayashi, *W. Macmahon Ball: Politics for the People* (Melbourne: Australian Scholarly Publishing, 2013), 82–9; W. Macmahon Ball, *Japan: Enemy or Ally?* (Melbourne: Cassell & Company, 1948), 21–2.
29  Macmahon Ball, *Japan*, 29.
30  Michael Schaller, *The American Occupation of Japan: The Origins of the Cold War in Asia* (Oxford, UK: Oxford University Press, 1985), 65–72.
31  '"Security in the Pacific", Address by H.V. Evatt to the Herald Tribune Forum, New York, 2 October 1945', in H.V. Evatt, *Australia in World Affairs* (Sydney: Angus & Robertson, 1946), 76.
32  Schaller, *The American Occupation of Japan*, 78–81; Macmahon Ball, *Japan*, 196–7.
33  Schaller, *The American Occupation of Japan*, 24–6, 82–3; 'Attachment, Speech by Royall (Secretary of the Army), 17 January 1948, Eckersley (Acting Head of Australian Mission in Tokyo) to Burton (DEA Secretary), 9 February 1948', NAA: A1838, 3103/11/161 Part 1.

the second in March–April 1948. Draper, who reportedly opposed heavy reparations and punitive peace, was joined by a retinue of prominent US businessmen charged with examining economic opportunities in Japan and the resources necessary to continue developing them.[34] Following the trips, the Army Department compiled a list of preliminary recommendations, including greater freedom of movement for Japanese businessmen, restoring power to the Japanese government and a revolving trade fund. The list of recommendations was presented to the State Department, which gave its 'unqualified support' to the rehabilitation of Japan and all associated funding.[35] This approach to the occupation of Japan was formalised in the National Security Council (NSC) policy paper 13/2, signed on 7 October 1948. NSC 13/2 planned for recovery driven by regional economic integration, arrangements for Japanese military security and the signing of a lenient peace treaty.[36] At this point, the State Department seized control of initiatives in Japan, MacArthur lost much of his administrative power and any opportunity for Australia to influence SCAP decision-making virtually disappeared.

The US considered Australia's endorsement of its policy towards Japan 'highly desirable' because of its role in the ACJ and membership of the Commonwealth, in which Australian support could 'usually be counted upon to involve New Zealand and often UK support'.[37] While Australian policymakers agreed that a stable Japanese economy was necessary for lasting peace, they feared the Reverse Course would place Japan 'in a position where her industries are built up to constitute a war potential'.[38] Patrick Shaw, the Commonwealth representative on the ACJ following Macmahon Ball's departure, was concerned by the thinly veiled justifications for the new US approach:

---

34  '"The Trend of United States Policy Towards Japan", [n.d. (April 1948)]' and 'Australian Mission in Tokyo to DEA, 31 March 1948', both in NAA: A1838, 3103/11/161 Part 1.
35  John Stenson-Wright, *Unequal Allies? United States Security and Alliance Policy Towards Japan, 1945–60* (Stanford, CA: Stanford University Press, 2005), 32–4; Schaller, *The American Occupation of Japan*, 122, 131–7; 'Doc. 651, Royall to Acting Secretary of State, 23 April 1948', in John G. Reid and David H. Stauffer (eds), Foreign Relations of the United States, 1948, *The Far East and Australasia*, Volume VI (Washington, DC: US Government Printing Office, 1974) [hereinafter *FRUS 1948*].
36  'Doc. 588, Attachment, "Recommendations with Respect to United States Policy toward Japan", Report by the NSC, 7 October 1948', in Reid and Stauffer, *FRUS 1948*.
37  'Doc. 1, Policy Statement of Department of State, 18 August 1948', in Reid and Glennon, *FRUS 1949*.
38  '"The Trend of United States Policy Towards Japan", [n.d. (April 1948)]', NAA: A1838, 3103/11/161 Part 1. Evatt reiterated these concerns in an address to Parliament, arguing that 'it will be an evil day for Australia if Japan is given capacity to rearm'. *CDP: Representatives*, 8 April 1948, No. 15, 747.

> The most frightening aspect of the present development of American policy is that while it is ostensibly aimed at 'lightening the burden of Occupation on the American taxpayer', everyone including the Japanese, knows the aim is the re-establishment of a strong Japan as the bulwark against the USSR. Strength implies military as well as economic revival.[39]

The Australian government was also concerned by America's concept of the Asia-Pacific region. Japanese economic rehabilitation relied on treating the Pacific and South-East Asia as a 'Japanese quarry', from which raw materials could be sourced, converted into manufactured goods and sold back to these same regional nations.[40] This arrangement undermined plans for a self-reliant regional system and relegated its immediate area of strategic concern to merely an appendage of US policy. Australia accordingly rejected US plans for Japan, promoting a just yet disciplinary peace treaty 'in which all participants in War had full voices'.[41] In the ACJ, Shaw doggedly resisted US attempts to relax restrictions on Japanese travel and commercial fishing.[42] The Chifley government's position, along with its reluctance to accept the Cold War world view, made for frigid Australian–US relations throughout the immediate postwar years.[43]

Australia's response to America's unacceptable concept for Asia-Pacific security was to promote a Commonwealth solution. The Chifley government acted quickly to coordinate new security arrangements with Britain. The Anglo-Australian Joint Project was established in 1946, leading to the development of the Woomera Range Complex in South Australia, where long-range missiles were to be tested.[44] As previously noted, at the 1946 Prime Ministers' Conference, it had been agreed that Commonwealth defence planning would be revised with a view to organising on a regional basis, although no definite machinery was established. In early 1947, Australia took preliminary steps towards

---

39  'Shaw to DEA, 24 March 1948', NAA: A1838, 3103/11/161 Part 1.
40  Reynolds, 'Imperial Defence After 1945', 125.
41  '"The Trend of United States Policy Towards Japan", [n.d. (April 1948)]', NAA: A1838, 3103/11/161 Part 1; 'Attachment, Evatt Address to ECOSOC, 30 July 1948, Australian Delegation at ECOSOC to DEA, 4 August 1948', NAA: A1838, 856/20 Part 3.
42  Buckley et al., *Doc Evatt*, 278.
43  These differences were not helped by suspicions about Soviet sympathisers within the Australian government. See, Frank Cain, 'Venona in Australia and its Long-Term Ramifications', *Journal of Contemporary History* 35, no. 2 (2000): 231–48.
44  Wayne Reynolds, *Australia's Bid for the Atomic Bomb* (Melbourne: Melbourne University Press, 2000), 74–91; Peter Morton, *Fire Across the Desert: Woomera and the Anglo-Australian Joint Project 1946–1980* (Canberra: AGPS, 1989), 52–7, 63–9, 103–33.

developing this machinery with a major defence review. The review, which considered national defence needs in the event of a global war, promoted the regionalisation of Commonwealth defence as the basis of a world system for security. As Defence Minister John Dedman explained:

> This means that each member of the Empire has a primary responsibility in regard to its own problem in its particular region, which requires working out, not only with the other members of the Empire concerned, but also with other nations with territorial and strategic interests in that area. If you piece these regional arrangements together you achieve a major contribution to an overall plan, whether on a British Commonwealth or a world basis.[45]

Within this system, Australia would be 'the main support area' for South-East Asia and the South Pacific and would, 'from time to time', act 'on behalf of the rest of the Commonwealth' in matters relating to the region.[46]

In 1947, Australia had been hopeful about securing a Commonwealth–US defence arrangement. By 1948, with the Reverse Course in Japan and America's refusal to make specific defence commitments, Australia was less optimistic and shifted its focus to a Commonwealth solution for Asia-Pacific security. In October, Evatt attended the 1948 Prime Ministers' Conference. Among his primary aims was determining the 'essential measures required … to allow Commonwealth countries to integrate successfully in the event of war'. This included high-level strategic planning, equipment standardisation and determining areas of strategic responsibility.[47] The British delegation tabled a memorandum that reaffirmed its commitment to the regionalisation of defence and the development of a machinery 'to prepare common strategic objectives and organise plans'.[48] Having read this memorandum, the Australian

---

45 *CPD: Representatives*, 4 June 1947, No. 23, 3336.
46 'Doc. 163, Council of Defence Meeting, 12 March 1947', in W.J. Hudson and Wendy Way (eds), *Documents on Australian Foreign Policy 1937–49. Volume 12: Australia and the Postwar World 1947* (Canberra: AGPS, 1995) [hereinafter *DAFP*, vol. 12]. See also, 'Doc. 160, "Appreciation of Certain Aspects of the Strategical Position of Australia", Joint Intelligence Committee Appreciation, 27 March 1947', in Hudson and Way, *DAFP*, vol. 12.
47 'Boase (Evatt's defence advisor during the 1948 Prime Ministers' Conference) to Shedden (Secretary Department of Defence), 27 September 1948', NAA: A816, 14/301/351.
48 '"Commonwealth Defence Co-operation", Memorandum by British COS, Prime Ministers' Conference, 23 September 1948', in Department of Defence: Correspondence files, multiple number series [Classified 301] [Main correspondence files series of the agency], 1928–62, NAA: A816, 14/301/351.

delegation proposed joint planning on a regional basis—a proposal that was 'given the "green light"' by the British.[49] It was on the basis of this joint planning that the Australian, New Zealand and Malayan (ANZAM) defence area was established.

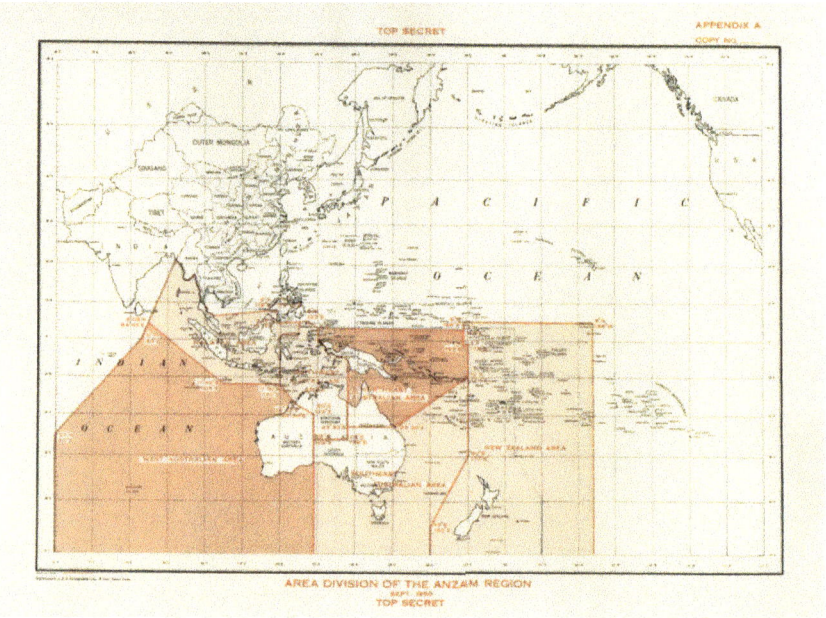

**Figure 6.1 ANZAM defence area**
Source: Courtesy of National Archives of Australia, NAA: A5954, 1419/13.

Established over a series of joint planning discussions in late 1948 and 1949, ANZAM was both an area of strategic responsibility and the machinery for Australian, British and New Zealand strategic planning. ANZAM provided the basis for defence responsibilities in peacetime and the command structure in the event of war. Effective consultation was achieved through the appointment of British and New Zealand liaison officers, stationed in Australia. Within the ANZAM area, Australia assumed overall responsibility for the lines of sea communication and home defence, New Zealand assumed responsibility for its home defence and Britain for the defence of Malaya and other possessions in the area. Regular consultation aimed to provide for relatively cohesive planning

---

49 'Boase to Shedden, 18 October 1948', NAA: A816, 14/301/351.

for 'co-ordination with overall planning in the Anzam Area'.[50] Spanning from the Indian Ocean across to the Cook Islands in the South Pacific Ocean and up from New Zealand to Malaya, the ANZAM area effectively codified Australia's strategic zone of responsibility as demarcated in the 1944 ANZAC Agreement.

## Responding to regional nationalism

America's declining interest in Australia's immediate region and the Reverse Course in the management of occupied Japan coincided with an upsurge of Asian nationalism, making regional engagement a more complicated and urgent task. Asian nationalism rendered trusteeship and the gradual move towards self-determination—the preferred method for trustee nations and the basis of Australia's plan for engaging with the islands to its north—effectively redundant. Australia's response was to reinforce its commitment to developing its diplomatic capabilities, principally in the role of a good neighbour and partner in realising the aspirations of its regional community.

Where the US and Britain tended to see the hand of the Soviet Union and ideological expansionism in the Asian nationalist movement, the Chifley government was broadly supportive and sought to accommodate the changing regional landscape within its foreign policy. This was particularly true of John Burton, Evatt's private secretary (1941–47) and DEA secretary (1947–50), who saw in the Asian nationalist movement legitimate aspirations worthy of support.[51] Australia's position on Asian nationalism has produced scholarly assessments pointing to a profound shift in Anglo-Australian relations. Christopher Waters, for instance, argues that Australia was 'bitterly to disappoint' the British government in its resistance to the narrative of a Soviet-inspired movement.[52] More critically, in supporting Indonesian independence and standing against

---

50   Hiroyuki Umetsu, 'The Origins of the British Commonwealth Strategic Reserve: The UK Proposal to Revitalise ANZAM and the Increased Australian Defence Commitment to Malaya', *Australian Journal of Politics and History* 50, no. 4 (2004): 509–25, at pp. 510–11; '"Procedure for Future Planning in Relation to British Commonwealth Defence in ANZAM Area", Defence Committee Report, revised copy following Joint Planning discussions, 26 August 1949', NAA: A5954, 1626/4.
51   Adam Hughes Henry, 'John Burton: Forgotten Mandarin?', in *The Seven Dwarfs and the Age of the Mandarins: Australian Government Administration in the Post-War Reconstruction Era*, ed. Samuel Furphy (Canberra: ANU Press, 2015), 221; Henry, *The Gatekeepers of Australian Foreign Policy*, 2–3.
52   Waters, *The Empire Fractures*, 168–9, 171–4.

the Netherlands at the UN—a move the British had cautioned against—Australia effectively undermined the legitimacy of Britain's own claims in South-East Asia and the South Pacific.[53] The Chifley and Clement Attlee governments certainly differed in their assessments of the USSR. When it came to Asian nationalism, Australia's response sought to deliver a regional system that reinforced the Commonwealth's influence.

Australia's response to Asian nationalism attempted to encourage stability and reform its regional identity. Supporting the economic aspirations of the nationalists was central to this task. In early 1947, the Australian economist and public servant H.C. Coombs wrote to the prime minister offering his personal suggestions on how best to respond to Asian nationalism. He believed it 'unwise' to allow political differences to lead Australia to 'oppose in any way the achievement of the legitimate economic aspirations of these peoples'. Coombs concluded that the Australian government 'should make a conscious attempt to identify herself with these developments'.[54] Coombs was by no means the first to note the relationship between economic development, diplomacy and regional stability. However, his position as director-general of the Department of Post-War Reconstruction and closeness to Chifley, as both an advisor and a friend, placed him among the most influential public servants in postwar Australia. It is significant, then, that these comments have been overlooked elsewhere.

While the Chifley government has been accused of betraying the Commonwealth in its response to Asian nationalism, there is much to suggest the government conceived of the changing political forces in South-East Asia and the Pacific as an opportunity to redefine and extend Commonwealth influence in the region. In a statement to the House of Representatives in June 1947, Evatt argued that Britain and the Pacific dominions had a responsibility to the region, calling on them to play their 'due part … in helping the peoples of these areas achieve their legitimate nationalist aspirations'. He made a clear link between these so-called regional responsibilities and safeguarding Commonwealth interests.

---

53   For discussion of Australia's role in Indonesian independence, see Peter Denis, 'Australia and Indonesia: The Early Years', in *Australia and the End of Empires: The Impact of Decolonisation on Australia's Near North, 1945–65*, ed. David Lowe (Geelong, Vic.: Deakin University Press, 1996), 43–52; George, *Australia and the Indonesian Revolution*.
54   'Coombs to Chifley, 11 February 1947', in Department of External Affairs: Correspondence files, multiple number series with year prefix [Main correspondence files series of the agency], 1933–71, NAA: A1068, ER47/70/7.

He encouraged Britain, Australia and New Zealand to cooperate in developing regional awareness, believing the two Pacific dominions were geographically positioned to provide 'special area knowledge' that could inform 'what is best likely to preserve British Commonwealth interests in this part of the world'.[55]

India was among the most important tests of Australia's support for Asian nationalism. While the Chifley government welcomed India's independence in 1947, it was vocal about its desire to see the nation remain a member of the Commonwealth. Evatt underscored the freedom and security Australia enjoyed as a dominion in a statement to the House of Representatives:

> The Australian Government, as a member of the British Commonwealth of Nations, enjoying a status of complete freedom and autonomy in both domestic and foreign policies, has looked forward to the achievement by India of a similar status and a similar freedom. The people of India should be fully aware of this free and autonomous position of Australia and other members of the British group of nations. On this view India could pursue all its national aspirations while still maintaining the link by which all members of the British Commonwealth are bound together.[56]

Australia ultimately supported Indian membership as a republic, owing no allegiance to the Crown but still committed to the Commonwealth and the British world system.

The Chifley government's enthusiasm for India's continuing Commonwealth membership rested on delivering strategic capabilities. Not only was India an important member of the Sterling Area and central to British commercial power; it was also defensively significant. As Commonwealth defence planning moved towards regionalisation, the Australian government identified an opportunity to draw India into a defence arrangement. India would act as 'a main support area', defending sea lines of communication adjacent to ANZAM and taking on greater responsibility in Middle Eastern defence.[57] Although the Chifley government did not successfully secure a defence arrangement with India,

---

55  *CPD: Representatives*, 5 June 1947, No. 23, 367–8.
56  *CPD: Representatives*, 26 February 1947, No. 9, 164–5.
57  Frank Bongiorno, 'British to the Bootstraps? H.V. Evatt, J.B. Chifley and Australian Policy on Indian Membership of the Commonwealth, 1947–49', *Historical Studies* 36, no. 125 (2005): 18–39; Reynolds, 'Imperial Defence After 1945', 124–6; Buckley et al., *Doc Evatt*, 296.

it continued to promote closer relations with this important neighbour. Australia consistently aligned itself with India on matters of regional importance at various meetings of Commonwealth ministers and at the 1947 and 1949 New Delhi conferences.[58]

By mid-1948, the Asian nationalist movement was gaining momentum: there was agitation in Malaya, India had gained independence from Britain and Burma and Ceylon (Sri Lanka) followed in 1948. The DEA acted on the ideas presented by Coombs, Evatt and others, appointing a goodwill mission to South-East and East Asia. The genesis of the mission was a tour of the region carried out by the British Council—a British government–funded body designed to promote greater international knowledge of British culture. Following this tour, Britain requested the Australian government contribute to a cultural diplomacy program that would 'ensure the spread of British ideas and influence … and prevent other foreign influences from supplanting British influence there'.[59] Macmahon Ball was appointed leader of the mission. As a prominent public intellectual, a close observer of Asian politics and an experienced diplomat, he was well suited to the task.[60] Australia committed to providing scholarships and relief aid; these plans were later broadened to include the provision of supplies under UN rehabilitation and development schemes.[61] The mission was also investigatory in nature, providing an opportunity to make contact with local officials and nationalist leaders to better understand the region and determine future development needs.

Macmahon Ball presented his report on the mission to the federal government in July 1948. Above all else, he recommended Australia invest in the economic aspirations of Asia, including the continued provision of scholarships and relief aid. Macmahon Ball was particularly focused on education:

---

58  David Fettling, 'An Australian Response to Asian Decolonisation: Jawaharlal Nehru, John Burton and the New Delhi Conference on Non-Western Nations', *Australian Historical Studies* 45, no. 2 (2014): 202–19; Julie Suares, 'Engaging with Asia: The Chifley Government and the New Delhi Conferences of 1947 and 1949', *Australian Journal of Politics and History* 57, no. 4 (2011): 495–510.
59  'Doc. 155, Cabinet Submission by Chifley and Pollard (Minister for Post-War Reconstruction), 12 January 1948', in Pamela Andre (ed.), *Documents on Australian Foreign Policy 1937–49. Volume 14: The Commonwealth, Asia and the Pacific, 1948–49* (Canberra: AGPS, 1998) [hereinafter *DAFP*, vol. 14].
60  Cotton, *The Australian School of International Relations*, 181, 187–8.
61  'Doc. 156, Press Statement by DEA, 16 May 1948', in Andre, *DAFP*, vol. 14.

> Technical and intellectual aid is singularly important in these countries since so many of the new governments are controlled by students. These are young men with enough intelligence to understand what they lack in training and experience. To win the friendship and goodwill of the students and technicians is to win the goodwill of people with great political influence.[62]

The key implication here was that Australia could demonstrate a shift from colonial overseer to a partner in regional affairs, signifying a commitment to engaging in the welfare of the peoples of South-East and East Asia.

Macmahon Ball's suggestions seemingly persuaded the DEA and, in September 1948, an appreciation of the recent developments in the region was carried out. The key theme emerging from this was that the Australian government 'should, by all possible means, encourage countries in the area to look to Australia as an impartial and sympathetic collaborator in their desire to develop stable governments and economic strength'. Existing scholarship programs were expanded and technical and administrative advice provided to local manufacturers and governments.[63] As we will see, there is a clear link between economic and technical assistance as a means of garnering political influence and the future Colombo Plan.[64]

Key Australian policymakers conceived of the Asian nationalist movement as an opportunity. They hoped to gain greater regional awareness and revitalise the Commonwealth presence in the area. More critically, they could piece together a strategic and diplomatic network in the region, countering America's disinterest in South-East Asia and the South Pacific and its ominous plans for Japan.[65]

Alongside diplomatic and strategic capabilities, Australia was seeking to develop its economic capabilities as part of a cohesive regional system. To fully appreciate the link between trade, diplomacy and security and the Chifley government's thinking on regional engagement, we must consider

---

62  'Report on a Mission to East Asia, 27 May – 6 July 1948, 27 July 1948', NAA: A6779, 17.
63  '"Survey of Political Events and Trends in South East Asia", 6 October 1948', NAA: A1068, DL47/5/6.
64  A number of scholars have noted this link, including: Christopher Waters, 'The Macmahon Ball Mission to East Asia 1948', *Australian Journal of Politics and History* 40, no. 3 (1994): 351–63, at pp. 351–2, 354; Daniel Oakman, *Facing Asia: A History of the Colombo Plan* (Canberra: Pandanus Books, 2004), 16–18.
65  'Cabinet Agendum Number 11, 2 July 1946, NAA: A6779, Volume 28', cited in Buckley et al., *Doc Evatt*, 295–6.

## The international economic situation

While the world had largely accepted US plans for multilateralism, there were conflicting views and major stumbling blocks on the path to achieving a global multilateral trading system. The greatest of these obstacles was the dollar gap and sterling convertibility crisis.

Before the war, Britain had generally been able to maintain its dollar deficit through surplus sales to other sterling countries. The war upended this balance as Britain's import needs from the US far outstripped its exports.[66] In July 1946, the Anglo-American loan was signed, granting US$3.75 billion to Britain to cover its dollar purchases. However, the US, which believed the removal of protectionist trade practices was the only way to achieve a multilateral world trade system, included the stipulation that the sterling must become convertible to dollars in July 1947.[67] Within the Sterling Area, Britain effectively acted as the banker, granting permission for members to convert their sterling reserves into dollars to purchase US goods. This system allowed Britain to artificially control the value of the sterling and ration US exports to the Sterling Area. By enforcing convertibility, the US would reduce the effectiveness of Sterling Area discrimination.[68]

When sterling became convertible on 15 July 1947, Britain's trading partners quickly sought to convert their sterling into dollars, for revenue and capital transactions alike. This forced Britain to draw on its dollar loan at a rate that would exhaust reserves by the end of the year. An emergency Cabinet meeting was called in mid-August and sterling convertibility was suspended indefinitely. Contrary to US hopes, Britain recommitted itself to the Sterling Area. Dollar pooling arrangements were reintroduced and Britain agreed to sell dollars for sterling to Sterling Area members that

---

66  Scott Newton, 'Britain, the Sterling Area and European Integration, 1945–50', in *Money, Finance and Empire, 1790–1960*, eds A.N. Porter and R.F. Holland (London: Frank Cass, 1985), 163–5.
67  Francine McKenzie, *Redefining the Bonds of Commonwealth*, 138–55.
68  Scott Newton, 'The Sterling Crisis of 1947 and the British Response to the Marshall Plan', *Economic History Review* 37, no. 3 (1984): 391–408, at pp. 392–3.

needed to balance deficits if those members drastically limited their dollar spending. The Sterling Area was reinstated as an insular and discriminatory system of trade and finance.[69]

Although Australia agreed to limit its dollar purchases—the rationing of foodstuffs and fuel saw imports from the US fall from 19.10 per cent to 10.03 per cent of total imports between 1946–47 and 1948–49—it adopted these measures with some reservations.[70] The war had driven home to Australia the dangers of dependency on foreign markets for defence goods, and the postwar reconstruction program was a long-term solution for greater industrial capacity.[71] To achieve industrial self-sufficiency, Australia needed new import and export markets. Even before the conversion crisis, there were those in Australian political circles mindful of the risk of economic dependency on Britain. In February 1947, Coombs, for example, warned Chifley against overdependence on the Sterling Area. He believed Britain faced a 'desperate economic situation'. The nation's purchasing power was depleted, economic growth was stagnant and it was already clear it was beyond its capacity to absorb the volume of Australian produce needed to avoid a deficit. Australia should continue to support the Sterling Area, Coombs argued, benefiting from preferential treatment while planning 'consciously to reduce our dependence on the United Kingdom market'. With British purchases making up 29 per cent of all Australian exports and more than 35 per cent of imports, this would have to be a gradual process. With this in mind, Coombs encouraged Chifley to explore trade opportunities with the newly independent Asian nations—namely, India, with hopes to build on existing goodwill between the two nations.[72]

By July 1947, Coombs was considering more hasty steps towards greater economic self-sufficiency. In his private notes, he anticipated a recession by the close of the year as well as Britain's retreat to the economies of Western Europe. Coombs believed Australia's policy must be 'to cushion the effects'

---

69   Lee, 'Protecting the Sterling Area', 183; Newton, 'The Sterling Crisis of 1947 and the British Response to the Marshall Plan', 394–401; 'Statement by Chifley in the House of Representatives, 4 December 1947', in John G. Crawford (ed.), *Australian Trade Policy 1942–66: A Documentary History* (Canberra: Australian National University Press, 1968), 105–9.
70   *Official Year Book of the Commonwealth of Australia*, No. 38 (Canberra: Commonwealth Government Printer, 1951), 483–5.
71   Tim Rooth, 'Imperial Self-Insufficiency Rediscovered: Britain and Australia, 1945–51', *Australian Economic History Review* 39, no. 1 (1999): 29–51, at pp. 29–32.
72   *Official Year Book of the Commonwealth of Australia*, No. 38 (1951), 483; 'Coombs to Chifley, 11 February 1947', NAA: A1068, ER47/70/7. Figures are for the financial year 1946–47.

of these developments—in other words, reducing dependency on Britain and the US. The principal cushion Coombs proposed was a long-term plan to develop a larger proportion of Australian trade with South-East Asian and Pacific countries. This included promoting Australian trade via increased trade representatives and providing technical education and finance. In theory, this assistance in the economic development of South-East Asian and Pacific nations would be remunerated in purchases from Australia.[73]

There is no evidence that Coombs shared these views with his colleagues, however, his suggestions mirrored the DEA's strategic interests in regional affairs and development initiatives such as the SPC. His ideas were also mirrored in the emerging Commonwealth policy that attempted to solve the dollar gap and safeguard the future of Commonwealth commercial interests in South-East Asia. To understand how this Commonwealth policy developed, we must look to Cold War tensions and the United States' economic attempts to secure Europe.

Following the 1947 sterling conversion crisis, the US feared economic crisis in Western Europe would create instability and opportunities for Soviet domination. The US government believed Europe's dire economic situation was the result of a 'failure … to produce', forcing these countries to buy from the US without any hope of selling enough in return.[74] The solution was, as Secretary of State George C. Marshall argued, to rehabilitate the European economic structure, allowing it to produce exports for the dollar market that would, in time, establish an equilibrium. Marshall's assessment was the origin of the European Recovery Program (ERP, or Marshall Plan), which aimed to stimulate production by way of dollar aid, thereby creating the conditions for an integrated Europe that was part of a global multilateral economy in which the dollar ruled.[75]

Facing a desperate economic situation, the British government welcomed dollar aid, although not without some reservations. Britain pinned its hopes of rebuilding global power on the Sterling Area and the restoration

---

73 'Rough Notes on Personal Letter, authored by Coombs, 3 July 1947', NAA: A1068, ER47/70/7.
74 'Doc. 164, Memorandum of Conversation, meeting of Clayton (Under Secretary of State) and British Cabinet Members, 25 June 1947', in Ralph E. Goodwin, Marvin W. Kranz, David H. Stauffer, Howard M. Smyth, O.N. Sappington, Fredrick Aandahl, Rogers P. Churchill and William Slany (eds), *Foreign Relations of the United States, 1947, The British Commonwealth; Europe, Volume III* (Washington, DC: US Government Printing Office, 1972) [hereinafter *FRUS 1947*].
75 Schaller, *The American Occupation of Japan*, 87, 96–7; 'Doc. 140, Press Release Issued by the Department of State, 4 June 1947, Remarks by Marshall', in Goodwin et al., *FRUS 1947*.

of its colonial empire in the Asia-Pacific. Britain's trading relationships were based on imperial links and the ability to offset dollar deficits through the dollar-earning capacity of the Sterling Area countries, many of which were British territories or former territories in South-East Asia. Britain provided sterling and soft currency credit to these nations, which exported raw materials and consumer goods to the US. The dollars earnt in these sales were used to repay the British, and then deposited in the dollar pool. If the underdeveloped Sterling Area countries did not develop concurrently with Europe, there was the risk of a rapid drain on the dollar pool, eventually leading to the sterling becoming unviable.[76] The ERP conceived of the dollar problem as a European problem and accordingly sought to solve it through a regional approach. Britain, along with much of the Commonwealth, not only believed the dollar problem was an international one in which global economic rehabilitation and US commitments to full employment and greater purchases would be more effective, but also did not wish to become fully integrated into a European economy. Despite Britain's insistence that the dollar problem was a global one, no dollar aid was granted to the Sterling Area for it fit within neither the United States' Cold War strategic outlook nor its vision for multilateralism, centred as it was on dismantling discriminatory trade practices.[77]

## South-East Asia, the solution to the dollar problem?

The problems apparent in the ERP were first discussed in depth by Australian and British officials when Chifley took part in economic discussions with British Cabinet ministers in July 1948 and Evatt attended the 1948 Commonwealth Prime Ministers' Conference. In the months preceding the conference, some in the Australian Treasury Department had raised concerns that the Marshall Plan would lead Britain to become increasingly reliant on Europe for both exports and imports. This would further limit Australia's export capabilities, leaving postwar reconstruction

---

76  Newton, 'The Sterling Crisis of 1947 and the British Response to the Marshall Plan', 391, 394–6; Newton, 'Britain, the Sterling Area and European Integration', 163, 167–9.
77  Tim Rooth, 'Economic Tensions and Conflict in the Commonwealth, 1945–1951', *Twentieth Century British History* 13, no. 2 (2002): 121–43, at pp. 133, 135–6; Newton, 'The Sterling Crisis of 1947 and the British Response to the Marshall Plan', 395–7; 'Doc. 164, Memorandum of Conversation, 25 June 1947', in Goodwin et al., *FRUS 1947*.

projects unfunded and contributing to rising unemployment.[78] The task for Chifley and Evatt while in London was to find a way to balance the need for dollar imports with the need to conserve dollar spending.[79]

In a meeting with Stafford Cripps, the British Chancellor of the Exchequer, Chifley was informed that, to maintain the sterling reserves at a 'safe level' of £500 million, Britain would continue to conserve dollar spending, with plans to reduce imports by a further 10 per cent in the coming year.[80] Cripps stressed that 'everything that Australia can do to reduce her dollar deficit will ease the cut in dollar imports which the UK must make'.[81] The expectation was clear: as a dominion and member of the Sterling Area, Australia should act to preserve Britain's dollar position, likely at the expense of domestic conditions.

Despite the grim economic outlook, a hopeful long-term solution was presented. The solution was predicated on the stimulation of economic growth in the non-dollar area to create a multilateral system that did not rely on the dollar. To achieve this, Britain and Australia would collaborate in developing the industries of non-dollar countries, prioritising commodities with dollar earning and saving capabilities.[82] This line of thinking formed the basis of the British government's economic forecast. The long-term economic program aimed to create a multilateral Sterling Area, stabilise sterling reserves and reduce Britain's per annum dollar deficit from £300 million in 1948 to £100 million by 1952. It was hoped these measures would protect the Sterling Area from any economic shock experienced when the ERP ended.[83]

---

78   'Doc. 6, Nimmo (ABS Officer) to Treasury, 1 March 1948' and 'Doc. 7, Beasley (Australian High Commissioner in London) to Chifley, 27 March 1948', both in Andre, *DAFP*, vol. 14; 'Questions Relating to the work of the Australian Mission, 5 July 1948', in Department of the Treasury: Correspondence files, multiple number series with year prefix [Main correspondence files series of the agency], 1901–78, NAA: A571, 1948/1840.
79   'Doc. 21, Nimmo to Department of Treasury, 28 June 1948', in Andre, *DAFP*, vol. 14; '"London Discussions", 2 July 1947', NAA: A571, 1948/1840.
80   'Notes on discussion with Cripps, 8 July 1948', NAA: A571, 1948/1840.
81   'Notes on meeting of Chifley, Australian officers and Cripps, 8 July 1948', NAA: A571, 1948/1840.
82   'Notes on meeting of Chifley, Australian officers and Cripps, 8 July 1948' and '"Long Term Policy", Attached note for Chifley, 8 July 1948', both in NAA: A571, 1948/1840; 'Doc. 22, Notes by Coombs, Notes on Prime Minister's visit to London as reported by Wheeler, 28 July 1948', in Andre, *DAFP*, vol. 14.
83   'Doc. 22, Notes on Prime Minister's visit to London, 28 July 1948' and 'Doc. 28, Notes by Coombs on First Discussion of Long-Term Program, 22 September 1948', both in Andre, *DAFP*, vol. 14; 'Minutes Second Meeting of Prime Ministers, 11 October 1948', NAA: A5954, 1790/1.

When setting out the long-term economic program, Cripps had noted opportunities to develop dollar earning and saving capabilities in South-East Asia.[84] This region not only was home to many of the Sterling Area members, whose exports were mostly the raw materials needed to service industrial output, but also was the main area of British interests caught up in the throes of the nationalist movement. The political and economic significance of South-East Asia was underscored during the Prime Ministers' Conference. The Secretary of State for Foreign Affairs reaffirmed Britain's commitment to the Asia-Pacific and the Middle East—an area he described as the 'middle planet'.[85] Bevin saw a critical role for Britain and the Commonwealth, arguing that, if this area was carefully organised, it could become

> an equilibrium between the United States on the one hand and Russia on the other. The great Powers represented rival ideologies … Between them was the United Kingdom, with her ties to the Commonwealth and with Europe. Here was an opportunity … to prevent the middle of the world from becoming embroiled in a conflict and to exert their [British Commonwealth] influence in preserving world peace.[86]

In this undertaking, Bevin encouraged interested Commonwealth members to establish a means of regular consultation 'with the object of helping to put the political and economic life of countries in South-East Asia on a firm footing'.[87] While Bevin was particularly concerned that the area would be drawn into the Soviet sphere—a consideration not yet dominating Australian policymaking—his emphasis on economic development as a means of garnering Commonwealth influence nevertheless resonated with earlier assessments made by Australian policymakers.

Evatt immediately seized on the link between Bevin's foreign policy appraisal and recent thinking on the dollar problem. He thanked Bevin for the attention given to 'the development of backward areas', describing

---

84  'Meeting of Chifley, Australian officers and Cripps, 8 July 1948' and '"Long Term Policy", 8 July 1948', both in NAA: A571, 1948/1840.
85  Geographical definitions remained relatively fluid during the 1940s, and it should be noted that Bevin actually referenced the Near and Middle East, which would suggest western Asia. However, he proceeded to discuss developments in both western Asia and South-East Asia.
86  'Minutes Third Meeting of Prime Ministers, 12 October 1948', NAA: A5954, 1790/1.
87  ibid.

it as going 'hand in hand' with the long-term economic program.[88] Evatt focused on the dollar problem and its implications on engagement with South-East Asian and South Pacific nations. While he supported the long-term economic program, he did have reservations about the uncertainty of plans to develop non-dollar industries for dollar earnings and savings. He called for a concrete framework for promoting growth in non-dollar countries, including the provision of capital equipment, which 'would facilitate industrial development' and, in turn, 'increase the domestic standard of living … [and] purchasing power to the advantage of Australia and other countries'. These suggestions received support from the other Commonwealth prime ministers—particularly India's Prime Minister Pandit Jawaharlal Nehru—but did not result in any coherent policy.[89]

Nevertheless, both the long-term economic program and discussions at the Prime Ministers' Conference are significant. They indicate the genesis of a Commonwealth response to the dollar problem—one centred on preserving British commercial power and the Sterling Area trade relationship in the face of challenges presented by the US-led economic order. Given the Chifley government's appreciation of the value of economic development for promoting regional stability and developing future markets, Australia's support for Commonwealth regional economic engagement as a solution to the dollar problem can be seen as intertwined with plans to develop the nation's strategic and diplomatic capabilities.

The dollar problem continued to intensify when the US experienced a sharp downturn in private sector investment and domestic consumption, sending the nation into a year-long recession from November 1948. The US restricted its already small non-dollar imports, while the Sterling Area continued to make dollar purchases. This situation led to a large drop in the Sterling Area's reserves—of some $300 million in the first quarter of 1949.[90] Unless the dollar gap was quickly corrected, the Sterling Area would face a recession, necessitating further protectionist measures and quashing all hopes for a multilateral world trading system.[91]

---

88   ibid.
89   'Minutes Fifth Meeting of Prime Ministers, 13 October 1948', NAA: A5954, 1790/1.
90   'Attachment, "Notes on the Dollar Problem", Coombs to Dedman, 7 July 1949', Papers of J.J. Dedman, NLA: MS 987/14/23–30.
91   Lee, 'Protecting the Sterling Area', 188–9.

In early July 1949, US–British treasury discussions were held, and the following week an emergency meeting of the Commonwealth finance ministers was convened in London to discuss the available options. The British government hoped to secure a long-term compromise with the US—one that acknowledged the importance of an equilibrium between the dollar and the Sterling Area in achieving a multilateral trading system. In the discussions with the US, the British tabled such a compromise, indicating it would improve expenditure and increase export sales in exchange for lower tariffs, continued recovery aid and increased purchases from the Sterling Area.[92] In the coming months, the US government realised the dollar problem was increasingly becoming a Cold War problem and there were no gains to be had in the collapse of the Sterling Area. The US eventually agreed to cooperate in the proposed compromise.[93]

Although the British government had emphasised the importance of establishing multilateralism in its negotiations with the US, the Sterling Area remained the priority. According to a report produced following the emergency meeting of the Commonwealth finance ministers, all ministers present agreed that 'rebuilding the sterling reserves as quickly as possible was of paramount importance' and they would make 'practicable contribution[s] to this end'. This involved making their economies as attractive as possible to dollar countries through the introduction of currency devaluation and tax incentives. As had been discussed in the long-term economic program and at the 1948 Prime Ministers' Conference, the underdeveloped Sterling Area countries had a key role to play. There were plans to invest in these countries so they could become competitive producers of 'those commodities which can earn dollars or which the sterling area would otherwise have to purchase for dollars'.[94] As the Cold War intensified during the closing months of 1949 and into 1950, the Commonwealth was finally offered an opportunity to integrate these tentative proposals into the United States' international outlook.

---

92  'Meeting of Commonwealth Finance Ministers, Recommendations to Governments, [n.d. (July 1949)]', NLA: MS 987/14/147–53; 'Doc. 440, Snyder (Secretary of the Treasury) to Acheson (Secretary of State), 9 July 1949' and 'Doc. 441, Snyder to Acheson, 10 July 1949', both in David H. Stauffer, Frederick Aandahl, Charles S. Sampson, Howard McGaw Smyth and Joan Ellen Corbett (eds), *Foreign Relations of the United States, 1949, Western Europe, Volume IV* (Washington, DC: US Government Printing Office, 1974) [hereinafter *FRUS 1949*].
93  Lee, 'Protecting the Sterling Area', 190–1; 'Doc. 449, Position Paper for the Discussions with the British and Canadians on Pound–Dollar Problems, Prepared by the Policy Planning Staff, 3 September 1949', in Stauffer et al., *FRUS 1949*.
94  'Meeting of Commonwealth Finance Ministers, Recommendations to Governments, [n.d. (July 1949)]', NLA: MS 987/14/147–53.

THE GENESIS OF A POLICY

# Opportunities for Australian–US cooperation as the Cold War enters Asia

On 1 October 1949, the Cold War swept dramatically into Asia when the Chinese Communist Party proclaimed the People's Republic of China. This development contributed to an increasing consensus between the Department of Defence and the DEA, the two departments having previously clashed over the strategic prioritisation of South-East Asia and the threat posed by communism.[95] On the basis of the changed strategic outlook, Burton organised a series of interdepartmental discussions to work towards consistency across departments when it came to regional policy. In addition to the ministers and senior officials from the departments of Trade and Customs, Commerce and Agriculture, Defence, and External Affairs, the Chifley government called home its diplomatic representatives from China, Indonesia, Japan, Malaya, the Philippines and Thailand. Officials from Britain and New Zealand were also invited to attend the plenary sessions as observers.[96]

Burton's working paper and final summary of the discussions clearly set out the framework for Australia's future policy approach in its region. These two documents detailed fears that communist forces would use the arc of islands to Australia's north as 'stepping stones' to the continent. Political and economic stability were central to the protection of this area, avoiding the development of an environment that would allow communism to take hold. It was agreed that Australia should implement positive measures in the region to aid the development of stable and moderate states that would act as a 'buffer region between us and the Asian mainland'. Proposed measures included expanding bilateral trade, new diplomatic appointments—contacts who would not only extend

---

95 'Joint Intelligence Committee Report 72/1949, 8 February 1949' and 'Moodie (Officer in Administrative and General Division, DEA) to Joint Intelligence Committee, 24 May 1949', both in NAA: A1068, DL 47/5/6. For a full account of DEA–Defence tensions, see Christopher Waters, 'The Great Debates: H.V. Evatt and the Department of External Affairs, 1941–49', in *Ministers, Mandarins and Diplomats: Australian Foreign Policy Making, 1941–1969*, eds Joan Beaumont, Christopher Waters, David Lowe and Gary Woodard (Melbourne: Melbourne University Press, 2003), 45–61.
96 '"Australian Policy in South East Asia", report prepared for Burton, 12 December 1949', NAA: A1068, DL 47/5/6.

goodwill, but also serve as a channel for intelligence 'gathered on the spot with an eye to specific Australian requirements'—and the provision of technical and financial assistance in the region.[97]

Considering the centrality of economic development to the Chifley government's previous responses to Asian nationalism and the dollar problem, Burton's emphasis on investing in regional economic development to combat communism was not particularly novel. What was new, however, was that Australia's plans for regional engagement were beginning to accommodate the US and its Cold War outlook. Not only was there an expressed willingness to cooperate with the US in providing assistance in South-East Asia, but also there was a changing assessment of Japan. The department heads agreed it was in Australia's strategic interest that the rehabilitation of the Japanese economy continue, at least in so far as the communist victory in China had resulted in the loss of a large market for South-East Asian and Pacific nations and Japan represented an alternative market.[98] Although Australia still treated Japan with caution, this softening position indicated a renewed willingness to cooperate with US plans. Fortuitously, the Truman administration was also reassessing its policy in the Asia-Pacific region, with outcomes overlapping with many of Australia's own priorities.

The US had developed a policy for Japan as the bulwark against the USSR. Following the communist victory in China, however, the fear was that it had been the neglect of the rest of Asia that had allowed Soviet influence to expand into China.[99] In November, the State Department presented President Truman with a brief considering how best to remedy this neglect. The communist victory in China was seen as emblematic of the new 'tool of ... Russian imperialism in the Far East', and it was feared that Soviet influence would spread from mainland Asia down through the 'weak and vulnerable' South-East Asian nations. The State Department advised the president to support a program of moral and material aid to strengthen the area against a communist insurgency. Japan's continued economic growth was fundamentally tied to this program. The nation's political and economic progress would demonstrate to others 'the advantages of

---

97  '"Australia and Southeast Asia", Burton working paper for Interdepartmental Discussions, 13 November 1949' and '"Australian Policy in South East Asia", 12 December 1949', both in NAA: A1068, DL47/5/6.
98  '"Australian Policy in South East Asia", 12 December 1949', NAA: A1068, DL47/5/6.
99  Claire L. Chennault, 'The Chinese Civil War: What We Face in the Far East', *Vital Speeches of the Day* 15, no. 15 (1949): 468–70.

close association with the United States'. More critically, as the South-East Asian nations developed and their purchasing power increased, Japan would offer an alternative regional market to China and the USSR.[100]

The State Department's November report stressed the urgency of settling the Japanese peace treaty. This advice reinforced earlier reports, including those from the NSC. The US recognised that the peace treaty would give Japan the legitimacy and implied reform necessary for the nation to take its place among the Asia-Pacific community. There was also the opportunity to formalise the use of Japanese territory for US bases in the peace treaty's terms.[101] The report went on to inform US Cold War policy in Asia—largely contained in NSC policy paper 48/2, approved on 30 December 1949. The central tenant of NSC 48/2 was that the US would provide economic, technical and military assistance to friendly Asia-Pacific nations in an attempt to 'increase the present Western orientation of the area and to assist, within our capabilities, its governments in their efforts to meet the minimum aspirations of their people and to maintain internal security'. Japan was at the top of the list of nations to be supported, with plans to include MFN status in the Pacific peace treaty to ensure Japan was positioned for economic recovery and its eventual development as a regional economic hub.[102]

By late 1949, not only was the US government ready to negotiate Japanese peace, but also it had acknowledged the significance of South-East Asian countries, both in the sustainability of a multilateral trade system and in containing the spread of communism. The US was willing to provide these countries with the economic aid for which the Commonwealth had been calling since the implementation of the ERP. This convergence of Australian and US interests marked a renewed opportunity for regional cooperation. We know that Australia was aware of these opportunities because of reports received from the Australian Embassy in Washington—with one such report remarking that US 'foreign policy has turned from

---

100 'Doc. 386, Memorandum by Jessup (Ambassador at Large) to Acheson, 16 November 1949, Attachment, "Outline of Far Eastern and Asian Policy for Review with the President", 14 November 1949', in John G. Reid and John P. Glennon (eds), Foreign Relations of the United States, 1949, *The Far East and Australasia, Volume VII, Part 2* (Washington, DC: US Government Printing Office, 1976) [hereinafter *FRUS 1949*].
101 'Doc. 70, "Recommendations with Respect to US Policy Toward Japan", Report by the NSC, 6 May 1949' and 'Doc. 386, "Outline of Far Eastern and Asian Policy for Review with the President", 14 November 1949', both in Reid and Glennon, *FRUS 1949*.
102 'Doc. 387, "The Position of the US with Respect to Asia", Report to the President by the NSC, 30 December 1949', in Reid and Glennon, *FRUS 1949*.

Europe to [the] Far East'—and because NSC 48/2 was mentioned either directly or in passing in a number of press releases and newspapers articles collected by the DEA.[103]

The Chifley government was never able to capitalise on these opportunities or transfer to tangible policy the strategies developed during the later half of 1949, being defeated by Robert Menzies' coalition government in the December election. Nevertheless, as David Lowe has noted, the foreign policy thinking of the Chifley government, particularly that which developed in the years 1948 to 1949, went on to inform the Menzies government's early position towards Australia's regional role and relationships with the Commonwealth and the US.[104]

## The Colombo Plan as a constructive approach to the dollar problem

In January 1950, the Commonwealth Foreign Ministers' Conference was held in the Ceylonese capital of Colombo to discuss the political and economic implications of the communist victory in China. Australia's representative was the new Minister for External Affairs, Percy Spender. Spender, who was ambitious and well versed in the geopolitics of Australia's region, began his 16-month stint as minister with gusto. He hoped to transform tentative aid proposals into a concerted Commonwealth plan. The meeting in Colombo was the ideal platform to achieve this. Spender proposed a cooperative assistance program in South-East Asia that would create a standard of living 'under which the ideological attractions which communism exerts will lose their force'.[105] Along with a similar proposal from Ceylon's Foreign Minister, Spender's proposal went on to form the Colombo Plan.

---

103 These press releases and newspaper articles can be found in NAA: A1838, 3103/11/161 Part 4; 'Crisis in Asia: An Examination of US Policy, Remarks by Acheson, 12 January 1950', *Department of State Bulletin: Far Eastern Series* 32 (1950): 111–18.
104 David Lowe, *Menzies and the 'Great World Struggle': Australia's Cold War, 1948–1954* (Sydney: UNSW Press, 1999), 37.
105 'Doc. 16, "Economic Policy in South and South-East Asia", Memorandum by Australian Delegation to the Commonwealth Meeting of Foreign Ministers, 11 January 1950', in David Lowe and Daniel Oakman (eds), *Documents on Australian Foreign Policy. Volume 24: Australia and the Colombo Plan, 1949–1957* (Canberra: DFAT, 2004) [hereinafter *DAFP*, vol. 24].

THE GENESIS OF A POLICY

As an anti-communist program, the Colombo Plan tends to be seen through a Cold War lens—designed to capitalise on the symbolic importance of cultural and economic engagement in fighting the Cold War in Asia as well as mirroring Australia's foreign policy with that of the US, like the Point Four Program, with hopes this would lead to a regional defence arrangement. Spender's emphasis on enlisting US support for the Colombo Plan—in particular, his private message to Menzies that this was 'the main tactical objective'—leaves little doubt the Colombo Plan was a strategic solution to Asia's sudden entrance into the Cold War.[106] A solely strategic assessment of the Colombo Plan, however, overlooks the ideas about diplomatic and economic capacity-building and Commonwealth influence that had evolved during the Chifley years. As the centre of gravity of world affairs began to shift towards South-East Asia, 1950 provided the moment in which this thinking could be shaped into policy and integrated within the United States' international outlook.

The principal evidence that the economic capacity of the Sterling Area played a role in the Colombo Plan can be found in some rather neglected discussions during the 1950 Foreign Ministers' Conference. During the second session of the conference, the dollar problem was described as a Cold War problem. All present agreed that if there was a sudden financial crisis because of the dollar problem, a drop in the standard of living would invariably follow, providing the communists with the political and economic environment in which to flourish. To combat this, production would have to be increased across the non-communist world, promoting a unified and stable trading system.[107] The link between the dollar problem, Commonwealth economic power and the Colombo Plan was more clearly noted in the eighth session of the conference. According to Spender:

> [T]he fuller economic development of South-East Asia would bring great benefits not only to the region itself but also to other parts of the world and, in particular, would contribute to the solution of the monetary problems of the sterling area. The negative policy of reducing dollar imports could not provide a permanent solution. The economic development of South-East Asia would provide a more constructive approach to this problem.[108]

---

106 'Doc. 17, Spender to Menzies, 11 January 1950', Lowe and Oakman, *DAFP*, vol. 24.
107 'Minutes Second Meeting of Foreign Ministers, 9 January 1950', NAA: A1838, 532/5/2/1.
108 'Minutes Eighth Meeting of Foreign Ministers, 12 January 1950', NAA: A1838, 532/5/2/1.

He went on to note promising opportunities for raw materials and food, 'for which there was a ready market in dollar countries'.[109] Spender echoed tentative Commonwealth plans presented in the long-term economic program, seeking to reorient finance away from Europe and build up the Sterling Area as a market for dollar earnings and savings. These revelatory documents have been overlooked in histories of the Colombo Plan; nor are they included in the DFAT volume on the plan or the single Australian-authored historical monograph dedicated to it.[110]

The Colombo Plan discussions were informed by the desire to invite the US to contribute to a region in which the weight of Commonwealth economic interests was evident. The US accepted in principle the strategic importance of greater dollar and sterling equilibrium and the need to incorporate technical assistance into its South-East Asian policy, but little progress had been made. This sluggishness was due to the State Department's reluctance to initiate the provision of material support to regional associations, lest it be accused of using Asian nationalism to further its strategic ambitions.[111] While there was an opportunity to attract dollar investment in an area that was so critical to Commonwealth commercial and strategic power, it had to be carried out prudently. In the memorandum outlining the Colombo Plan, Spender noted that South-East Asia's new significance in the Cold War 'make[s] timely a high-level approach to the United States Government to represent the views of [the] Commonwealth ... on the political and economic situation and the need for economic support'.[112] The conference delegates supported Spender's recommendations and plans were made to reconvene in the coming May to discuss the implementation of the Colombo Plan. However, it was cautioned that 'any published version of the recommendations should be carefully worded, so as to avoid any possibility of misunderstanding'.[113] Presumably, this meant placing Cold War imperatives rather than the dollar problem at the forefront of discussion, as well as avoiding a brash request for US financial assistance.

---

109 ibid.
110 Lowe and Oakman, *DAFP*, vol. 24; Oakman, *Facing Asia*.
111 Lowe, 'Percy Spender and the Colombo Plan 1950', 165; 'Spender to DEA, 14 January 1950', Papers of Percy Spender, NLA: MS 4875/1/1.
112 '"Economic Policy in South and Southeast Asia", Memorandum by the Australian Delegation to the Meeting of Foreign Ministers, 11 January 1950', in Department of Foreign Affairs and Trade: Unregistered files of the Department of External Affairs, 1920–64, NAA: A9992, 1950/1.
113 'Minutes Eighth Meeting of Foreign Ministers, 12 January 1950', NAA: A1838, 532/5/2/1.

Of course, the US did not miss the rather thinly veiled ulterior motives of the Colombo Plan. The US Ambassador at Large, Phillip Jessup, noted the problem of sterling balances was 'closely associated' with the Colombo Plan, along with the possibility of being 'presented with a staggering bill' if the US supported the plan. An article in a US newspaper described the upcoming conference in Sydney as

> much less a conference to discuss 'Aid to South East Asia' than it is a conference to discuss just how South East Asia can be made to continue its aid to the Commonwealth by supplying goods which the Empire can sell for much needed dollars.[114]

Despite these reservations, the US agreed to join the Colombo Plan in November 1950, officially being admitted in February the following year.

The United States' budding hub-and-spoke alliance system was an important factor contributing to its support for the Colombo Plan. As the Cold War entered Asia, the US was considering formal alliance opportunities in the Asia-Pacific region. In April 1950, the State Department conducted an appraisal of relations with Australia. This document noted that the Menzies government was more sensitive than its predecessor to the threat of communism and willing to cooperate with the US, concluding that this new attitude 'should not be undervalued nor taken for granted'. This being said, Australia's continued mistrust of Japan meant it could not necessarily be relied on to support US plans for a lenient peace treaty. The State Department, seeing a strategic opportunity in this insecurity, knew Australia was 'anxious to see the US military position in the western Pacific strengthened' and it believed the nation could not 'afford to oppose major US policy toward Japan'.[115] The hope here was that Australia could perhaps be convinced to support US policy towards Japan in return for security assurances. This logic was apparent in the future ANZUS Treaty signed in exchange for Australia's support of a lenient peace treaty with Japan. Australia's standing as a possible ally and, to that end, US support for the Colombo Plan were helped along by the outbreak of the Korean War and Spender's opportunistic offer to send

---

114 'Doc. 22, Record of the Conversation Between Jessup and Representatives of the British Foreign Office, London, 11 March 1950', in Neil H. Petersen, William Z. Slany, Charles S. Sampson, John P. Glennon and David W. Mabon (eds), *Foreign Relations of the United States, 1950, East Asia and the Pacific, Volume VI* (Washington, DC: US Government Printing Office, 1976) [hereinafter *FRUS 1950*]; 'Memorandum, Hodgson (Head of Australian Mission in Japan) to Spender, 20 April 1950', NAA: A1838, 3103/11/161 Part 4.
115 'Doc. 96, Department of State Policy Statement, 21 April 1950', in Petersen et al., *FRUS 1950*.

Australian ground troops to Korea. For that matter, the Korean War was also a major factor in closing the dollar gap as US military commitments necessitated increased purchases from the Sterling Area, although this did coincide with increased commercial and technical development in South-East Asia.[116]

Australia's postwar strategy for regional engagement was multifaceted and highly opportunistic. Economic development in South-East Asia and the Pacific would preserve the Sterling Area, provide a long-term investment in future markets for Australian exports, promote regional goodwill and stability and revive British influence in the region—all of which were critical in building Australia's capabilities. As the Cold War entered Asia and the United States' strategic outlook expanded to include South-East Asia, the Menzies government was provided with a chance to transform the strategy developed during the Chifley years into a tangible policy. Yet, as the next chapter explores, the shared Cold War outlook of Australia, Britain and the US did not necessarily secure a Commonwealth–US partnership that would safeguard Australia's national interests.

---

116 Oakman, *Facing Asia*, 56.

# 7

# A confluence of interests: Australia realigns with the US, 1951–57

The government of Robert Menzies oversaw the signing of the ANZUS Treaty in 1951, marking the realisation of the Pacific security pact long coveted by the Australian government. By 1957, Australia had announced its decision to standardise military equipment for cooperation with the US. Some have pointed to these developments bookending the period 1951–57 as key markers of Australia's realignment from imperial ties and the British sphere of influence to that of the US and Cold War dependency. Such assessments tend to depict Australia's realignment with the US as inevitable and seamless. Thereafter, Australia's foreign policy ostensibly paralleled US directives.[1] Joan Beaumont judges this to be a 'grossly simplistic' assessment.[2] The Menzies government's foreign policy, at least until the 1957 endpoint of this book, can best be understood as an uneven transition to the US order as the government was forced to make frank assessments of Britain and the US, their priorities and capabilities and which relationship best served Australia's national interest.

---

1  See T.B. Millar, *Australia's Foreign Policy* (Sydney: Angus & Robertson, 1968); Alan Renouf, *The Frightened Country* (Melbourne: Macmillan, 1979).
2  Joan Beaumont, 'Making Australian Foreign Policy, 1941–69', in *Ministers, Mandarins and Diplomats: Australian Foreign Policy Making, 1941–1969*, eds Joan Beaumont, Christopher Waters, David Lowe and Gary Woodard (Melbourne: Melbourne University Press, 2003), 3.

This chapter is grounded in the uncertain and incompatible strategic planning of Britain and the US, exploring Australia's efforts to forge a partnership between the British Commonwealth (specifically Australia, Britain and New Zealand) and the US, built around a common goal of South-East Asian security. In the wake of the 1954 crisis in South-East Asia, Australia came to accept the unfeasibility of coordinating US and British priorities in the region, deciding to put its faith in US-led regional defence arrangements, particularly the Southeast Asia Treaty Organization (SEATO), and its vision for the region. As Britain's declining global power became apparent to the world in a series of crises and policy realignments, the Australian government was forced to acknowledge that the nation could no longer provide for its defensive or economic security on its own. This realisation hastened Australia's move into the US sphere of influence, marking the departure from the Australian–British relationship of patronage and protection that had existed for 170 years.

## ANZUS, ANZAM and the search for strategic planning

Prime Minister Robert Menzies opened Parliament in 1951 with a warning that the nation had no more than three years in which to prepare for a global war. The establishment of the Department of Defence Production and the Department of Supply to oversee government-operated factories for the production of defence goods, the introduction of the *National Service Act 1951* and plans to commit a wartime expeditionary force to the Middle East to support British interests there are indicative of the real anticipation gripping Australian policymakers of a third world war.[3] In this war, Australia would be fighting alongside Britain and the US, and Menzies accordingly wanted to ensure close consultation in the formation of global strategy. Although the US was militarily more powerful than Britain, Australia continued to value Britain's experience in world leadership and the shared values of the Commonwealth—values that aligned with Australia's national interests more closely than did those of the US.[4] Accordingly, the Australian government—drawing on the

---

3   Lowe, *Menzies and the 'Great World Struggle'*, 48–50, 52–3, 88–100; *CPD: Representatives*, 7 March 1951, No. 10, 77–8; *Official Year Book of the Commonwealth of Australia*, No. 38 (1951), 1200–9.
4   For Australian Ambassador to the US Percy Spender's assessment of Britain's values and experience, see 'Spender to Casey, 10 July 1951', cited in David Lowe, *Australia Between Empires: The Life of Percy Spender* (London: Pickering & Chatto, 2010), 145–6.

rhetoric of an alliance of the great English-speaking nations—promoted the protection of the Asia-Pacific region through closer Commonwealth–US relations. For all these efforts, however, Australia faced US reluctance to make tangible commitments to the defence of the Asia-Pacific and struggled to reconcile the fundamentally different strategic priorities of the two major Western powers. The nation was left unable to define its role, in terms of both regional and global strategic planning, and uncertain about what commitments to expect from its two powerful allies.

The ANZUS Treaty, signed on 1 September 1951, was a partial disappointment for Australia. The treaty was a vague and limited commitment and Percy Spender, who negotiated the treaty as Minister for External Affairs (soon after this, he took up the post of Australian Ambassador to the US), lamented to his successor, Richard Casey, that it was 'difficult to find within the State Department here any real policy on these [Asia-Pacific] issues'.[5] The reality was that, while the US was conscious of the strategic threats in South-East Asia and the Pacific, it continued to prioritise developments further north.[6] Spender made it his ambitious personal mission as ambassador to strengthen the Australian–US relationship and encourage a strategic Commonwealth–US partnership. He sought to use the ANZUS framework as a pathway for the exchange of intelligence and strategic planning and to relate planning for South-East Asia and the Pacific to the global planning that took place in the North Atlantic Treaty Organization (NATO) and meetings of the US Joint Chiefs of Staff (USJCS).[7]

The annual meetings of the ANZUS Pacific Council presented the main opportunity to negotiate plans for greater coordination. At the first of these meetings, held in August 1952, Spender and Casey pushed for more details on the allocation of reserve forces to the Pacific and the machinery that would coordinate ANZUS defence planning. The two men hoped to see the creation of a 'military committee' of sorts, with a high-ranking Australian and New Zealand military representative attached to their

---

5   'Spender to Casey, 18 March 1952', NLA: MS 4875/1/1.
6   There is a view that the US used ANZUS to protect the Middle East—the treaty providing a sense of regional security for Australia and New Zealand and, in turn, freeing up forces to be sent to the Middle East. See, for instance, Philip Dorling, *The Origins of the ANZUS Treaty: A Reconsideration*, Flinders Political Monographs No. 4 (Adelaide: Flinders University, 1989).
7   David Lowe, 'Mr Spender Goes to Washington: An Ambassador's Vision of Australian–American Relations, 1951–58', *The Journal of Imperial and Commonwealth History* 24, no. 2 (1996): 278–95, at pp. 282–3, 286–7; 'Spender to Casey, 18 March 1952', NLA: MS 4875/1/1.

respective embassies in Washington and granted access to USJCS meetings to ensure the two nations had a voice in global planning.[8] It soon became clear, however, that the US did not regard the ANZUS Council as a body through which combined military plans would be made. Nor was the US willing to make concrete defence commitments.

Secretary of State Dean Acheson effectively quashed Australia's hopes of being involved in global planning when he declared 'there was no such animal' and, for the time being, the 'only real "plan" was that, on the outbreak of war, we should strike at the enemy's most vulnerable point as soon as he showed his hand'.[9] Instead, the US focused on political discussions and the importance of having in place a framework for information-sharing in the event of enemy aggression. Rather than the broad-ranging machinery for consultation and military planning that Spender and Casey had envisioned, discussions were narrowed to the annual ANZUS Council meetings, with a political body and a military body, represented by the three member nations' foreign affairs ministries and military chiefs.[10] Any military queries or recommendations put forward by Australia or New Zealand generally remained unresolved, bouncing back and forth between the two council bodies. What plans the US was willing to share were readymade without prior consultation or thought for the interests of the two junior partners.[11] With the US unwilling to give Australia and New Zealand equal status in ANZUS defence planning, there was a need to secure an Australian voice through a British Commonwealth–US partnership.

The lack of a military machinery and limited opportunities to participate in decision-making were not the only causes for concern when it came to ANZUS. The treaty also highlighted the British–US struggle for power

---

8   'Doc. 53, Minutes First Meeting of ANZUS Council, First Session, 4 August 1952', in David W. Mabon (ed.), *Foreign Relations of the United States, 1952–1954, East Asia and the Pacific, Volume XII, Part 1* (Washington, DC: US Government Printing Office, 1984) [hereinafter *FRUS 1952–54*, vol. XII].
9   '1 August 1952' and '4 August 1952', both in T.B. Millar (ed.), *Australian Foreign Minister: The Diaries of R.G. Casey* (London: Collins, 1972), 84–6.
10  'Doc. 69, Appendix A, Lovett (Secretary of Defense) to Acheson, 4 September 1954', in Mabon, *FRUS 1952–54*, vol. XII; '"A Note on ANZUS Military Machinery—Its Nature and Tasks", Department of Defence memorandum, 6 October 1952', in Prime Minister's Department: Correspondence files, annual single number series [classified] with occasional C [classified] suffix [Main correspondence files series of the agency], 1913–, NAA: A1209, 1957/4252.
11  Lowe, *Menzies and the 'Great World Struggle'*, 154–5; Andrew Kelly, *ANZUS and the Early Cold War: Strategy and Diplomacy Between Australia, New Zealand and the United States, 1945–56* (Cambridge, UK: Open Book Publishers, 2018), 95–7.

and tensions surrounding strategic priorities in the Far East. To understand these tensions, the ANZAM arrangement and British strategic assessments throughout 1951–52 must be examined. Originally formed in 1949, ANZAM was both an area of responsibility and a service-level organisation designed to coordinate Australian, British and New Zealand wartime command in South-East Asia and the South Pacific. The ANZAM area overlapped with the US Pacific Command and both Britain and Australia saw early on the need for basic coordination with the US. Attempts to coordinate planning began in 1948, when Australia's Chief of Naval Staff, Vice-Admiral John Collins, approached the US Pacific Fleet. After a series of discussions between Collins, who was acting on behalf of Australia, Britain and New Zealand, and Admiral Arthur Radford, Commander-in-Chief of the US Pacific Fleet, an agreement was signed in September 1951. The main feature of the Radford–Collins agreement was the creation of a maritime boundary of responsibility between the ANZAM area and Radford's area of command in which sea communications would be jointly surveyed during peacetime and protected in the event of war. In terms of administrative ease and open communication between Britain and its Pacific dominions and the US, the Radford–Collins agreement was a useful development. Beyond this, however, as both David Stevens and Alastair Cooper note, it did not offer access to the intelligence or high-level strategic planning that Australia desired.[12]

Despite its interests in the Asia-Pacific region, Britain had not been included in the ANZUS Treaty. This exclusion was largely due to the United States' refusal to assume responsibility for defending the nation's colonial interests. Throughout 1952, the British government campaigned for observer status at ANZUS Council meetings, warning against the appearance of weakened British–US and British–Antipodean relations as a result of its exclusion.[13] While both Australia and New Zealand lent their support to British association, the US was unswayed: ANZUS membership remained unchanged and Britain was not associated in any capacity.[14]

---

12   David Stevens, *The Australian Centenary History of Defence. Volume 3: The Royal Australian Navy* (Melbourne: Oxford University Press, 2001), 163–4; Alastair Cooper, 'At the Crossroads: Anglo-Australian Naval Relations, 1945–1971', *The Journal of Military History* 58, no. 4 (1994): 699–718, at pp. 704–5.
13   '"ANZUS: United Kingdom Pressure for Observer Status", 13 October 1952', NAA: A1209, 1957/4252.
14   'Doc. 54, Minutes First Meeting of ANZUS Council, Second Session, 4 August 1952', in Mabon, *FRUS 1952–54*, vol. XII.

Britain's failed campaign for association with ANZUS coincided with a major review of global strategy. The Chiefs of Staff Committee (COS) concluded that nuclear deterrence was the most effective way to avoid a hot war with the Soviets. This was not so in the case of the Chinese threat to mainland Asia and South-East Asia, which were the areas anticipated to be the most susceptible to aggressive communist insurgencies. Britain needed to establish long-term planning and expand its commitments in the Asia-Pacific region; however, it could not afford to do this alone while also investing in its nuclear capabilities. The COS accordingly recommended the reworking of ANZAM as a strategic planning body in which Australia and New Zealand would assume planning and operational responsibilities for the region.[15] The details of the review of ANZAM were first formally discussed in a December 1952 meeting between Menzies, British Prime Minister Winston Churchill and New Zealand Prime Minister Sidney Holland. The ANZAM review was not simply about negotiating a more equitable distribution of the cost of defending Commonwealth interests; it was also about seeking to counterbalance ANZUS and US domination of the determination of strategic priorities in South-East Asia and the Pacific. To Britain, the outside observer, its exclusion from ANZUS appeared to be a deliberate blow to its influence and an attempt to undermine the Commonwealth relationship. The British government feared that, in the event of conflict in South-East Asia or the Pacific, ANZUS would become the primary planning body—one in which it would have no voice.[16]

Neither Menzies nor Holland wanted to see ANZUS debased, and Churchill accordingly reassured them that his hope was to expand the strategic partnership between Australia, Britain, New Zealand and the US with the creation of a joint ANZAM–ANZUS committee as the central machinery for planning and operations in the Asia-Pacific area.[17] The Five-Power Staff Agency, established in 1952 and comprising military representatives from Australia, Britain, France, New Zealand and the US, was the potential framework for an ANZUS–ANZAM linkage. Menzies and Holland agreed that ANZUS, with its exclusion of Britain and broadly defined area of strategic concern, was an inadequate basis for the defence of the Asia-Pacific region as a whole. The men agreed to

---

15 '"Review of Defence Policy and Global Strategy", COS Report, 7 February 1952', in Records of the Ministry of Defence, Ministry of Defence: Chiefs of Staff Committee—Reports of the Joint Planning Staff and successors, TNA: DEFE 6/20/17.
16 Umetsu, 'The Origins of the British Commonwealth Strategic Reserve', 509–10.
17 'Minutes of Meeting between Churchill, Menzies and Holland, 12 December 1952', NAA: A1209, 1957/4252.

a future meeting of Britain's, Australia's and New Zealand's chiefs of staff committees to discuss ANZAM planning and how to convince the US of its significance. With all this in place, the three men agreed 'it would then follow that the [strategic] planning … should fall into the hands of a joint ANZUS/ANZAM Committee'.[18]

Despite initial support for revising ANZAM, developments were slow. The Australian government feared the Five-Power Staff Agency would subsume ANZAM, ANZUS or both, diminishing what little scope Australia had in regional strategic planning.[19] The government also feared it would offend the US or Britain—a situation that led Casey to question whether 'membership of the Commonwealth precludes any of us from having friends outside'.[20] To a certain extent, these concerns were warranted. Britain's vision of an ANZAM–ANZUS linkage failed to appreciate the fact that central to the significance of ANZAM was the protection of colonial interests—interests the US was not willing to defend. As will be discussed, this question of colonial interests and a willingness to defend broader South-East Asia was an early sign of the challenge Australia would face in integrating US and British interests into plans for regional defence.

The joint COS discussions were postponed until mid-1953, during which time it became clear that the Five-Power Staff Agency would not form the basis of military planning and command in South-East Asia and the Pacific. It was an ad hoc body designed to aid in information exchange and consider possible responses in the event of Chinese aggression.[21] Now was the time to revisit ANZAM and consider alternative approaches to joint US–Commonwealth strategic planning for South-East Asia and the Pacific. Over five days in October 1953, the Australian, British and New Zealand defence chiefs met in Melbourne to discuss ANZAM arrangements. It was decided the ANZAM area would be reworked as the machinery for strategic planning by way of a permanent ANZAM chief of staff established in Australia. It was also agreed that responsibility for the defence of Malaya—the epicentre of British Commonwealth power

---

18  'Minutes of Meeting, 12 December 1952', NAA: A1209, 1957/4252.
19  '"Some thoughts on the ANZUS–ANZAM Item in London", Watt memorandum, [n.d. (1952)]', NAA: A1209, 1957/4252.
20  '7 September 1953', in Millar, *Australian Foreign Minister*, 103.
21  'Foster to Matthews, 29 May 1953, NARA: RG 59, 790.5/5-2953', cited in Kelly, *ANZUS and the Early Cold War*, 109; 'Doc. 86, Memorandum, Allison (Assistant Secretary of State for Far Eastern Affairs) to Dulles (Secretary of State), 29 January 1953', in Mabon, *FRUS 1952–54*, vol. XII.

in the region—should be transferred solely from Britain to the ANZAM chief of staff. Crucial to the protection of Malaya was the creation of the British Commonwealth Far East Strategic Reserve (FESR)—an idea first tabled at the 1953 Commonwealth Prime Ministers' Conference—which required the three nations to train and equip a joint military force for forward deployment in the event of unrest in Malaya.[22] The FESR was not ready for deployment until 1955, and its implications for Australia's strategic relationship with Britain and the US will be returned to.

## Crisis in South-East Asia

From late 1953, the threat of a global war gradually receded, only to be replaced with the increasing chance of limited war in South-East Asia. The ongoing power struggle in Indochina reached its peak in the early months of 1954, when the Viet Minh launched an offensive against the French garrison at Dien Bien Phu. Although reconciliation talks were planned to commence in Geneva in April, the US government was sceptical about whether these would deliver a settlement for long-term stability in South-East Asia. The nation accordingly sought to prepare for a military intervention. In early April, Secretary of State John Foster Dulles approached the Australian and New Zealand ambassadors in Washington, encouraging their respective governments to participate in the prospective united action. Dulles also hoped that, in addition to their contribution, the Pacific dominions could push Britain 'in the right direction'—that is, towards participation.[23]

Spender was particularly buoyed by the United States' eagerness to finally commit forces to South-East Asia and encouraged his government to join the united action. This enthusiasm can be better understood in the context of fears about US isolationism. President Dwight D. Eisenhower's 'New Look' approach to foreign policy focused on closer working relationships within existing alliances like ANZUS and Spender was desperately looking for ways in which Australia could capitalise on this new approach and demonstrate its usefulness as an ally. Spender

---

22 'Defence Talks Melbourne 1953—Sir John Harding Chief of the Imperial General Staff/ Australia and New Zealand', NAA: A1209, 1957/5023.
23 'Doc. 687, Memorandum of Conversation, 3 April 1951', in Neil H. Petersen (ed.), *Foreign Relations of the United States, 1952–1954, Indochina, Volume XIII, Part 1* (Washington, DC: US Government Printing Office, 1982) [hereinafter *FRUS 1952–54*, vol. XIII].

feared inactivity on the proposed united action would offend the US and threaten prospects for future interest in the defence of Australia's area of strategic concern.[24] Casey shared some of Spender's anxieties, penning in his diary that Washington would not 'go in alone' and a failure to respond may see them 'change their Southeast Asia attitude'.[25] Despite genuine concerns surrounding both the situation in Indochina and maintaining US interest in South-East Asia, the Australian government declined to join the united action. Andrew Kelly notes that the uncertain extent of military commitments and the recent Petrov affair, which had heightened concerns about the threat of domestic communism, contributed to this decision.[26] Above all, however, Australia was guided by allegiance to Britain. London was not willing to act before the Geneva conference and peaceful alternatives had been considered and Canberra would not act without London, with a Cabinet document describing such a move as 'a terrible innovation for Australia to promote, for it would be the first cleavage in Commonwealth unity'.[27]

The Geneva conference opened on 26 April. While talks were under way, the Viet Minh achieved a decisive victory at Dien Bien Phu. The task now at hand was to settle on a diplomatic solution in Indochina. The conference closed on 21 July with the signing of the Geneva Accords, which stipulated a truce and a temporary partitioning of Indochina, with the French occupying the south and the Viet Minh the north. The US government refused to endorse the accords and, as far as it was concerned, this arrangement simply consolidated the communists' position in South-East Asia and provided a foothold from which to launch further attacks. In a pre-emptive effort to deter any further advances, the US government immediately began discussing options for a collective security pact in South-East Asia. Within six weeks of the delivery of the Geneva Accords, the members of the Five-Power Staff Agency and Pakistan, Thailand and the Philippines convened in Manila to sign SEATO.[28]

---

24  Lowe, *Australia Between Empires*, 152–3. The New Look approach to US foreign policy is outlined in 'Doc. 101, Report to the NSC by Lay (Executive Secretary of NSC), 30 October 1953', in Lisle A. Rose and Neal H. Petersen (eds), *Foreign Relations of the United States, 1952–1954, National Security Affairs, Volume II, Part 1* (Washington, DC: US Government Printing Office, 1984) [hereinafter *FRUS 1952–54*, vol. II].
25  '7 April 1954', in Millar, *Australian Foreign Minister*, 124.
26  Kelly, *ANZUS and the Early Cold War*, 122–4.
27  'Menzies and Casey to Spender, 24 June 1954', in Secretary to Cabinet/Cabinet Secretariat: Menzies and Holt Ministries—Cabinet files 'C' single number series, 1949–85, NAA: A4940, C987.
28  Damien Fenton, *To Cage the Red Dragon: SEATO and the Defence of Southeast Asia* (Singapore: NUS Press, 2012), 25–8.

SEATO was promoted as a NATO-like organisation for South-East Asia, and the Australian government approached the proposed treaty with clear expectations that it should provide the military machinery necessary for the exchange of intelligence and provisions for reserve forces for deployment in the event of a regional conflict.[29] Much to Australia's disappointment, SEATO was fundamentally different to NATO. While SEATO agreed to respond to armed aggression in the treaty area as a common threat, it did not earmark forces for commitments in the treaty area. Article 5 of SEATO provided for a consultative council through which the members could meet and discuss 'matters concerning the implementation of this treaty', but this did not actually constitute the command structure desired by Australia. Furthermore, the US included a provision that it would only respond to communist aggression in the treaty area.[30] The constrained nature of SEATO was a pragmatic step to protect US freedom of action, ensuring the nation did not have to make specific military commitments in South-East Asia and that it could respond to threats on a case-by-case basis.[31]

In private discussions and in Manila, senior DEA and defence officials questioned the narrow anti-communist scope and the usefulness of a defence organisation that did not actually offer specific military commitments, appearing as more of 'a simple political organisation'.[32] Despite these reservations, Australia lent its support to SEATO, conceding that it 'would not be prepared to press it with the Americans beyond a certain point'.[33] Menzies—no doubt mindful the opportunity may not present itself again—informed Parliament that Australia could not expect its 'great friends ... to accept commitments while our own attitude

---

29 '"Proposed Establishment of SEATO—Report on Defence Aspects", Joint Planning Committee report on meetings held 16, 21, 23 and 26 July 1954' and '"South-East Asian Collective Security Organisation", Discussion between McBride (Minister of Defence) and Casey, 19 August 1954', both in NAA: A816, 11/301/938.
30 'Southeast Asia Collective Defense Treaty (Manila Pact), September 8, 1954', in US Department of State, *American Foreign Policy, 1950–1955: Basic Documents. Volume 1* (Washington, DC: US Government Printing Office, 1957–58), 912–15.
31 Fenton, *To Cage the Red Dragon*, 26–7.
32 '"South-East Asian Collective Security Organisation", 19 August 1954', NAA: A816, 11/301/938; '"Drafting of SEATO—'Aggression' or 'Communist Aggression'?", DEA working paper, 24 August 1954', NAA: A1838, TS654, 8/14/4/1A. Casey voiced these reservations while in Manila. For details of this see '5 September 1954', '6 September 1954' and '7 September 1954', in Millar, *Australian Foreign Minister*, 178–83.
33 'Notes for Casey, SEATO Conference, 31 August 1954', NAA: A1838, TS654, 8/14/4/1A.

remains tentative or conditional'.[34] Ultimately, a limited security pact for South-East Asia that included the US and Britain was better than nothing at all.

Arguably the most important aspect of the creation of SEATO and the unfolding crisis in South-East Asia was the climate it created for British–US strategic cooperation. Lowe has argued that the lack of South-East Asian member nations underscores the true significance of SEATO. Rather than a symbol of regional cooperation, SEATO was 'an opportunity to integrate and expand on Australia's defence relationships with Britain and the United States'.[35] The earliest opportunity to pursue integrated US–British defence planning for South-East Asia came in the early months of 1955. Menzies was in London for the Commonwealth Prime Ministers' Conference, where he, Churchill and Holland discussed the revision of ANZAM. Along with the creation of the FESR, the ANZAM chiefs had developed a plan (codenamed Hermes) for the defence of Malaya. Hermes rested on the assessment that the Kra Isthmus was the key line of defence. In the event of communist aggression and threat to the isthmus, all ANZAM resources would be mobilised towards preserving this line.[36] Menzies was willing to endorse Hermes with the qualification that all planning for the defence of Malaya received US endorsement. This qualification was largely a continuation of the original approach to US–ANZAM linkages discussed in December 1952, whereby it was believed that if the US saw the significance of ANZAM and the Commonwealth members were making serious contributions rather than simply expecting the US to bear the bulk of the cost, it would be willing to commit to joint planning and action.[37]

Following the Prime Ministers' Conference, Menzies continued on to Washington, bringing with him a draft of a statement guaranteeing 'effective cooperation' in the event of the ANZAM powers deploying 'substantial forces for the defence of Malaya'.[38] The US government was not willing to approve such a strongly worded document and instead provided a statement that the US 'considers the defence of Southeast Asia,

---

34  *CPD: Representatives*, 5 August 1954, No. 31, 67.
35  Lowe, *Menzies and the 'Great World Struggle'*, 175.
36  'Operation "HERMES"', NAA: A1209, 1957/4250.
37  Edwards and Pemberton, *Crises and Commitments*, 162–8.
38  'Doc. 35, Menzies to Dulles, 16 March 1955', in Edward C. Keefer and David W. Mabon (eds), Foreign Relations of the United States, 1955–*1957, Vietnam, Volume I* (Washington, DC: US Government Printer, 1985) [hereinafter FRUS 1955–57, vol. I].

of which Malaya is an integral part, to be of very great importance' and 'effective cooperation' was implied in SEATO.[39] Menzies misunderstood the US statement, believing it to be a commitment to joint ANZAM–US action in the defence of Malaya. It was based on this misunderstanding that he triumphantly announced his government's decision to station Australian troops in Malaya as part of the FESR.[40]

The US government quickly clarified Menzies' misunderstanding. Radford, now serving as the Chairman of the USJCS, informed Canberra the US had in no way committed to joint ANZAM–US planning. US defence planning was directed towards deterring aggression and defending the whole of South-East Asia. The defence of Malaya could only be viewed in this context.[41] Casey was sent to plead Australia's case in Washington, where he, too, was informed the US would not prioritise the defence of Malaya—an approach Radford described as 'last-ditch' defeatism predicated on the loss of the rest of South-East Asia. In the wake of these revelations, Australian strategic planning was, by Casey's reckoning, 'left … in the air'.[42]

The State Department offered some suggestions about how to proceed. It believed the best way to defend Malaya from external communist threats was containment. Australia should now direct its energies towards SEATO and the broader regional fight against communism.[43] A similar proposal had also been floated in the Defence Committee with the view that the defence of Malaya should now be 'relegated to the category of a reserve objective' within a broader strategy of defending the whole of South-East Asia.[44] Realising the fundamental challenge of convincing the US to protect British possessions and the value of the United States' broad commitment to South-East Asian security as opposed to Britain's limited commitment to protecting Malaya, the Australian government took on

---

39   'Doc. 36, Memorandum of a Conversation by State Department, 18 March 1955' and 'Doc. 37, Dulles to Menzies, 18 March 1955', both in Keefer and Mabon, *FRUS 1955–57*, vol. I.
40   David Lee, 'Australia and Allied Strategy in the Far-East, 1952–1957', *Journal of Strategic Studies* 16 (1993): 511–38, at pp. 525–6.
41   'Doc. 65, Radford to Spender, 28 July 1955', in Keefer and Mabon, *FRUS 1955–57*, vol. I; '"Review of ANZAM Planning by US Joint Chiefs of Staff", Defence Committee Report, 30 August 1955', NAA: A1290, 1957/4857.
42   '12 September 1955' and '13 September 1955', in Millar, *Australian Foreign Minister*, 214–16.
43   'Doc. 71, US Minutes of the ANZUS Council Meeting, 24 September 1955', in Keefer and Mabon, *FRUS 1955–57*, vol. I; '24 September 1955', in Millar, *Australian Foreign Minister*, 217–19.
44   'McKnight to Brown, 30 August 1955', NAA: A1290, 1957/4857; 'Defence Committee Meeting, [n.d. (on or before 30 August 1955)]', NAA: A1290, 1957/4857.

these recommendations. Australia abandoned the Hermes plan, much to Britain's annoyance, and the FESR in Malaya was recast as a contribution to SEATO as a reserve force for the whole of South-East Asia.[45]

## Japan and the economic aspects of SEATO

The threat of communist insurgency in South-East Asia also shaped Australia's diplomatic outlook, forcing the nation to reconsider its policy towards Japan and the United States' regional strategy. In the containment of communism, the US saw the 'denial' of Japan to the Soviets and maintenance of Japanese goodwill towards the West as crucial. This was codified in NSC 48/2.[46] The US accordingly campaigned for a non-punitive peace treaty that signalled Japan's legitimacy as a reformed nation ready to return to the international community. Such a treaty would allow economic revival and remilitarisation in the future. In spite of ANZUS, the Australian government and public remained reluctant to embrace the former enemy, with racialised hostility and lingering misgivings about allowing Japan's economy to again reach a war potential.[47]

Under the leadership of Casey and his departmental secretary Alan Watt, the DEA continued to prioritise increasing Australia's representation in its region of strategic interest. Casey's first overseas trip as minister was to South-East and East Asia. Following this trip, new diplomatic postings were made in the newly independent nations in the region.[48] Casey was an ardent anti-communist and he saw the protection of the region from communist subversion as a central feature of regional engagement.[49] The Colombo Plan, accordingly, remained a significant tool and membership

---

45   Lee, 'Australia and Allied Strategy in the Far-East', 528–9.
46   'Doc. 145, Note by Souers (Executive Secretary NSC) to the NSC, 4 October 1949', in Reid and Glennon, *FRUS 1949*.
47   David Walton, *Australia, Japan and Southeast Asia: Early Post-War Initiatives in Regional Diplomacy* (New York: Nova Publishers, 2012), 27–9, 32–3.
48   Richard Casey, *Friends and Neighbours: Australia and the World* (Melbourne: Cheshire, 1954), 26; '19 August 1951', in Millar, *Australian Foreign Minister*, 37–40; '"Report on visit to South-East Asia and East Asia by Minister for External Affairs", 21 September 1951', NAA: A1838, 532/6/2.
49   Christopher Waters, 'Casey: Four Decades in the Making of Australian Foreign Policy', *Australian Journal of Politics and History* 51, no. 3 (2005): 380–8, at pp. 384–6; James Cotton, 'R.G. Casey and Australian International Thought: Empire, Nation, Community', *The International History Review* 33, no. 1 (2011): 95–113, at pp. 103–6.

was expanded throughout the early 1950s.[50] With new members being added and Japan's foreign economic policy directed towards rebuilding regional relationships through economic diplomacy, the Japanese government hoped to participate in the Colombo Plan. In the lead-up to the 1952 meeting of the Colombo Plan Consultative Committee, Britain raised the possibility of Japanese observer status. The following year, the Japanese government formally applied for membership. Both proposals were rejected following Australia's firm opposition.[51] In March 1954, with talk of Japan again seeking membership, Australia maintained its view that this would be 'premature'.[52] Meanwhile, Australia continued to restrict Japan's access to its markets, despite the nation being its second-largest export market. Japan was left to face a host of import restrictions, leading to a two-way trade relationship at a ratio of 18:1.[53] Along with straining its diplomatic and economic relationships with Japan, the Australian government's position countered NSC 13/2 and NSC 48/2. It denied Japan opportunities for economic growth and regional integration, so hindering its ability to become the bulwark against communism in the Asia-Pacific.

Given Australia's unwillingness to embrace Japan, it is somewhat surprising that, in October 1954, it sponsored the nation's entrance into the Colombo Plan as a donor nation.[54] Australia's softening attitude towards Japan is best understood in the context of the 1954 crisis in South-East Asia and the increasing threat posed by communist China. Both the US and Britain were acutely aware of the importance of maintaining friendly relations with Japan and developing the Japanese economy as an alternative to China. Throughout June–July 1954, both the US and Britain—the latter having recently adopted a new policy towards Japan that aimed to 'prevent economic distress which would foster communism by maintaining as high a level of trade between Japan and the sterling

---

50   New regional members were Laos (1951), Nepal and Burma (Myanmar) (1952), Indonesia (1953) and Thailand, Japan and the Philippines (1954).

51   Ai Kobayashi, 'Australia and Japan's Admission to the Colombo Plan', *Australian Journal of Politics and History* 60, no. 4 (2014): 518–33, at pp. 522–5; 'Australian High Commissioner's Office Karachi to DEA, 10 March 1952', NAA: A1838, 2080/13; '"Japan May Join Colombo Plan", *The Age*, [Melbourne], 6 October 1953', cutting, in NAA: A1838, 2080/13.

52   'Walker to Watt, 17 March 1954', NAA: A1838, 2080/13.

53   Peter Golding, *Black Jack McEwen: Political Gladiator* (Melbourne: Melbourne University Press, 1996), 173–5; *Official Year Book of the Commonwealth of Australia*, No. 42 (Canberra: Commonwealth Government Printer, 1956), 301. Figure for 1952–53.

54   '"Australia Got Japan Into Colombo Plan", *The Herald*, [Melbourne], 6 October 1954', cutting, in NAA: A1838, 3103/9/3/3.

area'—petitioned Australia to improve bilateral relations and do more to 'bring Japan into the community of nations'.[55] This pressure triggered a DEA submission to Cabinet reviewing Australian–Japanese relations, submitted by Casey on 28 July.

Casey's submission stressed that, with Japan's liberal democracy in its infancy and the nation's economy still rebuilding, the potential remained for economic and political crisis and, in turn, an environment that would encourage communist subversion. This situation would only worsen if Japan continued to face a hostile neighbourhood with limited opportunities for economic growth. Australia's policy towards Japan had to be designed to prevent a close relationship between it and China. This could be best achieved by providing Japan with the opportunities necessary for 'meeting her economic difficulties by expanding her export trade, and for developing her political and economic life and institutions in a way that will strengthen Japan's association with the West'.[56] On 17 August, the prime minister and Cabinet '*reluctantly*' agreed that Australia would 'adopt a more liberal policy towards Japan'. Cabinet also agreed that supporting the nation's membership of the Colombo Plan would be the most effective first step towards implementing this new policy; Casey described Japan's interest in the plan as a 'rather heaven-sent opportunity'.[57]

Strategic planning and the little-known economic aspects of SEATO also played a role in Australia's decision to support Japan's accession to the Colombo Plan. As the Australian government reviewed its policy towards Japan, SEATO was being finalised. The US had initially hoped Japan would be a member—an idea that was soon set aside due to the nation's lack of armed strength necessary to contribute to South-East Asian defence.[58] This was not the end of US hopes for Japan's association with SEATO.

---

55 '"Policy towards Japan", Cabinet Paper, TNA: FO 371/110413', cited in C.W. Braddick, 'Britain, the Commonwealth, and the Post-War Japanese Revival, 1945–70', *The Round Table* 99, no. 409 (2010): 371–89, at p. 374; '"Australia's Relations with Japan", Memorandum for Watt, 15 July 1954', NAA: A1838, 3103/10/1 Part 2; 'Australian Embassy in Washington to DEA, 12 August 1954', NAA: A1838, 2080/13.
56 '"Australian Policy towards Japan", Cabinet Submission by Casey, 28 July 1954', NAA: A1838, 2080/13.
57 'Doc. 66, Meeting Prime Minister's Committee of Cabinet, 17 August 1954', in Department of Foreign Affairs and Trade, *Documents on Australian Foreign Policy. Volume 19: The Australia Japan Agreement on Commerce, 1950–59* (Canberra: DFAT, 1997) [emphasis in original]; 'Casey to Tange, 16 August 1954', NAA: A1838, 2080/13.
58 'Doc. 267, Minutes of Meeting on Southeast Asia, 24 July 1954' and 'Doc. 288, New Zealand Embassy to Department of State, 5 August 1954', both in Mabon, *FRUS 1952–54*, vol. XII.

The State Department developed plans for the inclusion of an economic provision in SEATO for the purpose of a united economic strategy to counter communism. Plans were secretly made to link Colombo with this economic provision.[59] In an August meeting between Dulles and Harold Stassen, Director of the US Foreign Operations Administration, it was agreed that, if a Colombo–SEATO link was 'adopted as the basis of operations', it would be 'essential that Japan should be brought in to the Colombo Plan'.[60] The importance of Japan in this relates back to US plans to support the nation's regional economic integration. Japan's initial donor contributions to the Colombo Plan were modest, at only US$40,000.[61] Nevertheless, association was symbolically important in the rehabilitation of its regional image—a symbolism the State Department openly acknowledged, with one official noting 'political reason was as important as economic'.[62] The SEATO–Colombo Plan linkage was also strategically significant to the US as it fortified US diplomatic, military and economic influence in South-East Asia.

Australia's support for Japan's membership of the Colombo Plan and the economic aspects of SEATO was guided by anxiety about the United States' commitment to the defence of South-East Asia and the need to demonstrate its reliability as an ally. Australia was aware of plans to institute a SEATO–Colombo Plan linkage, and a planning brief for the Manila conference reveals the nation was 'chary' about the proposal.[63] Despite this, Australia went on to support Article 3 of SEATO, which made a general commitment to economic and technical assistance and cooperation. This cooperation took the form of SEATO aid being injected into the Colombo Plan by way of strategically prioritising the organisation's projects.[64] That Australia was mindful of relations with the US—perhaps even responding to US pressure, as David Walton has suggested—is evidenced in the DEA's Cabinet submission supporting Japan's admission to the Colombo Plan. The submission noted that if Australia continued to oppose Japanese membership it may face 'isolation

---

59 'Doc. 267, Minutes of Meeting on Southeast Asia, 24 July 1954', in Mabon, *FRUS 1952–54*, vol. XII; 'Australian Embassy in Washington to DEA, 23 August 1954', NAA: A1838, 3103/9/3/8.
60 'Doc. 321, Memorandum of Conversation by Dulles, 24 August 1954', in Mabon, *FRUS 1952–54*, vol. XII.
61 Oakman, *Facing Asia*, 110.
62 'Australian Embassy in Washington to DEA, 12 August 1954', NAA: A1838, 2080/13.
63 '"SEATO and Economic Aid to South East Asia", 25 August 1954', NAA: A1209, 1957/5846.
64 'Doc. 339, Memorandum of Conversation by Baldwin (Acting Deputy Assistant Secretary of State for Far Eastern Affairs), 1 September 1954', in Mabon, *FRUS 1952–54*, vol. XII.

among the Western donor countries'.[65] These Western members were Britain, New Zealand and the US—with all of which Australia had some form of regional security arrangement.

The Menzies government's shifting policy towards Japan in 1954 contributed in part to the 1957 Australia–Japan Agreement on Commerce, which heralded Australia's rapid integration into its regional markets. This marked a critical point in Australia's move towards alignment with the US, with the nation finally accepting, if not yet embracing, US plans to develop Japan as a regional economic hub and see it reintegrated into the Asia-Pacific community.

## The retreat from the British orbit

By the end of 1955, there were clear indicators that US-led strategic planning, rather than an integrated US–British system, offered Australia the greatest assurance for regional security. These strategic imperatives did not exist in a vacuum and revelations in 1956–57 of the true extent of Britain's military and economic capabilities expedited Australia's realignment from the British orbit to that of the US. In these years, the Australian government was forced to frankly assess Britain's capabilities and the value of the Commonwealth connection, finding they no longer met the nation's economic or defensive needs. These two pillars of the Commonwealth connection were quickly crumbling.

The Menzies government took office with a preference for a multilateral world trading system and the promise that it would do away with practices that protected the Sterling Area and British economic interests at the expense of Australia's national development. This led the government to abolish petrol rationing and approach the US for an individual loan of US$100 million within seven months of coming into power—steps that put pressure on the Sterling Area dollar reserves and, in turn, endangered Britain's vulnerable economy.[66] Throughout the early 1950s, Britain continued to struggle with its dollar trade and overall balance of payments,

---

65  Walton, *Australia, Japan and Southeast Asia*, 31; '"Japan and the Colombo Plan", Cabinet Submission by DEA, 27 August 1954', NAA: A4940, C1009.
66  Frank Bongiorno, 'The Price of Nostalgia: Menzies, the "Liberal" Tradition and Australian Foreign Policy', *Australian Journal of Politics and History* 51, no. 3 (2005): 400–17, at p. 412; David Lee, 'Australia, the British Commonwealth, and the United States, 1950–1953', *The Journal of Imperial and Commonwealth History* 20, no. 3 (1992): 445–69, at pp. 449–53.

leaving the nation to once again call on the members of the Sterling Area to introduce import restrictions in an attempt to maintain the Sterling Area reserves. While Australia did introduce import restrictions, there were general cuts to all sectors and from all sources, including the Sterling Area. Australia's finance and trade policymakers maintained that the Sterling Area as it existed was unsustainable and the import restrictions needed to stabilise its reserves were anathema to a multilateral world trading system. Australia unsuccessfully promoted the resumption of sterling–dollar convertibility and integration into the multilateral system.[67]

Australia's frustration with the discriminatory practices that sustained the British economy and the Sterling Area was heightened by problems in Australian–British bilateral trade. Since the end of World War II, Australian policymaking had been mobilised towards national development. The nation's primary and secondary industries steadily expanded, as did the markets to which goods were being sold.[68] With this rapid growth came the need for a larger population—to both service and purchase from the Australian economy. Encouraged by assisted passages and displaced persons programs, the annual population growth rate reached a postwar peak of 3.3 per cent per annum in 1950, compared with just 1 per cent at the outbreak of the war.[69] The national development program necessitated a high volume of imports but, despite expanding market opportunities, Australia was left with a balance-of-payments problem that threatened to trigger a recession.[70]

Britain, Australia's largest trading partner, was a significant contributor to the nation's balance-of-payments problem. British imports were expanding much faster than the exports Australia sold in return. By 1954–55, the disparity in two-way trade was upwards of £90 million annually.[71] There had always been periods of imbalance in the Australian–British trade relationship; by the mid-1950s, however, it was clear that this was a long-term trend. The British market for Australian goods was

---

67   Lee, 'Australia and the British Commonwealth', 455–9, 462.
68   'Speech by McEwen to House of Representatives, 28 February 1956', NAA: A5954, 64/1.
69   Australian Bureau of Statistics, 'Historical Population 2016', Cat. No. 3105.0.65.001 (Canberra: ABS), available from: www.abs.gov.au/AUSSTATS/abs@.nsf/Lookup/3105.0.65.001Main+Features12016?OpenDocument.
70   David Lee, 'Sir John Crawford: Agriculture and Trade', in *The Seven Dwarfs and the Age of the Mandarins: Australian Government Administration in the Post-War Reconstruction Era*, ed. Samuel Furphy (Canberra: ANU Press, 2015), 174.
71   *Official Year Book of the Commonwealth of Australia*, No. 41 (Canberra: Commonwealth Government Printer, 1955), 291.

shrinking. The 'disappointingly negative' state of Australian–British trade relations could largely be attributed to an unequal preference system.[72] In line with the 1932 Ottawa Agreements, Britain and Australia extended certain concessions to one another; however, these were not shared evenly. While 86 per cent of British exports received preference in Australia, only 43 per cent of Australian exports received preference in return. Britain also enjoyed a higher average margin of preference: 14 per cent compared with the 9 per cent afforded to Australia. The British government granted generous subsidies to domestic producers in an attempt to stimulate domestic and international sales. Agricultural producers were the principal benefactors of these subsidies and Australia, with agriculture among its largest exports, was left further disadvantaged in the British market.[73]

Politicians, economists and exporters alike called for a review of trade relations with Britain.[74] Preoccupation with the implementation of the General Agreement on Tariffs and Trade and the fact that responsibility for trade, tariffs and industry was spread across three different departments meant that little came from these appeals.[75] In January 1956, however, the Menzies ministry underwent a major restructure, including the creation of the Department of Trade. John McEwen and John Crawford, both previously of the Department of Commerce and Agriculture, were appointed minister and secretary, respectively. The two men immediately set out to address the imbalance in the Australian–British trading relationship with a proposal to renegotiate the Ottawa Agreements. Cabinet approved the renegotiation of the Ottawa Agreements on 10 May 1956 and, on 9 November, after several weeks of hard-fought bargaining, the new agreement was finalised.[76]

McEwen was careful to stress the revision of the Ottawa Agreements was not an attack on Britain or the imperial preference system. Rather, he believed the Australian–British trading relationship was a 'natural one' that had become unbalanced as a result of the immense changes in the

---

72  Crawford, *Australian Trade Policy*, 352.
73  Stuart Ward, *Australia and the British Embrace: The Demise of the Imperial Ideal* (Melbourne: Melbourne University Press, 1998), 34–5, 42; *Official Year Book of the Commonwealth of Australia*, No. 41 (1955), 217–19; '"Ottawa Agreement", Cabinet Submission by McEwen, 16 April 1956', in Department of Commerce and Agriculture: Miscellaneous items including alphabetical electorate, general filing, and personal items, 1915–82, NAA: M58, 219 Part 2.
74  Crawford, *Australian Trade Policy*, 321–6, 330–1, 334–6.
75  These three departments were the Department of Trade and Customs, the Department of Commerce and Agriculture and the Department of National Development.
76  Golding, *Black Jack McEwen*, 175–7.

international economic situation and in the individual economies of Australia and Britain in years since the Ottawa Agreements had originally been negotiated. The reappraisal of the agreements would ostensibly return equilibrium to the relationship.[77] Some are convinced by this argument. Stuart Ward, for instance, writes that the renewal of the Ottawa Agreements

> did not, in any fundamental sense, provoke a wider examination of the steadily widening gap between British commercial interests and Australian national aspirations ... Nor is there any evidence that the Ottawa renegotiation stimulated any ... reflection about the declining relevance of the old imperial ties.

He goes on to note the importance of British race patriotism to the Australian psyche well into the 1960s as evidence of this.[78] While it is true the revision of the Ottawa Agreements did not mark the end of Australian–British economic ties, it was an acknowledgement by Australia that it was no longer satisfied with the economic benefits offered in the imperial connection.

Much as he tried to soften it, McEwen could not hide the fact that Britain was a shrinking market for Australian goods. It will be recalled that F.H. Stewart had warned of this development as early as 1935 and H.C. Coombs echoed his concerns in 1947. Australia could not maintain its national development program with a continuing and widening payments imbalance. Parenthetically, as McEwen observed in a February statement to the House of Representatives, if imports were restricted as a cost-saving measure, employment and industrialisation would stagnate, exports would decline—particularly as foreign markets would likely respond to Australia's import restrictions with their own such restrictions—and the standard of living would decline.[79]

Australia's balance-of-payments problem was not simply a matter of improving the nation's standard of living, it was also linked to national defence. Although he was the Minister for Trade, McEwen took a great deal of interest in defence developments. He believed Australia needed

---

77 'Cabinet Submission by McEwen, 16 April 1956' and '"Proposals concerning the United Kingdom and Australia Trade Agreement", Cabinet Submission by McEwen, 7 May 1956', both in NAA: M58, 219 Part 2; John McEwen and Robert V. Jackson, *John McEwen: His Story* (Canberra: Printed privately, 1983), 49–51.
78 Ward, *Australia and the British Embrace*, 36–8.
79 'Speech by McEwen to House of Representatives, 28 February 1956', NAA: A5954, 64/1.

a robust economy with employment opportunities to entice migrants who, in turn, would service Australia's emerging defence goods industry and could be called on to defend the nation in the event of another war.[80] Frederick Shedden, the influential Secretary of Defence, shared this view, writing in a private letter to McEwen that

> immigration is a long-term defence measure … our Immigration Policy makes considerable demands for imports of both capital and consumption goods, but to keep this going we must export more to balance overseas expenditure with export earnings. A further aid would be greater investment from overseas in Australia.[81]

Shedden had been privately contacting official and business acquaintances in Britain, sending them copies of McEwen's statements regarding Australia's trade problem in the hope that he could impress on them the important link between Australian trade, immigration and defence.[82] Facing a difficult situation, the Menzies government could not afford to ignore any opportunity for export development.

As McEwen detailed in a number of Cabinet submissions concerning the Ottawa problem, there were considerable opportunities in a number of foreign markets. To capitalise on these opportunities, it was necessary for Australia to offer 'both good customer and good supplier countries a fairer share of our expanding market', with McEwen noting that some countries had already begun pressuring Australia to improve its imports. However, the ambit of preferences Australia was required to grant under the existing Ottawa system left the nation with little scope to offer other countries greater access to its markets.[83] Accordingly, among the main provisions secured in the new Ottawa Agreement was the reduction of the preference margin afforded to British exports, from between 12.5 and 17.5 per cent to 7–10 per cent.[84] This provision preserved the traditional imperial preference system while reducing margins enough to allow Australia greater freedom to negotiate a better position in multilateral and

---

80  Lee, *Search for Security*, 155; Golding, *Black Jack McEwen*, 166–7; Crawford, *Australian Trade Policy*, 353.
81  'Personal, Shedden to McEwen, 9 March 1956' and 'Personal, Shedden to McEwen, 26 April 1956', both in NAA: A5954, 64/1.
82  'Personal, Shedden to McEwen, 9 March 1956', NAA: A5954, 64/1.
83  'Cabinet Submission by McEwen, 16 April 1956' and 'Cabinet Submission by McEwen, 7 May 1956', both in NAA: M58, 219 Part 2.
84  Golding, *Black Jack McEwen*, 175–8; Crawford, *Australian Trade Policy*, 19–25.

bilateral trade relationships. In this, there was a recognition that the days of the closed and economically integrated Commonwealth were coming to an end.

McEwen acknowledged the broader implications of the reappraisal of the Ottawa Agreements. In a May Cabinet submission, he observed: 'I am not unmindful of the fact that our trading relationship with the United Kingdom is so great that any substantial proposals on it can impinge on wider issues of high policy.'[85] The British government, too, appreciated the divergence of Australian and British economic interests that had been brought to light by the renewal of the Ottawa system. Harold Macmillan, Chancellor of the Exchequer, concluded:

> Australia's changed attitude to the preference system reflected the fact the United Kingdom was no longer able to fulfil her traditional role of providing the capital needed for the industrial development of the Commonwealth ... It would now be necessary ... to re-examine, in light of the Australian attitude, the relative importance and future prospects of our trade with Australia and the Commonwealth, and with Europe and other overseas markets.[86]

Imperial sentiment could no longer outweigh national development needs. Crawford, who was involved in the renegotiation process, later stated as much: 'Britain was a declining rather than a growing market', necessitating 'a retreat from the political concept of an integrated Empire'.[87]

## Turning points: Malayan independence, the Suez Crisis and equipping the Australian defence forces

As Australia acknowledged the limitations of the British market, so, too, did the limitations of Britain's global power become apparent. The year 1956 opened with the British government's announcement that Malaya would be granted independence, with 31 August 1957 the target date for elections and the handing over of control. With the recent decision

---

85 'Cabinet Submission by McEwen, 7 May 1956', NAA: M58, 219 Part 2.
86 'Cabinet Minute, 12 July 1956', in Records of the Cabinet Office, Cabinet: Minutes (CM and CC Series), TNA: CAB 128/30/49.
87 Crawford, *Australian Trade Policy*, 319–20.

to recast the FESR as part of a broader contribution to SEATO and the defence of the whole of South-East Asia, the Australian government was most concerned by the possibility that it would be unable to maintain these forces in Malaya following independence.[88] These concerns triggered British–Malayan defence discussions and the eventual signing of the Anglo-Malayan Defence Agreement (AMDA, signed in October 1957). Britain reserved the right to maintain forces in Malaya after independence and to use and reinforce these forces to counter regional threats, subject to consultation with and the approval of the Malayan government. The FESR, including Australian and New Zealand commitments, was explicitly named in AMDA among the forces permitted to be maintained in Malaya.[89] There remained the symbolic implication of Britain ceding control to one of its few remaining footholds in the Pacific, giving way to suspicions in Australian government circles that Malayan independence marked Britain's retreat from the region.[90]

The year closed with the Suez Crisis. On 26 July 1956, Egyptian President Gamal Abdel Nasser announced the nationalisation of the Suez Canal and the immediate seizure of control from the Suez Canal Company. Egyptian forces occupied the canal, the Suez Canal Company's assets were frozen and the canal was closed to some foreign shipping. With private French and British nationals making up most company shareholders, it was in the two nations' interest to maintain private ownership and unrestricted access to the canal. The two governments approached Israel, which had been denied access to the waterway, and conspired with it to regain control of the canal. When Israel invaded Egypt in October, France and Britain responded with a military intervention, which was framed as a mediation force between the two combatants. Australia supported the military intervention in Egypt—a move one historian describes as 'blind

---

88   Edwards and Pemberton, *Crises and Commitments*, 188–92; 'Cabinet Minute, 16 January 1956', NAA: A4940, C1473 Part 1.
89   '"The Future of the Commonwealth Strategic Reserve in relation to the Malayan Defence Agreement", Cabinet Submission by Casey and Beale (Acting Minister for Defence), [n.d. (June 1957)]' and '"A Defence Appreciation on the Future of the Commonwealth Strategic Reserve in relation to the Malayan Defence Agreement", Department of Defence, [n.d. (June 1957)]', both in NAA: A4940, C1473 Part 1.
90   Wayne Reynolds, 'Menzies and the Proposal for Nuclear Weapons', in *Menzies in War and Peace*, ed. Frank Cain (Sydney: Allen & Unwin, 1997), 124–5; Lee, 'Australia and Allied Strategy in the Far-East', 530.

loyalty' to Britain—but it was one of only a handful of countries, with the UN Security Council deeming the action unwarranted and demanding the withdrawal of forces.[91]

The Suez Crisis not only damaged Britain's international prestige, but also revealed the nation's economic vulnerability. Britain relied on the canal for access to oil, and the high cost of oil elsewhere and stockholder speculation triggered a plummet in Sterling Area foreign currency reserves.[92] The British government sought financial assistance from the International Monetary Fund (IMF) to fortify the sterling. The US government—the largest single donor to the fund—feared Soviet intervention if the situation in Egypt continued and informed Britain that it would categorically block any attempts to seek assistance from the IMF for the purpose of maintaining forces in Egypt.[93] Facing a financial crisis and entirely reliant on the support of the US to continue its Suez operations, Britain was forced to withdraw from Egypt.

From the outset, Casey had misgivings about Britain's response to the Suez situation, which he freely shared with Menzies.[94] Along with correctly predicting the international backlash Britain would face if it resorted to the use of force, Casey appreciated the inference of British vulnerability if an apparently great power had to 'use force on a small Afro-Asian nation to deal with a political problem'. He continued:

> The use of force in the Suez issue would be 'life or death' to Britain—and more likely death than life, by reason of the overwhelming volume of world opinion against her that the use of force would generate, which would greatly diminish her influence in world affairs.[95]

---

91  W.J. Hudson, *Blind Loyalty: Australia and the Suez Crisis, 1956* (Melbourne: Melbourne University Press, 1989).
92  James Boughton, *Northwest of Suez: The 1956 crisis and the IMF*, IMF Working Papers 2000/192 (Washington, DC: International Monetary Fund, 2000): 3–5, 11–14.
93  'Caccia (British Ambassador to the US) to Foreign Office, 27 November 1956, TNA: T236/4190', cited in ibid., 20; 'Doc. 500, Memorandum of Conversation with Eisenhower, 5 November 1956' and 'Doc. 583, US Embassy in London to State Department, 17 November 1956', both in Nina J. Noring (ed.), *Foreign Relations of the United States, 1955–1957, Suez Crisis, July 26–December 31, 1956, Volume XVI* (Washington, DC: US Government Printing Office, 1990) [hereinafter *FRUS 1955–57*, vol. XVI].
94  '24 September 1956', in Carl Bridge (ed.), *A Delicate Mission: The Washington Diaries of R.G. Casey, 1940–1942* (Canberra: National Library of Australia, 2008), 245–6.
95  '7 September 1956', in ibid., 243–4 [emphasis in original].

Casey clearly grasped Britain's economic and defensive vulnerability and how the situation in Egypt would bring this into focus for an international audience.

Amid Malayan independence and the Suez Crisis, Australia's defence policy underwent a major review. In June 1956, Menzies travelled to London for the Commonwealth Prime Ministers' Conference. There he learnt that Britain's future defence policy in the event of a global war would include the use of thermonuclear weapons—previously treated as weapons of last recourse. Global war, however, was far less likely than a limited war in South-East Asia. It remained unclear what level of support Britain would offer in a limited war.[96] Britain's decision to focus on developing its massive force capabilities led to the 1957 Duncan Sandys defence white paper and the decision to reduce conventional forces in the Asia-Pacific region—seemingly confirming Australia's fears that Britain was retreating from the region.[97]

On his trip home, Menzies visited Washington, where he pressed Eisenhower for details of the US policy for the use of nuclear weapons and other new strategic defence technologies in the event of a limited war in South-East Asia. New technologies like intercontinental missiles would be essential in maintaining Australia's strategic isolation; however, as Menzies informed Eisenhower, a small country like Australia would be 'unable to afford these new weapons and would probably have to get along with conventional weapons'. Eisenhower assured Menzies that Australian military forces well-armed with conventional weapons would be adequate, believing 'the real deterrent in the eyes of the common man is not the number of atomic bombs which might be stored in some unknown place … but rather the man in uniform who can be seen'.[98] With both Britain and the US committed to nuclear deterrence and the expectation

---

96  'Minutes First Meeting of Commonwealth Prime Ministers, 27 June 1956', NAA: A1838, 899/6/3/1. The Commonwealth Prime Ministers' Conference was not the first news of Britain's move towards nuclear-based defence; it had received some attention at the 1955 Commonwealth Prime Ministers' Conference. See 'Meeting of Commonwealth Prime Ministers, January–February 1955, Minutes of Meetings and Memoranda', NAA: A5954, 1562/12.
97  Andrea Benvenuti, 'Australian Reactions to Britain's Declining Presence in Southeast Asia, 1955–63', *The Journal of Imperial and Commonwealth History* 34, no. 3 (2006): 407–29, at pp. 412–13; '"Statement on Defence", Cabinet Submission by Sandys (Minister for Defence), 1 April 1957', in Records of the Cabinet Office, Cabinet: Memoranda (CP and C Series), TNA: CAB 129/86.
98  'Doc. 112, Memorandum of Conversation, 3 August 1956', in Keefer and Mabon, *FRUS 1955–57*, vol. I.

that Australia would make a meaningful contribution to the defence of South-East Asia, there was a clear need for the nation to reconsider its strategic position.

The revelations in London and Washington triggered a Defence Committee review of Australian defence policy in October 1956, with Cabinet approving its recommendations the following February. The 1957 Defence Review was a careful assessment of Australia's capabilities and the relationships and strategies that would best serve the nation's interests in the event of a limited war in South-East Asia. The review argued that, as a small and isolated nation, Australia was 'dependent on the Western Powers, in particular the United States, for her ultimate security'. To achieve this security, Australia had to 'relate' its defence planning to the 'global strategy of the Western Powers' and seek to make a meaningful contribution to the implementation of this strategy. This approach would both contribute to the defence of the Western bloc and 'strengthen her case for the support of her allies' should a direct threat to Australian security present itself. The review identified participation in regional collective security arrangements as 'the best means' available to integrate Australian defence planning into the strategy of the Western powers. SEATO was 'the most important' of the regional arrangements and 'the most practicable organisation in which Australian strategic plans can be coordinated with those of the US'.[99]

The Eisenhower administration's New Look policy towards foreign and defence issues shaped the United States' approach to SEATO. The New Look policy reduced US defence costs by expanding the nation's nuclear deterrent and reducing the size of its conventional armed forces. At the same time, the US encouraged its allies to build up their own conventional forces for local security, allowing the US to provide massive retaliation rather than expensive and inflexible long-term commitments. The core tenets of the New Look policy were promoted by the US in the formation of the strategic concepts for the defence of the SEATO area.[100] Broadly outlined, the SEATO strategic concepts planned for an immediate response to a communist threat—likely isolated guerilla

---

99   '"The Strategic Basis of Australian Defence Policy", Defence Committee report, [n.d. (October 1956)]', in Department of Defence: Correspondence files, multiple number series [Class 501] [501–539] [Classified] [Main correspondence files series of the agency], 1936–60, NAA: A1196, 15/501/378.
100  Fenton, *To Cage the Red Dragon*, 96–101, 112–13; 'Doc. 101, Report to the NSC, 30 October 1953', in Rose and Petersen, *FRUS 1952–54*, vol. II.

activities. This initial phase would be followed up by 'supporting actions' to protect the lines of communication and contribute to counteroffensives when necessary. The nature of this warfare—liable to erupt anywhere and with little or no warning—and the size of the treaty area necessitated that SEATO members maintain highly mobile and flexible forces.[101]

On 4 April 1957, Menzies presented the 1957 Defence Review to the House of Representatives and announced his government's decision to adopt its recommendations. In preparing for a limited war, the review recommended a move away from the traditional organisation and deployment of large 'ineffective' divisions of multipurpose forces that had received general training. Instead, it was recommended that Australia focus its efforts on the creation of 'hard-hitting, flexible, mobile and readily available forces'.[102] In his 4 April address, Menzies called into question his government's own policy of national service, arguing that capability had been sacrificed to the sheer number of men trained. For this reason, the national service intake would be reduced from 34,000 to 12,000 annually for the AMF, while the RAN and RAAF programs were terminated. Menzies, anticipating criticism, pointed out that savings would be diverted to the creation of a Mobile Brigade Group. The new group of 4,000 regular forces would be highly trained and specialised for immediate deployment in the event of limited war in South-East Asia. Able to be deployed quickly to respond to an immediate threat and, if need be, supported by additional forces drawn from the citizen and regular forces, this contingent was consistent with the strategic concepts for the defence of the SEATO area.[103]

The 1957 Defence Review identified a critical lack of modern defence equipment, calling for the defence forces to be rearmed 'with the most modern conventional weapons available'.[104] There was, as Casey noted in an October 1956 diary entry, 'only one country from which we could get equipment of consequence … and that is the United States'. 'I realise,' he continued, 'that this means a departure from our traditional

---

101 'Report, First Meeting of SEATO Military Staff Planners, 5 May 1955', NAA: A1209, 1957/5850; 'Report, Third Meeting of Military SEATO Staff Planners, 5 July 1956', NAA: A1209, 1957/4260.
102 'Defence Committee report, [n.d. (October 1956)]', NAA: A1196, 15/501/378; '"Composition of the Australian Defence Forces", Cabinet Submission by Defence Committee, 19 February 1957', NAA: A4940, C2466.
103 *CPD: Representatives*, 4 April 1957, No. 14, 571–5; *Official Year Book of the Commonwealth of Australia*, No. 44 (Canberra: Commonwealth Government Printer, 1958), 1048–50.
104 'Defence Committee report, [n.d. (October 1956)]', NAA: A1196, 15/501/378.

standardisation with the United Kingdom—but we have to face up to this break sometime.'[105] Menzies faced this break on 4 April, announcing his government's decision to standardise AMF and RAAF equipment with that of the US. Preliminary plans included the local production of FN rifles (used by the US Army), the acquisition of 12 US C-130 Hercules-type modern transport aircraft and the formation of Australia's first surface-to-air weapons unit.[106] Having traditionally cooperated with Britain's defence industries, Menzies was conscious of the implications that US standardisation may have on the Australian–British relationship. The decision, he argued, was 'not a heresy', rather it recognised 'the facts of war'. By virtue of SEATO and ANZUS, Australia would fight any future war in South-East Asia alongside the US. The US had the capacity to maintain a supply of defence goods, while Britain would find it 'manifestly difficult'; although not specified, this conclusion was no doubt drawn as a result of the ongoing economic challenges faced by Britain and its embarrassing exit from Egypt.[107] Britain was struggling to maintain a major defence role east of Suez and Australia's reliance on the US increased accordingly.

Australia's transition to the US and adherence to its global strategy were not inevitable. Rather, maintaining British world power via cooperation with the US was a priority for the Menzies government. It was only through a careful and forthright assessment of the capabilities and priorities of Britain and the US that Australian policymakers concluded that the latter would best serve the national interest in the future. Britain's economic and defensive capabilities were unequivocally limited and it appeared to be retreating from South-East Asia. Conversely, the US seemed finally to be interested in the region and appreciative of its importance within global strategy. The developments covered in this chapter, particularly those during the years 1955–57, can be seen as a culmination of the lessons learnt and experimentation in foreign policy approaches in the previous three and a half decades as Australia made astute appreciations as to what the national interest was and the relationships that would best protect it. The final decision by Australia to realign with the US reveals

---

105 '10 October 1956', in Millar, *Australian Foreign Minister*, 247.
106 *CDP: Representatives*, 4 April 1957, No. 14, 575–6; *Official Year Book of the Commonwealth of Australia*, No. 44 (1958), 1048.
107 *CDP: Representatives*, 4 April 1957, No. 14, 572–3.

a level of autonomy and forward thinking that has been underappreciated in existing assessments of these crucial years in the development of the Australian foreign policy tradition.

The year 1957 was not the end of Australian–British high-level relations, with the RAN operating in line with British standards until 1961 and the two nations cooperating in 1964–65 in the defence of the Federation of Malaysia in the face of Indonesia's policy of *Konfrontasi*.[108] Britain and the Sterling Area also remained Australia's most significant commercial links into the 1960s. However, the Australian government was aware of an urgent need to diversify its trade relations, as the British government sought greater economic engagement with Western Europe via membership of the European Economic Community. The Australia–Japan Commerce Agreement, which was renewed and expanded in 1963, and a burgeoning commodities export trade formed the foundation of Australia's economic adjustment. By 1966, the Australian dollar was introduced, signalling the nation's withdrawal from the Sterling Area, and Japan had become Australia's largest export market.[109] In spite of these enduring links, developments and policy decisions made in the period 1951–57 marked a distinct departure from the traditional Australian–British relationship of patronage and protection. With this, there was the acknowledgement that the imperial connection could no longer provide for Australia's material interests nor its defensive security.

---

108 Cooper, 'At the Crossroads', 709–10; David Goldsworthy, *Losing the Blanket: Australia and the End of Britain's Empire* (Melbourne: Melbourne University Press, 2002), 95–8, 142–3.
109 Ward, *Australia and the British Embrace*, 41–68, 230, 247–8.

# Conclusion

The 36 years between the apparent settlement of Asia-Pacific peace and the assertion of US power in the region at the 1921–22 Washington Naval Conference and Australia's economic and military reorientation to the US order in 1957 wrought immense change in the Australian government's approach to regional and great-power relations. Yet, nowhere in the existing literature is there a comprehensive study of Australia's policy response. Instead, classic works and more recent contributions alike have tended to dismiss the proposition that Australia had a foreign policy before 1941. To the extent that a distinct Australian perspective has been identified, it has been compartmentalised or merely gestured to. This book offers a reassessment of Australia's foreign policy origins and maturation in the twentieth century. It identifies a marked continuity in how Australia's political elite approached foreign policy over the period 1921–57. Policymakers were attentive to the nation's strategic position, the changing international context and the forces of trade, diplomacy and defence. The policy that emerged in response was an integrated one that sought—with varying levels of success—to build a system that balanced geography with dependency on great powers. The integrated aspects of this policy extended to the theoretical level, with Australian actors demonstrating a keen appreciation of the interrelation between trade, diplomacy and defence when forming policy. This book successfully demonstrates that it was pragmatism, rather than naive loyalty or toadying to Britain and the US, that drove Australia's Asia-Pacific policy in this period.

First among its two aims, this book set out to examine the development of a distinct Australian approach to foreign policy. In so doing, the absolute importance of the interwar years has been established. Many thought the interwar years were a period of relative complacency as Australia relied uncritically on the imperial connection and new international arrangements to provide for its material security. By contrast, this study holds that it was the combined effect of economic crisis, regional instability, US isolationism and, most critically, the shortcomings of the imperial connection during the period 1921–31 that forced on Australian policymakers the need to reassess relations with regional and great powers alike and to seek greater influence in Asia-Pacific affairs.

In focusing on how Australia navigated great-power relations and the systems through which they interacted with the world, this study challenges the ideas espoused by Hugh White and others that Australia has historically taken great-power protection and representation for granted.[1] Australia's relations with Britain and the US over the period 1921–57 are marked by an acknowledgement among policymakers and intellectuals that the difference of Australia's economic and geopolitical considerations from those of Britain and the US meant neither of these nations could necessarily be relied on to provide for Australia's national interest. In response, policymakers attempted to draw attention to the importance of Australia's region and tie its unique interests and material needs to those of the great powers.

As a small power with limited influence in international decision-making, Australia was required to carefully assess methods for projecting its influence. For instance, in the 1934 AEM and the Pacific pact proposals of 1935 and 1937, Latham and Prime Minister Joseph Lyons characterised Australian and British interests in the Asia-Pacific as entangled and harmonious. The hope—although not realised—was that the imperial framework could be employed to deliver regional security outcomes. Richard Casey's activities in Washington are a particularly pertinent example of Australia's pragmatic—indeed, opportunistic—approach to great-power relations. Cognisant of Australia's limited influence in high-level strategic planning, Casey employed alternative measures to promote common Australian–US interests. He sought to use the United States' economic policy towards Japan and US–Japanese negotiations to underscore the Australian government's commitment to a coordinated response to war in the Pacific and to prolong relative peace, providing vital time in which to secure a US military guarantee. Herein are examples of the maturation of Australia's policy apparatus, as policymakers experimented with channels through which to voice their

---

1   White, *The China Choice*, 12.

opinion and exert influence. This study has accordingly highlighted an intuitive and explicitly pragmatic approach to foreign policy that has not previously been identified.

There was also a pragmatism in Australia's contracting and expanding relationships with the US and Britain as the government carefully assessed which partnership would best serve its national interest. In the years immediately preceding the Pacific War, Australia was increasingly willing to challenge Britain when it was seen to threaten relations with Japan, including proposed economic sanctions following the outbreak of the Second Sino-Japanese War and a partial trade embargo targeting neutral countries in the early months of World War II. In these instances, the Australian government can be seen to have made pragmatic appraisals of the benefits of the imperial connection and Britain's questionable diplomatic approach as it related to the deteriorating situation in the Far East. Concurrently, the Australian government turned its attention to the US for defence assurances beyond the Empire. This heralded a period of intense Australian–US collaboration and, on Australia's part, strategic dependence. However, as the crisis years of the Pacific War passed, the Curtin government acknowledged the US could not be relied on to build a postwar order in the Asia-Pacific that was conducive to the national interest. The ANZAC Agreement and the Fourth Empire proposal signified a return to Britain and the Commonwealth connection as the foundational framework through which Australia would interact with the world in the immediate future. By 1957, the centre of gravity in Australian foreign policy and future planning had shifted decisively to the US, as the Menzies government made a series of frank assessments about the material value of the Commonwealth connection and Britain's fading resolve and capacity to provide for its economic and defensive security.

In examining the opportunistic and pragmatic nature of Australia's interactions with Britain and the US, it becomes apparent that the nation has not been a passive player, nor has it taken for granted that the great powers would provide for its security. Australia gradually developed and experimented with tools to project its influence in international affairs and carefully assessed the strategies and capabilities of the great powers, considering which relationship best served its trade, defence and diplomatic interests.

THE GENESIS OF A POLICY

The second aim of this book has been to highlight the absolute importance of trade in Australia's foreign policy conceptualisations and approaches. In integrating the themes of trade, diplomacy and defence throughout, this book has highlighted the value of trade as a tool of diplomacy and its effect on strategic decision-making. This methodology augments existing studies, such as Neville Meaney's landmark 1976 volume of *A History of Australian Defence and Foreign Policy 1901–23*, subtitled *The Search for Security in the Pacific*, which challenged the orthodoxy that Australia was without a distinct foreign policy outlook or approach yet dismissed entirely trade and economic policy as they related to national security. The effect has been to expand the historical understanding of how Australian actors approached foreign policy in the twentieth century.

Amid the economic and strategic uncertainty of the 1930s, regional trade relations provided the basis for a policy designed to expand Australia's regional presence, strategically engage Japan in a bid to reduce the likelihood of hostilities and meet the urgent need for new export markets brought on by the Great Depression. This astute appreciation of the varied and complementary benefits to be had in increased regional trade is quite remarkable given the view that Australia had 'few ideas and policies of its own' and had not 'shuffled its way into a foreign policy' until 1941–42.[2] This book establishes that the comprehensive and integrated understanding of foreign policy that was institutionalised for Australia in 1987 was, in fact, a feature of the way Australian actors had been approaching policymaking from as early as the 1930s.

Australia's postwar plans for the Asia-Pacific region drew together threads from interwar and wartime policy thinking. In 1943, William D. Forsyth of the DEA Pacific Division called attention to the need for a self-subsisting system that would foster political and economic stability in South-East Asia and the South Pacific. These economic development plans were in concert with Australia's desire to see the arc of islands to its north developed as a defence perimeter. This regional concept went on to inform policymaking in the period 1946–50 as the Chifley and Menzies governments supported economic development in South-East Asia and the South Pacific. As in the 1930s, regional economic development had the manifold goal of expanding Australia's strategic, economic and diplomatic capabilities. In Australia's process of increased

---

2   Andrews, *Isolationism and Appeasement in Australia*, 25; Gyngell, *Fear of Abandonment*, 18.

regional economic engagement, there was a tacit acknowledgement that the British market was not without its limits and an extensive economic adjustment was at hand. This situation was acknowledged as early as 1931, when the Great Depression forced on Australian policymakers the reality that there were limited opportunities for growth in the British market. Herbert Gepp subsequently explored regional opportunities on behalf of the Prime Minister's Department. Two years later, the Advisory Committee on Eastern Trade was established, with trade commissioner appointments throughout the region following soon after. In 1947, with the British economy in crisis, economist and director-general of the Department of Post-War Reconstruction, H.C. Coombs, recommended the Australian government begin to cushion the effects of Britain's waning economic capabilities—the principal cushion being the markets in Australia's immediate region. A decade later, the Ottawa Agreements were renegotiated to allow foreign countries greater access to the Australian market—signalling that Britain, the natural market, could no longer meet Australia's development needs—and the Australia–Japan Commerce Agreement was signed.

The period 1921–57, then, is part of a longer history of the multifaceted role of trade relations in Australian foreign policy and the nation's economic disengagement from the British world and integration into its regional markets—a process that continued in Bob Hawke's North-East Asian ascendency and 'enmeshment' with Asia, the Rudd–Gillard governments' rhetoric of the Asian Century and, most recently, the 'stepping-up' of Australia's engagement in the Pacific.[3]

Granted, Australia's efforts were not without significant challenges and failures.

As global powers, the strategic outlooks of Britain and the US have predominated. Australia's status as a junior and strategically dependent partner contributed to an expectation of commitment to the great powers' world view. A tension ultimately exists when Australia's geographical considerations are not served by the strategic outlooks of its security

---

3   Ross Garnaut, *Australia and the Northeast Asian Ascendancy: Report to the Prime Minister and the Minister of Foreign Affairs and Trade* (Canberra: AGPS, 1989); Department of the Prime Minister and Cabinet, *Australia in the Asian Century: White Paper* (Canberra: Commonwealth of Australia, 2012); Department of Foreign Affairs and Trade, 'Stepping-Up Australia's Engagement with Our Pacific Family', *Pacific Step-Up* (Canberra: DFAT, n.d.), available from: dfat.gov.au/geo/pacific/engagement/Pages/stepping-up-australias-pacific-engagement.aspx.

partners. Australia did not exclusively kowtow to the directives of the great powers. Indeed, as this study has established, often the inadequacies of US and British policy were what led Australia to assume a more assertive posture, doggedly refusing to engage in activities it saw as threatening its economic and regional security. Nevertheless, there were points at which Australia was forced to make damaging or disappointing compromises—most readily observed in the Trade Diversion Policy and the US only allowing Australia partial insight into and a limited voice in ANZUS and SEATO decision-making. This brings into sharp focus one of the dominant themes of this study and, indeed, of Australia's foreign policy tradition more broadly: the liability of constructing a foreign policy within an asymmetrical relationship, particularly one centred on two different geopolitical outlooks and considerations.

# Bibliography

## Primary sources

### Archival collections

National Archives of Australia, Canberra. Material from the series:

A1. Department of External Affairs: Correspondence files, annual single number series [Main correspondence files series of the agency], 1890–1968.

A425. Department of Trade and Customs: Correspondence files, annual single number series [Main correspondence files series of the agency], 1935–.

A432. Attorney-General's Department: Correspondence files, annual single number series [Main correspondence files series of the agency], 1857–.

A463. Prime Minister's Department: Correspondence files, annual single number series with occasional 'G' [General Representations] infix [Main correspondence files series of the agency], 1903–.

A518. Prime Minister's Department: Correspondence files, multiple number series with alphabetical prefix, 1899–1983.

A571. Department of the Treasury: Correspondence files, multiple number series with year prefix [Main correspondence files series of the agency], 1901–78.

A601. Department of Commerce: Correspondence files, multiple number series, 1935–48.

A816. Department of Defence: Correspondence files, multiple number series [Classified 301] [Main correspondence files series of the agency], 1928–62.

A981. Department of External Affairs: Correspondence files, alphabetical series, 1927–42.

A989. Department of External Affairs: Correspondence files, multiple number series with year prefix [Main correspondence files series of the agency], 1927–45.

A1068. Department of External Affairs: Correspondence files, multiple number series with year prefix [Main correspondence files series of the agency], 1933–71.

A1196. Department of Defence: Correspondence files, multiple number series [Class 501] [501–539] [Classified] [Main correspondence files series of the agency], 1936–60.

A1209. Prime Minister's Department: Correspondence files, annual single number series [classified] with occasional C [classified] suffix [Main correspondence files series of the agency], 1913–.

A1667. Department of Trade and Customs: International trade relations files, multiple number series [Main correspondence files series of the agency], 1925–56.

A1838. Department of External Affairs: Correspondence files, multiple number series with year prefix [Main correspondence files series of the agency], 1914–93.

A2694. Secretary to Cabinet/Cabinet Secretariat: Lyons and Page Ministries— Folders and bundles of minutes and submissions, 1932–39.

A2910. Australian High Commission, United Kingdom [London]: Correspondence files, multiple number series (Class 400), 1913–60.

A3196. Prime Minister's Department: Master sheets (used stencils) of outwards cables, annual single number series, 1939–49.

A3300. Australian Legation United States of America: Correspondence files, annual alphabetical series (Washington), 1939–87.

A4355. Australian Mission, Political Representative to Allied Forces, Netherlands East Indies [Batavia], Correspondence files, multiple number series [first system, Djakarta/Jakarta] [Main correspondence files series of the agency], 1946–50.

A4719. Department of External Affairs: Volumes of microfilm printout of the personal papers of Sir George Pearce (compiled by Dr J.S. Cumpston), 1907–37.

A4940. Secretary to Cabinet/Cabinet Secretariat: Menzies and Holt Ministries— Cabinet files 'C' single number series, 1949–85.

A5954. Department of Defence: 'The Shedden Collection' [Records collected by Sir Frederick Shedden during his career with the Department of Defence and in researching the history of Australian defence policy], two number series, 1937–71.

A6494. Department of External Affairs: Correspondence files, multiple number system with SPTS [South Pacific Top Secret] prefix, 1943–54.

A6661. Governor-General: Correspondence and printed matter arranged according to subject ('Special Portfolio'), 1888–1936.

A9992. Department of Foreign Affairs and Trade: Unregistered files of the Department of External Affairs, 1920–64.

AWM36. Department of Defence: Official History, 1914–18 War—Naval records of Arthur W. Jose, 1912–30.

B6121. Department of Defence: Naval historical files, single number series with alphabetical suffixes.

CP290/1. Prime Minister's Department: Papers collected in the offices of the Secretary and the Prime Minister, 1901–39.

CP290/6. Prime Minister's Department: Miscellaneous cables, 1937–43.

CP4/2. Prime Minister's Department: Records relating to the Imperial Conference, 1937.

CP78/32. Governor-General: Decoded copies of telegrams exchanged between the Governor-General and the Secretary of State in connection with the 'Chanak Incident' with Turkey, 1922–24.

M58. Department of Commerce and Agriculture: Miscellaneous items including alphabetical electorate, general filing, and personal items, 1915–82.

M100. Australian High Commission London: Monthly War Files, 1939–45.

M2236. Australian High Commission, United Kingdom [London]—Office of the High Commissioner: Official papers and correspondence maintained by Stanley Melbourne Bruce in London, 1932–45.

## The National Archives, Kew. Material from the series:

ADM 116. Records of the Admiralty, Naval Forces, Royal Marines, Coastguard, and related bodies, Admiralty: Record Office: Cases.

CAB 2. Records of the Cabinet Office, Committee of Imperial Defence and Standing Defence Sub-committee: Minutes.

CAB 21. Records of the Cabinet Office, Cabinet Office and predecessors: Registered Files (1916 to 1965).

CAB 23. Records of the Cabinet Office, War Cabinet and Cabinet: Minutes.

CAB 32. Records of the Cabinet Office, Records of Imperial, Commonwealth and International Conferences, etc.

CAB 99. Records of the Cabinet Office, War Cabinet and Cabinet: Commonwealth and International Conferences: Minutes and Papers.

CAB 128. Records of the Cabinet Office, Cabinet: Minutes (CM and CC Series).

CAB 129. Records of the Cabinet Office, Cabinet: Memoranda (CP and C Series).

CO 323. Records of the Colonial Office, Commonwealth and Foreign and Commonwealth Offices, Empire Marketing Board, and related bodies, Colonies, General: Original Correspondence.

DEFE 6. Records of the Ministry of Defence, Ministry of Defence: Chiefs of Staff Committee—Reports of the Joint Planning Staff and successors.

DO 35. Records created or inherited by the Dominions Office, and of the Commonwealth Relations and Foreign and Commonwealth Offices, General Records of the Dominions Office.

FO 141. Records created or inherited by the Foreign Office, Foreign Office and Foreign and Commonwealth Office: Embassy and Consulates, Egypt— General Correspondence.

FO 371. Records created or inherited by the Foreign Office, Foreign Office: Political Departments—General Correspondence from 1906–66.

## Manuscript collections

### National Library of Australia, Canberra. Material from the series:

MS 987. Papers of J.J. Dedman.

MS 1009. Papers of John Latham.

MS 4851. Papers of J.A. Lyons.

MS 4875. Papers of Percy Spender.

MS 5700. Papers of William Douglass Forsyth.

TRC 121/27. William Douglass Forsyth interviewed by Mel Pratt, January–February 1972, Corrected transcript.

## Hansard

### Material from the series:

Australia. *Commonwealth Parliamentary Debates: House of Representatives.* Canberra: Australian Government Publishing Service.

Australia. *Commonwealth Parliamentary Debates: Senate.* Canberra: Australian Government Publishing Service.

United Kingdom. *Parliamentary Debates: House of Commons.* Available from: api.parliament.uk/historic-hansard/commons/index.html.

## Published documents

Aandahl, Frederick, Franklin, William M. and Slany, William, eds. *Foreign Relations of the United States: The Conferences at Washington, 1941–1942, and Casablanca, 1943.* Washington, DC: United States Government Printing Office, 1958.

Andre, Pamela, ed. *Documents on Australian Foreign Policy 1937–49. Volume 14: The Commonwealth, Asia and the Pacific, 1948–49.* Canberra: Australian Government Publishing Service, 1998.

Axton, Matilda F., Churchill, Rogers P., Sappington, N.O., Reid, John G., Prescott, Francis C. and Phillips, Shirley L., eds. *Foreign Relations of the United States Diplomatic Papers, 1936, General, British Commonwealth, Volume I.* Washington, DC: United States Government Printing Office, 1953.

Churchill, Rogers P. and Sappington, N.O., eds. *Foreign Relations of the United States Diplomatic Papers, 1935, The British Commonwealth; Europe, Volume II.* Washington, DC: United States Government Printing Office, 1952.

Churchill, Rogers P., Axton, Matilda F., Landau, Shirley L., Sappington, N.O. and Carroll, Kieran J., eds. *Foreign Relations of the United States Diplomatic Papers, 1934, General, the British Commonwealth, Volume I.* Washington, DC: United States Government Printing Office, 1950.

Churchill, Rogers P., Sappington, N.O., Carroll, Kieran J., Giffen, Morrison B. and Prescott, Francis C., eds. *Foreign Relations of the United States Diplomatic Papers, 1940, The British Commonwealth, The Soviet Union, The Near East and Africa, Volume III.* Washington, DC: United States Government Printing Office, 1958.

Copland, D.B. and Janes, C.V., eds. *Australian Trade Policy: A Book of Documents.* Sydney: Angus & Robertson, 1937.

Crawford, John G., ed. *Australian Trade Policy 1942–66: A Documentary History.* Canberra: Australian National University Press, 1968.

Crowley, F.K., ed. *Modern Australia in Documents. Volume 2: 1939–1970.* Melbourne: Wren Publishing, 1973.

Department of Foreign Affairs and Trade. *Documents on Australian Foreign Policy. Volume 19: The Australia Japan Agreement on Commerce, 1950–59.* Canberra: Department of Foreign Affairs and Trade, 1997.

Fuller, Joseph V. ed. *Papers Relating to the Foreign Relations of the United States 1922, Volume I.* Washington, DC: United States Government Printing Office, 1938.

Goodwin, Ralph E., Kranz, Marvin W., Stauffer, David H., Smyth, Howard M., Sappington, O.N., Aandahl, Fredrick, Churchill, Rogers P. and Slany, William, eds. *Foreign Relations of the United States, 1947, The British Commonwealth; Europe, Volume III.* Washington, DC: United States Government Printing Office, 1972.

Hudson, W.J., ed. *Documents on Australian Foreign Policy, 1937–49. Volume 7: 1944.* Canberra: Australian Government Publishing Service, 1988.

Hudson, W.J. and Stokes, H.J.W., eds. *Documents on Australian Foreign Policy 1937–49. Volume 5: July 1941 – June 1942.* Canberra: Australian Government Publishing Service, 1982.

Hudson, W.J. and Way, Wendy, eds. *Documents on Australian Foreign Policy 1937–49. Volume 9: January–June 1946.* Canberra: Australian Government Publishing Service, 1991.

Hudson, W.J. and Way, Wendy, eds. *Documents on Australian Foreign Policy 1937–49. Volume 10: July–December 1946.* Canberra: Australian Government Publishing Service, 1993.

Hudson, W.J. and Way, Wendy, eds. *Documents on Australian Foreign Policy 1937–49. Volume 12: Australia and the Postwar World 1947.* Canberra: Australian Government Publishing Service, 1995.

Kay, Robin, ed. *Documents of New Zealand External Relations. Volume 1: The Australian–New Zealand Agreement, 1944.* Wellington: A.R. Shearer Government Printer, 1972.

Keefer, Edward C. and Mabon, David W., eds. Foreign Relations of the United States, 1955–1957, *Vietnam, Volume I.* Washington, DC: United States Government Printer, 1985.

Keith, Arthur B., ed. *Speeches and Documents on International Affairs, 1918–1937. Volume 1.* London: Oxford University Press, 1938.

Lowe, David and Oakman, Daniel, eds. *Documents on Australian Foreign Policy. Volume 24: Australia and the Colombo Plan, 1949–1957.* Canberra: Department of Foreign Affairs and Trade, 2004.

Mabon, David W., ed. *Foreign Relations of the United States, 1952–1954, East Asia and the Pacific, Volume XII, Part 1.* Washington, DC: United States Government Printing Office, 1984.

Mansergh, Nicholas, ed. *Documents and Speeches on British Commonwealth Affairs, 1931–52.* London: Oxford University Press, 1953.

Neale, R.G., ed. *Documents on Australian Foreign Policy, 1937–49. Volume 1: 1937–1938.* Canberra: Australian Government Publishing Service, 1976.

Neale, R.G., ed. *Documents on Australian Foreign Policy, 1937–49. Volume 2: 1939.* Canberra: Australian Government Publishing Service, 1976.

Neale, R.G., ed. *Documents on Australian Foreign Policy, 1937–49. Volume 3: January–June 1940.* Canberra: Australian Government Publishing Service, 1979.

Neale, R.G., ed. *Documents on Australian Foreign Policy, 1937–49. Volume 4: July 1940 – January 1941.* Canberra: Australian Government Publishing Service, 1980.

Neale, R.G., ed. *Documents on Australian Foreign Policy, 1937–1949. Volume 6: July 1942 – December 1943.* Canberra: Australian Government Publishing Service, 1983.

Noring, Nina J., ed. *Foreign Relations of the United States, 1955–1957, Suez Crisis, July 26–December 31, 1956, Volume XVI.* Washington, DC: United States Government Printing Office, 1990.

*Peace and War: United States Foreign Policy, 1931–1941.* Washington, DC: United States Government Printing Office, 1943.

Perkins, E. Ralph, Gleason, S. Everett, Reid, John G., Glennon, John P., Sappington, N.O., Slany, William, Cassidy, Velma Hastings and Reynolds, Warren H., eds. *Foreign Relations of the United States: Diplomatic Papers, 1944, The British Commonwealth and Europe, Volume III*. Washington, DC: United States Government Printing Office, 1965.

Petersen, Neil H., ed. *Foreign Relations of the United States, 1952–1954, Indochina, Volume XIII, Part 1*. Washington, DC: United States Government Printing Office, 1982.

Petersen, Neil H., Slany, William Z., Sampson, Charles S., Glennon, John P. and Mabon, David W., eds. *Foreign Relations of the United States, 1950, East Asia and the Pacific, Volume VI*. Washington, DC: United States Government Printing Office, 1976.

Reid, John G. and Glennon, John P., eds. Foreign Relations of the United States, 1949, *The Far East and Australasia, Volume VII, Part 2*. Washington, DC: United States Government Printing Office, 1976.

Reid, John G. and Stauffer, David H., eds. Foreign Relations of the United States, 1948, *The Far East and Australasia, Volume VI*. Washington, DC: United States Government Printing Office, 1974.

Reid, John G., Goodwin, Ralph R. and Gates, Louis E., eds. *Foreign Relations of the United States Diplomatic Papers, 1940, The Far East, Volume IV*. Washington, DC: United States Government Printing Office, 1955.

Rose, Lisle A. and Petersen, Neil H., eds. *Foreign Relations of the United States, 1952–1954, National Security Affairs, Volume II, Part 1*. Washington, DC: United States Government Printing Office, 1984.

Stauffer, David H., Aandahl, Fredrick, Sampson, Charles S., McGaw Smyth, Howard and Ellen Corbett, Joan, eds. *Foreign Relations of the United States, 1949, Western Europe, Volume IV*. Washington, DC: United States Government Printing Office, 1974.

United States Department of State. *American Foreign Policy, 1950–1955: Basic Documents. Volume 1*. Washington: United States Government Printing Office, 1957–58.

# Contemporary government publications, statistical collections and records of proceedings

*Congressional Record*, 67th Congress, 2nd Session. Washington, DC: The United States Congress, 1923.

Gepp, Herbert. *Report on Trade between Australia and the Far East*. Canberra: Parliament of the Commonwealth of Australia, 1932.

*Imperial Conference of Prime Ministers and Representatives of the United Kingdom, the Dominions and India Held in June, July and August 1921: Summary of Proceedings and Documents*. London: J.J. Keliher & Co. for His Majesty's Stationery Office, 1921.

Melbourne, A.C.V. *Report on Australian Intercourse with Japan and China*. Brisbane: Fredrick Phillips, Government Printer, 1932.

*Official Year Book of the Commonwealth of Australia*. No. 26. Canberra: Commonwealth Government Printer, 1933.

*Official Year Book of the Commonwealth of Australia*. No. 28. Canberra: Commonwealth Government Printer, 1935.

*Official Year Book of the Commonwealth of Australia* No. 30. Canberra: Commonwealth Government Printer, 1937.

*Official Year Book of the Commonwealth of Australia*. No. 31. Canberra: Commonwealth Government Printer, 1938.

*Official Year Book of the Commonwealth of Australia*. No. 32. Canberra: Commonwealth Government Printer, 1939.

*Official Year Book of the Commonwealth of Australia*. No. 33. Canberra: Commonwealth Government Printer, 1940.

*Official Year Book of the Commonwealth of Australia*. No. 38. Canberra: Commonwealth Government Printer, 1951.

*Official Year Book of the Commonwealth of Australia*. No. 41. Canberra: Commonwealth Government Printer, 1955.

*Official Year Book of the Commonwealth of Australia*. No. 42. Canberra: Commonwealth Government Printer, 1956.

*Official Year Book of the Commonwealth of Australia*. No. 44. Canberra: Commonwealth Government Printer, 1958.

*Statistics of the Military Effort of the British Empire During the Great War 1914–1920*. London: His Majesty's Stationery Office, 1922.

## Treaty

The World War I Document Archive. 'Peace Treaty of Versailles, 28 June 1919: Articles 1–30 and Annex—The Covenant of the League of Nations.' Available from: net.lib.byu.edu/~rdh7/wwi/versa/versa1.html.

## Historical speeches, diaries and memoirs

Bridge, Carl, ed. *A Delicate Mission: The Washington Diaries of R.G. Casey, 1940–1942*. Canberra: National Library of Australia, 2008.

Evatt, H.V. *Australia in World Affairs*. Sydney: Angus & Robertson, 1946.

Evatt, H.V. *Foreign Policy of Australia: Speeches*. Sydney: Angus & Robinson, 1945.

McEwen, John and Jackson, Robert V. *John McEwen: His Story*. Canberra: Printed privately, 1983.

Millar, T.B., ed. *Australian Foreign Minister: The Diaries of R.G. Casey*. London: Collins, 1972.

Museum of Australian Democracy. 'Australian Federal Election Speeches, Joseph Lyons, 23 October 1937, United Australia Party. Delivered at Deloraine, Tas., 28 September 1937.' Available from: electionspeeches.moadoph.gov.au/speeches/1937-joseph-lyons.

Page, Earl. *Truant Surgeon: The Inside Story of Forty Years of Australian Political Life*. Ann Mozley, ed. Sydney: Angus & Robertson, 1963.

## Newspapers/magazines

*The Age* (Melbourne)
*The Argus* (Melbourne)
*Army News* (Darwin)
*The Australian Worker* (Sydney)
*The Brisbane Courier* (Brisbane)
*The Courier-Mail* (Brisbane)
*Daily Commercial News and Shipping List* (Sydney)
*The Gazette Times* (Pittsburgh)
*The Herald* (Melbourne)
*The New York Times* (New York)
*The Sun* (Sydney)

*Sunday Times* (Perth)
*Sydney Morning Herald* (Sydney)
*Telegraph* (Brisbane)
*The Times* (London)
*Tweed Daily* (Murwillumbah, NSW)

## Secondary sources

### Books

Allison, Graham. *Destined for War: Can America and China Escape Thucydides's Trap?* New York: Houghton Mifflin Harcourt, 2017.

Andrews, Eric M. *A History of Australian Foreign Policy: From Dependence to Independence*. Melbourne: Longman Cheshire, 1979.

Andrews, Eric M. *Isolationism and Appeasement in Australia: Reactions to the European Crisis, 1935–1939*. Canberra: Australian National University Press, 1970.

Andrews, Eric M. *The Writing on the Wall: The British Commonwealth and Aggression in the East, 1931–1935*. Sydney: Allen & Unwin, 1987.

Australian Association of British Manufacturers. *One-Way Traffic: Australia's Trade with the United States*. Melbourne: Australian Association of British Manufacturers, 1931.

Barnett, Correlli. *The Collapse of British Power*. London: Eyre Methuen, 1972.

Bell, Coral. *Dependent Ally: A Study in Australian Foreign Policy*. 2nd edn. Melbourne: Oxford University Press, 1988.

Bell, Roger J. *Unequal Allies: Australian–American Relations and the Pacific War*. Melbourne: Melbourne University Press, 1977.

Bird, David S. *J.A. Lyons: The 'Tame Tasmanian'—Appeasement and Rearmament in Australia, 1932–39*. Melbourne: Australian Scholarly Publishing, 2008.

Bridge, Carl. *William Hughes: Australia*. London: Haus, 2011.

Buckley, Ken, Dale, Barbara and Reynolds, Wayne. *Doc Evatt: Patriot, Internationalist, Fighter and Scholar*. Melbourne: Longman Cheshire, 1994.

Butlin, S.J. *Australia in the War of 1939–45. Series 4: Civil. Volume III: War Economy, 1939–1942*. Canberra: Australian War Memorial, 1955.

Butlin, S.J. and Schedvin, C.B. *Australia in the War of 1939–1945. Series 4: Civil. Volume IV: War Economy, 1942–1945*. Canberra: Australian War Memorial, 1977.

Casey, Richard. *Australia's Place in the World*. Melbourne: Robertson & Mullens, 1931.

Casey, Richard. *Friends and Neighbours: Australia and the World*. Melbourne: Cheshire, 1954.

Cotton, James. *The Australian School of International Relations*. New York: Palgrave Macmillan, 2013. doi.org/10.1057/9781137308061_11.

Curran, James. *Curtin's Empire*. Melbourne: Cambridge University Press, 2011.

Curran, James and Ward, Stuart. *The Unknown Nation: Australia After Empire*. Melbourne: Melbourne University Press, 2010.

Darwin, John. *The Empire Project: The Rise and Fall of the British World System, 1830–1970*. Cambridge, UK: Cambridge University Press, 2009. doi.org/10.1017/CBO9780511635526.

Day, David. *The Great Betrayal: Britain, Australia and the Onset of the Pacific War, 1939–42*. Melbourne: Oxford University Press, 1992.

Department of Defence. *2020 Defence Strategic Update*. Canberra: Commonwealth of Australia, 2020.

Department of the Prime Minister and Cabinet. *Australia in the Asian Century: White Paper*. Canberra: Commonwealth of Australia, 2012.

Dorling, Philip. *The Origins of the ANZUS Treaty: A Reconsideration*. Flinders Political Monographs No. 4. Adelaide: Flinders University, 1989.

Drummond, Ian M. *Imperial Economic Policy, 1917–1939: Studies in Expansion and Protection*. London: Allen & Unwin, 1974. doi.org/10.3138/9781442653948.

Drummond, Ian M. *The Floating Pound and the Sterling Area: 1931–1939*. Cambridge, UK: Cambridge University Press, 1981. doi.org/10.1017/CBO9780511895623.

Edwards, Peter Geoffrey. *Prime Ministers and Diplomats: The Making of Australian Foreign Policy, 1901–1949*. Melbourne: Oxford University Press for the Australian Institute of International Affairs, 1983.

Edwards, Peter and Pemberton, Gregory. *Crises and Commitments: The Politics and Diplomacy of Australia's Involvement in Southeast Asian Conflicts 1948–1965*. Sydney: Allen & Unwin, 1992.

Eggleston, Frederic William. *Reflections on Australian Foreign Policy*. Melbourne: F.W. Cheshire for Australian Institute of International Affairs, 1957.

Esthus, Raymold A. *From Enmity to Alliance: US–Australian Relations, 1931–1941*. Melbourne: Melbourne University Press, 1964.

Fenton, Damien. *To Cage the Red Dragon: SEATO and the Defence of Southeast Asia*. Singapore: NUS Press, 2012. doi.org/10.2307/j.ctv1qv2pf.

Fraser, Malcolm with Roberts, Cain. *Dangerous Allies*. Melbourne: Melbourne University Press, 2014.

Frei, Henry P. *Japan's Southward Advance and Australia: From the Sixteenth Century to World War II*. Melbourne: Melbourne University Press, 1991.

Garnaut, Ross. *Australia and the Northeast Asian Ascendancy: Report to the Prime Minister and the Minister of Foreign Affairs and Trade*. Canberra: Australian Government Publishing Service, 1989.

Gelber, Harry. *The Australian–American Alliance: Costs and Benefits*. Melbourne: Penguin Books, 1968.

George, Margaret. *Australia and the Indonesian Revolution*. Melbourne: Melbourne University Press, 1980.

Golding, Peter. *Black Jack McEwen: Political Gladiator*. Melbourne: Melbourne University Press, 1996.

Goldsworthy, David. *Losing the Blanket: Australia and the End of Britain's Empire*. Melbourne: Melbourne University Press, 2002.

Grant, Bruce. *Crisis of Loyalty: A Study in Australian Foreign Policy*. Sydney: Angus & Robertson for Australian Institute of International Affairs, 1972.

Gyngell, Allan. *Fear of Abandonment: Australia in the World Since 1942*. Melbourne: Black Inc., 2017.

Hamill, Ian. *The Strategic Illusion: The Singapore Strategy and the Defence of Australia and New Zealand, 1919–1942*. Singapore: NUS Press, 1981.

Hamilton, Clive. *Silent Invasion: China's Influence on Australia*. Melbourne: Hardie Grant Books, 2018.

Harper, Norman. *A Great and Powerful Friend: Australia and the United States, 1900–1975*. Brisbane: University of Queensland Press, 1986.

Harper, Norman. *Australia and the United States*. Melbourne: Thomas Nelson, 1971.

Hasluck, Paul. *Australia in the War of 1939–1945. Series 4: Civil. Volume I: The Government and the People, 1939–1941*. Canberra: Australian War Memorial, 1970.

Hasluck, Paul. *Diplomatic Witness: Australian Foreign Affairs, 1941–1947*. Melbourne: Melbourne University Press, 1980.

Hastedt, Glenn P. *American Foreign Policy: Past, Present, Future*. Upper Saddle River, NJ: Pearson Education Inc., 2006.

Henry, Adam Hughes. *The Gatekeepers of Australian Foreign Policy*. Melbourne: Australian Scholarly Publishing, 2015.

Horner, David. *High Command: Australia's Struggle for an Independent War Strategy, 1939–45*. 2nd edn. Sydney: Allen & Unwin, 1992.

Hudson, W.J. *Blind Loyalty: Australia and the Suez Crisis, 1956*. Melbourne: Melbourne University Press, 1989.

Hudson, W.J. *Casey*. Oxford, UK: Oxford University Press, 1986.

Hudson, W.J. *Towards a Foreign Policy, 1914–1941*. Melbourne: Cassell, 1967.

Kelly, Andrew. *ANZUS and the Early Cold War: Strategy and Diplomacy Between Australia, New Zealand and the United States, 1945–56*. Cambridge, UK: Open Book Publishers, 2018.

Kennedy, Paul. *The Rise and Fall of British Naval Mastery*. London: A. Lane, 1976.

Kennedy, Paul. *The Rise and Fall of the Great Powers: Economic Change and Military Conflict from 1500 to 2000*. London: Fontana Press, 1988.

Knock, Thomas J. *To End All Wars: Woodrow Wilson and the Quest for a New World Order*. Princeton, NJ: Princeton University Press, 1995.

Kobayashi, Ai. *W. Macmahon Ball: Politics for the People*. Melbourne: Australian Scholarly Publishing, 2013.

Lee, Bradford A. *Britain and the Sino-Japanese War, 1937–1939: A Study in the Dilemmas of British Decline*. Stanford, CA: Stanford University Press, 1973.

Lee, David. *Australia and the World in the Twentieth Century: International Relations Since Federation.* Melbourne: Circa, 2006.

Lee, David. *Search for Security: The Political Economy of Australia's Postwar Foreign and Defence Policy.* Sydney: Allen & Unwin, 1995.

Lee, David. *Stanley Melbourne Bruce: Australian Internationalist.* Sydney: Bloomsbury, 2010.

Lockwood, R. *War on the Waterfront: Menzies, Japan and the Pig Iron Dispute.* Sydney: Hale & Iremonger, 1987.

Louis, William Roger. *Imperialism at Bay 1941–1945: The United States and the Decolonization of the British Empire.* Oxford, UK: The Clarendon Press, 1977.

Lowe, David. *Australia Between Empires: The Life of Percy Spender.* London: Pickering & Chatto, 2010.

Lowe, David. *Menzies and the 'Great World Struggle': Australia's Cold War, 1948–1954.* Sydney: UNSW Press, 1999.

McCarthy, John. *Australia and Imperial Defence 1918–39: A Study in Air and Sea Power.* Brisbane: University of Queensland Press, 1976.

Macintyre, Stuart. *Australia's Boldest Experiment: War and Reconstruction in the 1940s.* Sydney: NewSouth, 2015.

McKenzie, Francine. *Redefining the Bonds of Commonwealth, 1939–1948: The Politics of Preference.* London: Palgrave Macmillan, 2002. doi.org/10.1057/9780230554689.

Macmahon Ball, W. *Japan: Enemy or Ally?* Melbourne: Cassell & Company, 1948.

Masey, Edward. *Is It Necessary? An Examination of the Commonwealth Government's Trade Diversion Policy.* Sydney: Stafford Printing, 1936.

Meaney, Neville. *A History of Australian Defence and Foreign Policy 1901–23. Volume 1: The Search for Security in the Pacific, 1901–1914.* 2nd edn. Sydney: Sydney University Press, 2009.

Meaney, Neville. *A History of Australian Defence and Foreign Policy 1901–23. Volume 2: Australia and World Crisis, 1914–1923.* Sydney: Sydney University Press, 2009.

Meaney, Neville. *Fears and Phobias: E.L. Piesse and the Problem of Japan, 1909–39.* Canberra: National Library of Australia, 1996.

Meredith, David and Dyster, Barrie. *Australia in the Global Economy: Continuity and Change*. Melbourne: Cambridge University Press, 1999.

Millar, T.B. *Australia in Peace and War: External Relations Since 1788*. Canberra: Australian National University Press, 1978.

Millar, T.B. *Australia's Foreign Policy*. Sydney: Angus & Robertson, 1968.

Miller, Edward S. *Bankrupting the Enemy: The US Financial Siege of Japan Before Pearl Harbor*. Annapolis: Naval Institute Press, 2007.

Mitchell, B.R. *British Historical Statistics*. Cambridge, UK: Cambridge University Press, 1988.

Morton, Peter. *Fire Across the Desert: Woomera and the Anglo-Australian Joint Project 1946–1980*. Canberra: Australian Government Publishing Service, 1989.

Oakman, Daniel. *Facing Asia: A History of the Colombo Plan*. Canberra: Pandanus Books, 2004.

Orders, P.G.A. *Britain, Australia, New Zealand and the Challenge of the United States, 1939–46*. New York: Palgrave Macmillan, 2003. doi.org/10.1057/9780230289079.

Prior, James. *America Looks to Australia: The Hidden Role of Richard Casey in the Creation of the Australia–America Alliance, 1940–1942*. Melbourne: Australian Scholarly Publishing, 2017.

Renouf, Alan. *Let Justice Be Done: The Foreign Policy of Dr H.V. Evatt*. Brisbane: University of Queensland Press, 1983.

Renouf, Alan. *The Frightened Country*. Melbourne: Macmillan, 1979.

Reynolds, Wayne. *Australia's Bid for the Atomic Bomb*. Melbourne: Melbourne University Press, 2000.

Ross, A.T. *Armed and Ready: The Industrial Development and Defence of Australia, 1900–1945*. Sydney: Turton & Armstrong, 1995.

Schaller, Michael. *The American Occupation of Japan: The Origins of the Cold War in Asia*. Oxford, UK: Oxford University Press, 1985.

Schedvin, Boris. *Australia and the Great Depression: A Study of Economic Development and Policy in the 1920s and 1930s*. Sydney: Sydney University Press, 1970.

Schedvin, Boris. *Emissaries of Trade: A History of the Australian Trade Commissioner Service*. Canberra: Department of Foreign Affairs and Trade, 2008.

Shepherd, Jack. *Australia's Interests and Policies in the Far East*. New York: International Secretariat, Institute of Pacific Relations, 1940.

Shimazu, N. *Japan, Race and Equality: The Racial Equality Proposal of 1919*. London: Routledge, 1998.

Stenson-Wright, John. *Unequal Allies? United States Security and Alliance Policy Towards Japan, 1945–60*. Stanford, CA: Stanford University Press, 2005.

Stevens, David. *The Australian Centenary History of Defence. Volume 3: The Royal Australian Navy*. Melbourne: Oxford University Press, 2001.

Thorne, Christopher. *Allies of a Kind: The United States, Britain and the War Against Japan, 1941–1945*. London: Hamish Hamilton, 1978.

Tow, Shannon. *Independent Ally: Australia in an Age of Power Transition*. Melbourne: Melbourne University Press, 2017.

Trotter, A. *Britain and East Asia, 1933–1937*. London: Cambridge University Press, 1975.

Tsokhas, Kosmas. *Markets, Money and Empire: The Political Economy of the Australian Wool Industry*. Melbourne: Melbourne University Press, 1990.

Tweedie, Sandra. *Trading Partners: Australia and Asia, 1790–1993*. Sydney: UNSW Press, 1994.

Walker, David. *Anxious Nation: Australia and the Rise of Asia 1850–1939*. Brisbane: University of Queensland Press, 1999.

Wallis, Joanne. *Pacific Power? Australia's Strategy in the Pacific Islands*. Melbourne: Melbourne University Press, 2017.

Walton, David. *Australia, Japan and Southeast Asia: Early Post-War Initiatives in Regional Diplomacy*. New York: Nova Publishers, 2012.

Ward, Stuart. *Australia and the British Embrace: The Demise of the Imperial Ideal*. Melbourne: Melbourne University Press, 1998.

Waters, Christopher. *Australia and Appeasement: Imperial Foreign Policy and the Origins of World War II*. London: I.B. Tauris, 2012. doi.org/10.5040/9780755625871.

Waters, Christopher. *The Empire Fractures: Anglo-Australian Conflict in the 1940s*. Melbourne: Australian Scholarly Publishing, 1996.

Watt, D.C. *How War Came: The Immediate Origins of the Second World War, 1938–1939*. New York: Pantheon Books, 1989.

White, Hugh. *The China Choice: Why America Should Share Power*. Melbourne: Black Inc., 2013.

Wigmore, Lionel. *Australia in the War of 1939–1945: The Japanese Thrust. Series 1: Army. Volume 4*. Canberra: Australian War Memorial, 1957.

## Edited collections

Attard, Bernard. 'Financial Diplomacy.' In *Between Empire and Nation: Australia's External Relations from Federation Until the Second World War*, edited by Carl Bridge and Bernard Attard, 92–109. Melbourne: Australian Scholarly Publishing, 2000.

Beaumont, Joan. 'Australia's War: Asia and the Pacific.' In *Australia's War, 1939–45*, edited by Joan Beaumont, 26–53. Sydney: Routledge, 1996. doi.org/10.4324/9781003115007-2.

Beaumont, Joan. 'Making Australian Foreign Policy, 1941–69.' In *Ministers, Mandarins and Diplomats: Australian Foreign Policy Making, 1941–1969*, edited by Joan Beaumont, Christopher Waters, David Lowe and Garry Woodard, 1–18. Melbourne: Melbourne University Press, 2003.

Bridge, Carl. '"The Other Blade of the Scissors": Richard Gardiner Casey, Australia's First Minister to the United States, 1940–1942.' In *Diplomats at War: British and Commonwealth Diplomacy in Wartime*, edited by Christopher Baxter and Andrew Stewart, 127–48. Leiden: Martinus Nijhoff, 2008.

Carroll, Peter. 'Australia, ECOSOC and the UN Specialised Agencies.' In *Australia and the United Nations*, edited by James Cotton and David Lee, 191–227. Canberra: Longueville Books with the Department of Foreign Affairs and Trade, 2012.

Day, David. '27 December 1941 Prime Minister Curtin's New Year Message: Australia "Looks to America".' In *Turning Points in Australian History*, edited by Martin Crotty and David Roberts, 129–42. Sydney: UNSW Press, 2008.

Day, David. *Brave New World: Dr H.V. Evatt and Australian Foreign Policy, 1941–1949*. Brisbane: University of Queensland Press, 1996.

Day, David. 'Pearl Harbour to Nagasaki.' In *Munich to Vietnam: Australia's Relations with Britain and the United States Since the 1930s*, edited by Carl Bridge, 52–69. Melbourne: Melbourne University Press, 1991.

Dennis, Peter. 'Australia and Indonesia: The Early Years.' In *Australia and the End of Empires: The Impact of Decolonisation on Australia's Near North, 1945–65*, edited by David Lowe, 43–52. Geelong, Vic.: Deakin University Press, 1996.

Dennis, Peter. 'Australia and the "Singapore Strategy".' In *Sixty Years On: The Fall of Singapore*, edited by B. Farrell and S. Hunter, 29–41. Singapore: Eastern Universities Press, 2002.

Eccles, R. 'Australian Perspectives and the Balfour Declaration of 1926.' In *Dependency? Essays in the History of Australian Defence and Foreign Policy*, edited by John McCarthy, 23–37. Canberra: University College, University of New South Wales, Australian Defence Force Academy, 1989.

Edwards, P.G. 'The Rise and Fall of the High Commissioner: S.M. Bruce in London 1933–1945.' In *Australia and Britain: Studies in a Changing Relationship*, edited by A.F. Madden and W.H. Morris-Jones, 39–56. Sydney: Sydney University Press, 1980.

Evans, Gareth. 'The Labor Tradition: A View From the 1990s.' In *From Evatt to Evans: The Labor Tradition in Australian Foreign Policy*, edited by David Lee and Christopher Waters, 11–22. Canberra: Allen & Unwin with the Department of International Relations, Research School of Pacific and Asian Studies, The Australian National University, 1997.

Fitzpatrick, John. 'European Settler Colonialism and National Security Ideologies in Australian History.' In *Middling, Meddling, Muddling: Issues in Australian Foreign Policy*, edited by Richard Leaver and David Cox, 91–119. Sydney: Allen & Unwin, 1997.

Fry, Gregory E. 'International Cooperation in the South Pacific: From Regional Integration to Collective Diplomacy.' In *The Political Economy of Regional Cooperation: Comparative Case Studies*, edited by W. Andrew Axline, 136–77. London: Pinter Publishers, 1994.

Fry, Gregory E. 'The Politics of South Pacific Regional Cooperation.' In *The South Pacific: Problems, Issues and Prospects*, edited by Ramesh Thakur, 169–81. London: Palgrave Macmillan, 1991. doi.org/10.1007/978-1-349-12519-7_11.

Hajime, Shimizu. 'Japanese Economic Penetration into Southeast Asia and the Southward Expansion School of Thought.' In *International Commercial Rivalry in Southeast Asia in the Interwar Period*, edited by Shinya Sugiyama and Milagros C. Guerrero, 11–39. Newhaven, CT: Yale University Southeast Asia Studies, 1994.

Harris, Stuart. 'The Separation of Economics and Politics: A Luxury We Can No Longer Afford.' In *Academic Studies and International Politics: Papers of a Conference Held at The Australian National University, June 1981*, edited by Coral Bell, 75–83. Canberra: Department of International Relations, The Australian National University, 1982.

Henry, Adam Hughes. 'John Burton: Forgotten Mandarin?' In *The Seven Dwarfs and the Age of the Mandarins: Australian Government Administration in the Post-War Reconstruction Era*, edited by Samuel Furphy, 219–32. Canberra: ANU Press, 2015. doi.org/10.22459/sdam.07.2015.12.

Jones, Paul. 'Trading in a "Fool's Paradise"? White Australia and the Trade Diversion Dispute of 1936.' In *Relationships: Japan and Australia, 1870s – 1950s*, edited by Vera Mackie and Paul Jones, 133–62. Melbourne: University of Melbourne, Department of History, 2001.

Jordan, Matthew. 'Decolonisation.' In *Australia and the United Nations*, edited by James Cotton and David Lee, 34–65. Canberra: Longueville Books with the Department of Foreign Affairs and Trade, 2012.

Lee, David. 'Australia's Defence Policy: A Historical Overview.' In *Australia's Security in the 21st Century*, edited by J. Mohan Malik, 8–31. Sydney: Allen & Unwin, 1999.

Lee, David. 'Sir John Crawford: Agriculture and Trade.' *The Seven Dwarfs and the Age of the Mandarins: Australian Government Administration in the Post-War Reconstruction Era*, edited by Samuel Furphy, 169–82. Canberra: ANU Press, 2015. doi.org/10.22459/sdam.07.2015.08.

Lee, David. 'Sir John Latham and the League of Nations.' In *League of Nations: Histories, Legacies and Impact*, edited by Joy Damousi and Patricia O'Brien, 86–91. Melbourne: Melbourne University Press, 2018.

Macintyre, Stuart. 'Reading Post-War Reconstruction Through National and Transnational Lenses.' In *Transnationalism, Nationalism and Australian History*, edited by Anna Clark, Anne Rees and Alecia Simmonds, 133–45. Singapore: Palgrave Macmillan, 2017. doi.org/10.1007/978-981-10-5017-6_9.

McKenzie, Francine. 'Imperial Solutions to International Crises: Alliances, Trade and the Ottawa Imperial Economic Conference of 1932.' In *The Foreign Office, Commerce and British Foreign Policy 1900–2000*, edited by John Fisher, Effie G.H. Pedaliu and Richard Smith, 165–87. London: Palgrave Macmillan, 2016. doi.org/10.1057/978-1-137-46581-8_7.

Macmahon Ball, W. *Intermittent Diplomat: The Japan and Batavia Diaries of W. Macmahon Ball*, edited by Alan Rix. Melbourne: Melbourne University Press, 1988.

May, Andrew. 'Fortress Australia.' In *Between Empire and Nation: Australia's External Relations from Federation Until the Second World War*, edited by Carl Bridge and Bernard Attard, 188–204. Melbourne: Australian Scholarly Publishing, 2000.

Meaney, Neville. 'Dr H.V. Evatt and the United Nations: The Problems of Collective Security and the Liberal International Order.' In *Australia and the United Nations*, edited by James Cotton and David Lee, 105–46. Canberra: Longueville Books with the Department of Foreign Affairs and Trade, 2012.

Murfett, Malcolm. 'The Singapore Strategy.' In *Between Empire and Nation: Australia's External Relations from Federation Until the Second World War*, edited by Carl Bridge and Bernard Attard, 168–87. Melbourne: Australian Scholarly Publishing, 2000.

Newton, Scott. 'Britain, the Sterling Area and European Integration, 1945–50.' In *Money, Finance and Empire, 1790–1960*, edited by A.N. Porter and R.F. Holland, 163–82. London: Frank Cass, 1985.

Nish, Ian. 'Relations with Japan.' In *Between Empire and Nation: Australia's External Relations from Federation Until the Second World War*, edited by Carl Bridge and Bernard Attard, 130–41. Melbourne: Australian Scholarly Publishing, 2000.

Palazzo, Albert. 'The Overlooked Mission: Australia and Home Defence.' In *Australia 1942: In the Shadow of War*, edited by Peter J. Dean, 53–69. Cambridge, UK: Cambridge University Press, 2013. doi.org/10.1017/CBO9781139540681.007.

Pemberton, Gregory. 'An Imperial Imagination: Explaining the Post-1945 Foreign Policy of Robert Gordon Menzies.' In *Menzies in War and Peace*, edited by Frank Cain, 154–75. Sydney: Allen & Unwin, 1997.

Reynolds, Wayne. 'Dr H.V. Evatt: Foreign Minister for a Small Power.' In *Brave New World: Dr H.V. Evatt and Australian Foreign Policy, 1941–1949*, edited David Day, 146–57. Brisbane: University of Queensland Press, 1996.

Reynolds, Wayne. 'Imperial Defence After 1945.' In *Australia and the End of Empires: The Impact of Decolonisation on Australia's Near North, 1945–65*, edited by David Lowe, 119–35. Geelong, Vic.: Deakin University Press, 1996.

Reynolds, Wayne. 'Menzies and the Proposal for Nuclear Weapons.' In *Menzies in War and Peace*, edited by Frank Cain, 116–37. Sydney: Allen & Unwin, 1997.

Rooth, Tim. 'Ottawa and After.' In *Between Empire and Nation: Australia's External Relations from Federation Until the Second World War*, edited by Carl Bridge and Bernard Attard, 110–29. Melbourne: Australian Scholarly Publishing, 2000.

Smith, Shannon L. 'Towards Diplomatic Representation.' In *Facing North: A Century of Australian Engagement with Asia. Volume 1: 1901 to the 1970s*, edited by David Goldsworthy, 61–96. Melbourne: Melbourne University Press and Department of Foreign Affairs and Trade, 2001.

Stewart, F.H. 'Australian Commercial Representation Abroad.' In *Australian Foreign Policy, 1934*, edited by H. Dinning and J. Holms. Melbourne: Melbourne University Press for Australian Institute of International Affairs, 1935.

Waters, Christopher. 'The Great Debates: H.V. Evatt and the Department of External Affairs, 1941–49.' In *Ministers, Mandarins and Diplomats: Australian Foreign Policy Making, 1941–1969*, edited by Joan Beaumont, Christopher Waters, David Lowe and Garry Woodard, 46–61. Melbourne: Melbourne University Press, 2003.

## Journal articles

Andrews, Eric M. 'The Australian Government and the Manchurian Crisis, 1931–3.' *Australian Outlook* 35, no. 3 (1981): 307–16.

Attard, Bernard. 'The Limits of Influence: The Political Economy of Australian Commercial Policy After the Ottawa Conference.' *Australian Historical Studies* 29, no. 111 (1998): 325–43. doi.org/10.1080/10314619808596076.

'Australia and Japan Seek Trade Treaty.' *Far Eastern Survey* 4, no. 11 (1935): 86–7. doi.org/10.2307/3023029.

Bairoch, P. 'International Industrialisation Levels from 1750–1980.' *Journal of European Economic History* 11 (1982): 269–333.

Barnes, Felicity. 'Lancashire's "War" with Australia: Rethinking Anglo-Australian Trade and the Cultural Economy of Empire, 1934–36. *The Journal of Imperial and Commonwealth History* 46, no. 4 (2018): 707–30. doi.org/10.1080/03086534.2018.1452539.

Benson, Erik. 'Suspicious Allies: Wartime Aviation Developments and the Anglo-American International Airline Rivalry, 1939–45.' *History and Technology* 17 (2000): 21–42. doi.org/10.1080/07341510008581981.

Benvenuti, Andrea. 'Australian Reactions to Britain's Declining Presence in Southeast Asia, 1955–63.' *The Journal of Imperial and Commonwealth History* 34, no. 3 (2006): 407–29. doi.org/10.1080/03086530600826140.

Best, Antony. 'Economic Appeasement or Economic Nationalism? A Political Perspective on the British Empire, Japan, and the Rise of Intra-Asian Trade, 1933–37.' *The Journal of Imperial and Commonwealth History* 30, no. 2 (2002): 77–101. doi.org/10.1080/03086530208583142.

Best, Antony. 'The "Ghost" of the Anglo-Japanese Alliance: An Examination into Historical Myth-Making.' *The Historical Journal* 49, no. 3 (2006): 811–31. doi.org/10.1017/s0018246x06005528.

Bongiorno, Frank. '"British to the Bootstraps?" H.V. Evatt, J.B. Chifley and Australian Policy on Indian Membership of the Commonwealth, 1947–49.' *Historical Studies* 36, no. 125 (2005): 18–39. doi.org/10.1080/10314610508682909.

Bongiorno, Frank. 'The Price of Nostalgia: Menzies, the "Liberal" Tradition and Australian Foreign Policy.' Australian Journal of Politics and History 51, no. 3 (2005): 400–17. doi.org/10.1111/j.1467-8497.2005.0382a.x.

Boughton, James. *Northwest of Suez: The 1956 crisis and the IMF*. IMF Working Papers 2000/192. Washington, DC: International Monetary Fund, 2000. doi.org/10.5089/9781451859751.001.

Braddick, C.W. 'Britain, the Commonwealth, and the Post-War Japanese Revival, 1945–70.' *The Round Table* 99, no. 409 (2010): 371–89. doi.org/10.1080/00358533.2010.498975.

Bridge, Carl. 'Appeasement and After: Towards a Re-assessment of the Lyons and Menzies Governments' Defence and Foreign Policies, 1931–41.' *Australian Journal of Politics and History* 51, no. 3 (2005): 372–9. doi.org/10.1111/j.1467-8497.2005.0379a.x.

Bridge, Carl. 'R.G. Casey, Australia's First Washington Legation, and the Origins of the Pacific War, 1940–42.' *Australian Journal of Politics and History* 28, no. 2 (1982): 181–89. doi.org/10.1111/j.1467-8497.1982.tb00176.x.

Cain, Frank. 'Venona in Australia and its Long-Term Ramifications.' *Journal of Contemporary History* 35, no. 2 (2000): 231–48. doi.org/10.1177/002200940003500205.

Chennault, Claire L. 'The Chinese Civil War: What We Face in the Far East.' *Vital Speeches of the Day* 15, no. 15 (1949): 468–70.

Cooper, Alastair. 'At the Crossroads: Anglo-Australian Naval Relations, 1945–1971.' *The Journal of Military History* 58, no. 4 (1994): 699–718. doi.org/10.2307/2944275.

Cooper, Richard N. 'Fettered to Gold? Economic Policy in the Interwar Period.' *Journal of Economic Literature* 30, no. 4 (1992): 2120–8.

Cotton, James. 'R.G. Casey and Australian International Thought: Empire, Nation, Community.' *The International History Review* 33, no. 1 (2011): 95–113. doi.org/10.1080/07075332.2011.555380.

Cotton, James. 'William Morris Hughes, Empire and Nationalism: The Legacy of the First World War.' *Australian Historical Studies* 46, no. 1 (2016): 100–18. doi.org/10.1080/1031461x.2014.995114.

'Crisis in Asia: An Examination of US Policy, Remarks by Acheson, 12 January 1950.' *Department of State Bulletin: Far Eastern Series* 32 (1950): 111–18.

Cumpston, I.M. 'The Australian–Japanese Dispute of the Nineteen-Thirties.' *The Australian Quarterly* 29, no. 2 (1957): 45–55.

Curran, James. '"An Organic Part of the Whole Structure": John Curtin's Empire.' *The Journal of Imperial and Commonwealth History* 37, no. 1 (2009): 51–75. doi.org/10.1080/03086530902757704.

Curthoys, R.L. 'Australia in the Changing East.' *Foreign Affairs* 15, no. 4 (1937): 750–6. doi.org/10.2307/20028817.

Devetak, Richard. 'An Australian Outlook on International Affairs? The Evolution of International Relations Theory in Australia.' *Australian Journal of Politics and History* 55, no. 3 (2009): 335–59. doi.org/10.1111/j.1467-8497.2009.1521a.x.

Dobson, Alan P. 'The Other Air Battle: The American Pursuit of Post-War Civil Aviation Rights.' *Historical Journal* 22, no. 2 (1985): 429–39. doi.org/10.1017/s0018246x00003216.

Eggleston, Frederic. 'Washington and After: An Australian View.' *The Nineteenth Century and After* 92 (1922): 455–65.

Evatt, H.V. 'Risks of a Big-Power Peace.' *Foreign Affairs* 24, no. 2 (1946): 195–209. doi.org/10.2307/20029959.

Fettling, David. 'An Australian Response to Asian Decolonisation: Jawaharlal Nehru, John Burton and the New Delhi Conference on Non-Western Nations.' *Australian Historical Studies* 45, no. 2 (2014): 202–19. doi.org/10.1080/1031461x.2014.911758.

Gurry, Meg. 'Identifying Australia's "Region": From Evatt to Evans.' *Australian Journal of International Affairs* 49, no. 1 (1995): 17–31. doi.org/10.1080/10357719508445143.

Harris, Stuart. 'The Linking of Politics and Economics in Foreign Policy.' *Australian Outlook* 40, no. 1 (1986): 5–10. doi.org/10.1080/10357718608444895.

Kobayashi, Ai. 'Australia and Japan's Admission to the Colombo Plan.' *Australian Journal of Politics and History* 60, no. 4 (2014): 518–33. doi.org/10.1111/ajph.12073.

Lee, David. 'Australia and Allied Strategy in the Far-East, 1952–1957.' *Journal of Strategic Studies* 16 (1993): 511–38. doi.org/10.1080/01402399308437531.

Lee, David. 'Australia, the British Commonwealth, and the United States, 1950–1953.' *The Journal of Imperial and Commonwealth History* 20, no. 3 (1992): 445–69. doi.org/10.1080/03086539208582880.

Lee, David. 'Britain and Australia's Defence Policy, 1945–49.' *War and Society* 13, no. 1 (1995): 61–80. doi.org/10.1179/072924795791200178.

Lee, David. 'Protecting the Sterling Area: The Chifley Government's Response to Multilateralism 1945–9.' *Australian Journal of Politics* 25 (1990): 178–95. doi.org/10.1080/00323269008402117.

Lowe, David. 'Mr Spender Goes to Washington: An Ambassador's Vision of Australian–American Relations, 1951–58.' *The Journal of Imperial and Commonwealth History* 24, no. 2 (1996): 278–95. doi.org/10.1080/03086539608582979.

Lowe, David. 'Percy Spender and the Colombo Plan 1950.' *Australian Journal of Politics and History* 40, no. 2 (1990): 162–76. doi.org/10.1111/j.1467-8497.1994.tb00098.x.

McLean, David. 'Australia in the Cold War: A Historiographical Review.' *The International History Review* 23, no. 2 (2001): 299–321. doi.org/10.1080/07075332.2001.9640932.

Meaney, Neville. 'Australia, the Great Powers and the Coming of the Cold War.' *Australian Journal of Politics and History* 38, no. 6 (1992): 316–33. doi.org/10.1111/j.1467-8497.1992.tb00678.x.

Megaw, Ruth. 'The Australian Goodwill Mission to the Far East in 1934: Its Significance in the Evolution of Australian Foreign Policy.' *Journal of the Royal Australian Historical Society* 59, no. 4 (1973): 247–63.

Nanto, Dick K. and Takagi, Shinju. 'Korekiyo Takahashi and Japan's Recovery from the Great Depression.' *The American Economic Review* 75, no. 2 (1985): 369–74.

Newton, Scott. 'The Sterling Crisis of 1947 and the British Response to the Marshall Plan.' *Economic History Review* 37, no. 3 (1984): 391–408. doi.org/10.2307/2597288.

O'Brien, J.B. 'Empire v. National Interest in Australian–British Relations During the 1930s.' *Historical Studies* 22, no. 89 (1987): 569–86. doi.org/10.1080/10314618708595769.

Plimsoll, James. 'Australia and Ottawa.' *The Australian Quarterly* 13, no. 4 (1941): 14–21. doi.org/10.2307/20630973.

Reynolds, Wayne. 'Beyond White Australia: Australian Education and the Engagement of Asia After the Second World War.' *International Journal of Learning* 13, no. 3 (2006): 7–14. doi.org/10.18848/1447-9494/CGP/v13i03/44690.

Robertson, John. 'Australia and the "Beat Hitler First Strategy", 1941–1942: A Problem in Wartime Consultation.' *Journal of Imperial and Commonwealth History* 11, no. 3 (1983): 300–21. doi.org/10.1080/03086538308582644.

Rooth, Tim. 'Economic Tensions and Conflict in the Commonwealth, 1945–c. 1951.' *Twentieth Century British History* 13, no. 2 (2002): 121–43. doi.org/10.1093/tcbh/13.2.121.

Rooth, Tim. 'Imperial Self-Insufficiency Rediscovered: Britain and Australia, 1945–51.' *Australian Economic History Review* 39, no. 1 (1999): 29–51. doi.org/10.1111/1467-8446.00037.

Rosenstein-Rodan, P.N. 'The International Development of Economically Backward Areas.' *International Affairs* 20, no. 2 (1944): 157–65. doi.org/10.2307/3018093.

Sissons, D.C.S. 'Manchester v. Japan: The Imperial Background of the Australian Trade Diversion Dispute with Japan, 1936.' *Australian Outlook* 30, no. 3 (1976): 480–502. doi.org/10.1080/10357717608444583.

Sissons, D.C.S. 'Private Diplomacy in the 1936 Trade Dispute with Japan.' *Australian Journal of Politics and History* 27, no. 2 (1981): 143–59. doi.org/10.1111/j.1467-8497.1981.tb00548.x.

Strating, Rebecca. 'Should Australia Be in the South China Sea?' *The La Trobe Asia Brief* 2 (2019): 3–4.

Suares, Julie. 'Engaging with Asia: The Chifley Government and the New Delhi Conferences of 1947 and 1949.' *Australian Journal of Politics and History* 57, no. 4 (2011): 495–510. doi.org/10.1111/j.1467-8497.2011.01610.x.

Tsokhas, Kosmas. 'Anglo-Australian Relations and the Origins of the Pacific War.' *History* 80, no. 260 (1995): 400–20. doi.org/10.1111/j.1468-229x.1995.tb01677.x.

Tsokhas, Kosmas. 'Dedominionization: The Anglo-Australian Experience, 1939–1945.' *Historical Journal* 37, no. 4 (1994): 861–83. doi.org/10.1017/s0018246x00015120.

Tsokhas, Kosmas. 'The Wool Industry and the 1936 Trade Diversion Dispute Between Australia and Japan.' *Australian Historical Studies* 23, no. 93 (1989): 442–61. doi.org/10.1080/10314618908595823.

Umetsu, Hiroyuki. 'The Origins of the British Commonwealth Strategic Reserve: The UK Proposal to Revitalise ANZAM and the Increased Australian Defence Commitment to Malaya.' *Australian Journal of Politics and History* 50, no. 4 (2004): 509–25. doi.org/10.1111/j.1467-8497.2004.00350.x.

Valkoun, Jaroslav. 'Great Britain, the Dominions and Their Position On Japan in the 1920s and Early 1930s.' *Prague Papers on the History of International Relations* 2 (2017): 32–46.

Ward, Stuart. 'Sentiment and Self-Interest: The Imperial Ideal in Anglo-Australian Commercial Culture.' *Australian Historical Studies* 32, no. 116 (2001): 91–108. doi.org/10.1080/10314610108596149.

Waterhouse, Richard. 'Empire and Nation: Australian Popular Ideology and the Outbreak of the Pacific War.' *History Australia* 12, no. 3 (2015): 30–54. doi.org/10.1080/14490854.2015.11668585.

Waters, Christopher. 'Casey: Four Decades in the Making of Australian Foreign Policy.' *Australian Journal of Politics and History* 51, no. 3 (2005): 380–8. doi.org/10.1111/j.1467-8497.2005.0380a.x.

Waters, Christopher. 'The Macmahon Ball Mission to East Asia 1948.' *Australian Journal of Politics and History* 40, no. 3 (1994): 351–63. doi.org/10.1111/j.1467-8497.1994.tb00109.x.

Westmore, R.D. 'Japan and the Trade Diversion Policy.' *The Australian Quarterly* 9, no. 1 (1937): 93–6. doi.org/10.2307/20629413.

White, Hugh. 'Powershift: Australia's Future Between Washington and Beijing.' *Quarterly Essay* 39 (2010): 1–74.

White, Hugh. 'The Limits to Optimism: Australia and the Rise of China.' *Australian Journal of International Affairs* 59, no. 4 (2005): 469–80. doi.org/10.1080/10357710500367273.

White, Hugh. 'Without America: Australia in the New Asia.' *Quarterly Essay* 68 (2017): 1–81.

## Theses

Kilmister, Michael. 'Antipodean imperialist: Sir John Latham, a political biography, 1902 to 1934.' PhD thesis, University of Newcastle, 2018.

Reed, J. 'American diplomatic relations with Australia during the Second World War.' PhD thesis, University of Southern California, Los Angeles, 1969.

Sissons, D.C.S. 'Attitudes to Japan and defence, 1890–1923.' MPhil thesis, University of Melbourne, 1956.

## Online content

Australian Bureau of Statistics. 'Historical Population 2016.' Cat. No. 3105.0.65.001. Canberra: Australian Bureau of Statistics. Available from: www.abs.gov.au/AUSSTATS/abs@.nsf/Lookup/3105.0.65.001Main+Features12016?OpenDocument.

Churchill, Winston. 'Sinews of peace.' Speech, Westminster College, Fulton, Missouri, 5 March 1946. Fulton, MO: National Churchill Museum, 2021. Available from: www.nationalchurchillmuseum.org/sinews-of-peace-iron-curtain-speech.html.

Davidson, Remy. 'Australia is Hedging its Bets on China with the Latest Foreign Policy White Paper.' *The Conversation*, 23 November 2017. Available from: theconversation.com/australia-is-hedging-its-bets-on-china-with-the-latest-foreign-policy-white-paper-88009.

Department of Foreign Affairs and Trade. 'Stepping-Up Australia's Engagement with Our Pacific Family.' *Pacific Step-Up*. Canberra: DFAT, n.d. Available from: dfat.gov.au/geo/pacific/engagement/Pages/stepping-up-australias-pacific-engagement.aspx.

Doran, Matthew and Dziedzic, Stephen. 'Australian Correspondents Bill Birtles and Mike Smith Pulled Out of China After Five-Day Diplomatic Standoff Over National Security Case.' *ABC News*, 8 September 2020. Available from: www.abc.net.au/news/2020-09-08/bill-birtles-mike-smith-evacuated-china-safety-concerns/12638786.

'Enhancing Australia's role in Pacific infrastructure projects.' Joint media release, Senator the Hon. Marise Payne, Minister for Foreign Affairs, Canberra, 4 April 2019. Available from: www.foreignminister.gov.au/minister/marise-payne/media-release/enhancing-australias-role-pacific-infrastructure-projects.

'Ensuring a consistent Australian foreign policy.' Joint media release, Prime Minister, Minister for Foreign Affairs, Minister for Women, Canberra, 27 August 2020. Available from: www.pm.gov.au/media/ensuring-consistent-australian-foreign-policy.

Greste, Peter. 'China Rising: The Challenges for Australia as China and the US Struggle for Supremacy in Asia.' *Four Corners*, ABC TV, 3 October 2016. Available from: www.abc.net.au/4corners/four-corners-china-rising-promo/7890504.

'Joint Statement Australia–U.S. Ministerial Consultations (AUSMIN) 2020.' Joint statement, Senator the Hon. Marise Payne, Canberra, 28 July 2020. Available from: www.foreignminister.gov.au/minister/marise-payne/media-release/joint-statement-australia-us-ministerial-consultations-ausmin-2020.

Lavelle, Alex. 'Australia Doesn't Have to Choose US Over China or Vice Versa.' *The Age*, [Melbourne], 1 March 2018. Available from: www.theage.com.au/national/australia-doesn-t-have-to-choose-us-over-china-or-vice-versa-20180301-p4z2cd.html.

Lowy Institute. 'In Conversation: Hugh White on How to Defend Australia.' Lowy Institute, Sydney, 16 July 2019. Available from: www.lowyinstitute.org/news-and-media/multimedia/audio/conversation-hugh-white-how-defend-australia.

Lyon, Rod. 'What Happened to the "Canberra Consensus" On Australia–China Relations?' *The Strategist*, 3 July 2019. Canberra: Australian Strategic Policy Institute. Available from: www.aspistrategist.org.au/what-happened-to-the-canberra-consensus-on-australia-china-relations.

Morrison, Scott. 'Address: Launch of the 2020 Defence Strategic Update.' Speech, Royal Military College, Duntroon, ACT, 1 July 2020. Available from: www.pm.gov.au/media/address-launch-2020-defence-strategic-update.

National Library of Australia. 'South Pacific Commission.' Canberra: NLA, 2008 [revised 2019]. Available from: www.nla.gov.au/selected-library-collections/south-pacific-commission.

National Museum of Australia. 'Stanley Bruce.' *Prime Ministers of Australia*. Canberra: NMA, 2021. Available from: www.nma.gov.au/primeministers/stanley_bruce.

'Realising the Pacific's vision for stability, security and prosperity.' Speech, Ewen McDonald, Head of the Office of the Pacific, Department of Foreign Affairs and Trade, Canberra, 7 June 2019. Available from: www.dfat.gov.au/news/speeches/Pages/realising-the-pacifics-vision-for-stability-security-and-prosperity.

Srinivasan, Prianka. 'China's Trade War with Australia Is Affecting A Growing Number of Industries. How Did We Get Here?' *ABC News*, 10 December 2020. Available from: www.abc.net.au/news/2020-12-10/chinas-trade-war-with-australia-export-industry/12967190.

# Index

A page number containing 'n.' indicates a reference appearing in a footnote on that page; numbers in bold are illustrations.

Abbott, Joseph P. 63, 64
ABDACOM, see American–British–Dutch–Australian Command
Acheson, Dean 174
Advisory War Council 98, 105, 106
AEM, see Australian Eastern Mission
Allied Council for Japan (ACJ) 143, 144, 145, 146
America, see United States of America
American Samoa 122
American–British–Dutch–Australian Command (ABDACOM) 110, 111, 112
Anglo-American 6, 101, 154
  alliance 6, 21, 24, 101, 102, 175, 181
Anglo-Australian Joint Project 146
Anglo-Japanese Alliance 18–22, 24, 52, 53, 76, 103, 104
Anglo-Japanese Treaty of Commerce and Navigation 103, 104
Anglo-Malayan Defence Agreement (AMDA) 193
ANZAC Agreement, see Australian–New Zealand Agreement
ANZAM, see Australian, New Zealand and Malayan
ANZUS, see Australia, New Zealand, United States Security Treaty
appeasement 9, 82, 84–8, 90, 91–4, 103–8

Arcadia Conference 110
Atlantic Charter 115
Attlee, Clement 121, 150
Australia
  accommodation of Japan 47, 51, 78
  appeasement of Japan 82, 85, 86, 89, 92, 103, 104
  approval of peace treaty with Japan 144, 146, 168
  Britain's defence of 18, 24–5, 28, 96, 111–12, 114, 136
  Britain's inability to protect 14, 35, 75–6, 82, 95–6, 103, 109, 203
  British markets for 38, 39, 40, 60, 65, 66, 188–9, 190, 192
  British military directives to 14, 95, 111–12, 172
  British pressure over Japan 66–9, 203
  challenge to US Pacific hegemony 120, 125, 127, 131
  change in attitude to Japan 163, 183, 184
  declaration of war with Japan 102, 107
  disagreements with US 6, 131, 146
  economic pressure from Britain 60–1, 70–1
  'Fourth Empire' concept 6n.15, 130, 131, 132, 203

237

iron embargo against Japan
89–90, 91
Japan as threat to 4, 16, 19, 53,
75, 90, 114
Japanese markets for 35, 42, 43,
44, 53, 59, 163, 164, 199
lack of British consultation with
32, 95, 130, 196
legation in Japan 96–7, 98
legation in US 96–7, 99, 102,
116, 164, 174, 178, 202
'looks to' US 109, 132
policy divergence with Britain
9, 93–4, 98, 111–12, 136,
149–50
potential of war with Japan 81,
85, 91–2, 98
problems in relations with Britain
82, 93, 98, 111–12, 125, 137,
179, 188
realignment with US 171–99,
201, 203
rebuilding of relations with Japan
184, 185, 186–7
relations with Britain 4, 8, 9, 14,
28, 84, 130, 131–2, 137, 198,
202
relations with Japan 1, 7, 16, 32,
33, 36, 42, 45, 46, 48, 49–51,
56, 66, 68, 98, 204
relations with US 4, 5, 9, 59, 103,
105, 186
reliance on US 5, 109, 156, 196,
198
reluctance to act against Japan 45,
46, 47–8, 66–8, 69, 88, 93,
203
retreat from Sterling Area 187–8,
199
role in Japanese peace settlement
118, 122–4, 127
role in postwar occupation of
Japan 136, 143–4, 145, 146

rupture in relations with Japan
74, 75, 85, 184
security relations with US 101,
122, 136, 181, 187, 197
shift in relations with Britain 4, 5,
6, 109, 149, 171–2, 175, 187,
198, 199, 205, 206
suspicion of Japan 16, 23–4, 32,
163, 168, 183
trade agreements with Japan 68,
69, 88, 93, 104
trade embargo with Japan 104
trade war with Japan 8, 60, 63,
64, 71, 72, 73–4
trade with Britain 35, 65, 66,
68–70, 71, 72, 155, 188–92,
199, 205
trade with Japan 44–8, 49–50,
53–7, 66, 67–8, 74, 86, 93,
184
trade with US 3, 40–2, 62–3, 70
Treaty of Friendship, Commerce
and Navigation with Japan
55, 61
US alliance 6, 18, 24, 132, 137
US antagonism 9, 118, 146
US military cooperation 113,
163, 171, 172, 198
Australia–Japan Agreement on
Commerce (1957) 187, 199, 205
Australia, New Zealand, United States
Security Treaty (ANZUS) 10,
109, 178, 183, 198
and ANZAM 176–7
Australia signs 6, 168, 171, 173
Australian disappointment with
173, 174–5
British exclusion from 175, 176
Council 173, 174, 175
US dominance of 174, 176, 206
Australian Eastern Mission (AEM)
48–53, 54, 55, 56, 58, 63, 68,
97, 202

Australian–New Zealand Agreement (ANZAC Agreement) 9, 123, 124–6, 127, 128, 130, 132, 138, 140, 141, 149, 203
   ANZAC Area 110, 111
   ANZAC Conference 123, 124–6, 128
Australian, New Zealand and Malayan (ANZAM) (arrangement and area) 148, 149, 151, 172, 175, 176–8, 181–2

Balfour, Arthur 31
Balfour Declaration (1926) 31, 32
Britain
   and AEM 48, 51
   and ANZAC Agreement 125, 127–8
   and ANZAM 148, 172, 175, 176–8
   and Asian nationalism 136–7, 149, 150, 151, 152, 159, 179
   and Australian legation in Japan 96–7, 98
   and Australian legation in US 96–7
   and Cold War 162, 169, 171
   and Colombo Plan 137, 184, 187
   and imperial economic reciprocity 68, 71, 72
   and Indochina 178, 179
   and Manchukuo 47, 52, 53
   and Manchurian Crisis 45, 47, 85, 86, 91–2
   and Marshall Plan 157, 158
   and Ottawa Agreements 37, 38, 68, 189–90, 191, 192
   and Pacific pact 76, 202
   and SEATO 181–3
   and Singapore Strategy 24–8, 101–2, 107
   and status of dominions 28, 30–1, 32
   and Suez Crisis 193–5, 198
   and US encroachment in Pacific 125, 129, 146
   and Washington System 20–2, 23–4
   as 'Fourth Empire' 6n.15, 130, 131, 132, 203
   as global power 4, 8, 9, 131, 156, 159
   as market for Australian goods 38, 39, 40, 60, 65, 66, 188–9, 190, 192
   Asia-Pacific defence policy 47, 52, 53, 75–6, 111, 147–8, 176, 177–8
   competition with US 6, 174–5
   decline in global power 6, 8, 10, 13, 14, 15, 127, 130–1, 156, 172, 187, 192
   defence expenditure 15, 19, 26
   defence of Australia 18, 24–5, 28, 96, 111–12, 114, 136
   defence policy 26–7, 52, 82, 95, 195, 198
   economic pressure on Australia 60–1, 70–1
   economic reliance on US 14, 154–5
   exclusion from ANZUS 175–6, 177
   foreign policy 3, 32, 46, 76, 81, 172, 175, 203, 205
   inability to protect Australia 14, 35, 75–6, 82, 95–6, 103, 109, 203
   Japan as threat to influence of 4, 6, 60
   lack of consultation with Australia 32, 95, 130, 196
   maintenance of global power 129, 131, 160, 198
   markets 35, 38, 39, 68
   military directives to Australia 14, 95, 111–12, 172

military presence in Pacific 22, 24–5, 128, 139
naval power 15, 19, 20, 23, 72, 100
Pacific postwar planning 8–9, 108, 121, 123, 127, 147–8
Pacific War 5, 107, 111, 112, 127
policy divergence with Australia 9, 93–4, 98, 111–12, 136, 149–50
policy divergence with US 6, 104, 175
presence in Asia-Pacific 24, 120, 140, 146, 150–2, 159, 169, 176, 202
pressure on Australia over Japan 66–9
problems in relations with Australia 82, 93, 98, 111–12, 125, 137, 179, 188
relations with Australia 4, 8, 9, 14, 28, 84, 130, 131–2, 137, 198, 202
relations with dominions 125, 127, 128, 129, 130, 139, 157, 178
relations with Japan 16, 18–19, 21, 24, 26, 36, 52, 53, 76, 91, 92, 94, 98, 110, 123
relations with Russia/USSR 13, 92, 136, 149
renewal of global power 130, 156–7
retreat from Asia-Pacific 112, 114, 195, 198
sanctions against Japan 46, 47, 92–3, 103, 104
shift in relations with Australia 4, 5, 6, 109, 149, 171–2, 175, 187, 198, 199, 205, 206
Sterling Area as basis of power 6, 9, 37, 154, 156–7, 160
trade diversion 64–6, 71, 72
trade policy 38, 44n.31, 68, 69–72, 104, 154–5, 157
trade with Australia 35, 65, 66, 68–70, 71, 72, 155, 188–92, 199, 205
trade with dominions 37, 38, 64, 68, 71
US security alliance 6, 24, 100–3, 107, 142–3, 144, 169, 172, 174, 181, 182
waning of power in Asia-Pacific 7, 8, 20–1, 112, 176
war in Europe 92, 95, 100, 102, 103, 108
wartime strategy 8, 9, 108
world system 6, 9, 137, 147, 151, 152, 154, 205
World War I 13, 14–15
see also American–British–Dutch–Australian Command; Anglo-American; Anglo-Australian Joint Project; Anglo-Japanese Alliance; Anglo-Japanese Treaty of Commerce and Navigation; Anglo-Malayan Defence Agreement; Commonwealth; Sterling Area
British Admiralty 24, 25, 26, 111
British Air Ministry 84
British Commonwealth Far East Strategic Reserve (FESR) 178, 181, 182, 183, 193
British Commonwealth Occupation Force in Japan 144
British Council 152
British Foreign Office 49, 50, 67, 96, 131n.105
British Tariff Board 67–8, 69
Bruce, Stanley Melbourne 46, 48, 73n.62, 92, 97
  and legation in Washington 99, 100
  and Manchurian Crisis 46, 47, 48
  and Ottawa Agreements 53, 67, 68–9

and trade with Japan 53, 67, 93
and US support for war 100, 107
criticism of defence planning 22, 27, 95
Burma 107, 111, 152
Burton, John 149, 162, 163

Cairo Conference 122–3, 125
Canberra Pact, *see* ANZAC Agreement
Casey, Richard
  and Cordell Hull 101, 105, 106
  and engagement with Asia 32–3, 185
  and Percy Spender 173, 174
  and Sumner Welles 100, 104, 107
  and US support for war 99–100, 101, 102, 107, 182
  as anti-communist 183, 185
  diplomacy 99, 106, 183
  on ANZUS 173, 174, 177, 179
  on Suez Crisis 194–5
  on US alliance 197–8, 202
Chamberlain, Neville 92
Chanak Crisis (1922) 29, 30, 31
Chiefs of Staff Committee (COS) 47, 75, 176, 177
Chifley, Ben 5, 146
  and Anglo-Australian relationship 137, 146, 150
  and Asian nationalism 149, 150, 151–2, 163
  and Cold War 162, 169
  and Colombo Plan 9–10
  and Commonwealth relations 150, 151–2
  and H.C. Coombs 150, 155
  and regional leadership 136, 138, 139, 141, 154, 204
  and USSR 149, 150
  defence policy 141, 142, 143, 151
  economic policy 155, 157–8, 160, 163, 166
  foreign policy 136, 137, 152, 165
  ideas about diplomacy 162, 166
China
  Belt and Road Initiative 94, 140
  communist 'threat' 176, 177, 184
  communist victory in 163, 165
  international relations 33, 51, 94n.49, 107
  Japan as alternative market to 163, 164, 184, 185
  Japanese invasion of 33, 45, 77, 89, 90, 97
  Pacific territory 123
  postwar relations with Japan 121, 123, 144
  proclamation of People's Republic 162
  relations with Australia 1–2, 3, 42, 47, 48, 49, 50, 59, 76, 94, 97, 162
  relations with Britain 26, 91–2, 97
  relations with Japan 48, 51, 76, 85, 91
  relations with US 2, 59, 89
  rise of 2, 3, 59
  Soviet influence in 163
  Tientsin incident 91–2, 94
  trade with Australia 3, 43, 49, 55n.83
  war with Japan 77, 82, 85, 90, 91–2, 97, 105, 107, 203
  *see also* Manchukuo; Manchuria; Manchurian Crisis; Second Sino-Japanese War
Chinese Communist Party 162
Churchill, Winston 96, 111, 115, 121, 123, 142, 176, 181
Colombo Plan for Cooperative Economic Development in South and South-East Asia 10, 137, 153, 165–9, 183–4, 185, 186
Committee of Imperial Defence (CID) 22, 46

Commonwealth 6, 9, 31, 127, 151
  and ANZAM review 176, 178, 181
  and ANZUS 176
  and Australian regional policy 137, 165, 177
  and Colombo Plan 165–9
  as basis of British power 6, 129
  as counterweight to US 9, 110, 118, 129
  Australia in 9, 99, 127, 129, 131, 135, 145, 147, 151, 165, 172, 203
  Australian retreat from 179, 187, 192
  aviation 118, 125
  defence cooperation 9, 110, 122–9, 132, 136, 146–7, 151
  defence policy 130, 142, 143, 144, 146–7
  economic policy 156, 157, 160, 161, 164, 166–8
  foreign policy 130, 140, 142
  influence in Asia-Pacific 51, 139, 159, 166, 167
  influence on global affairs 130, 131, 150, 159, 161
  interests in Asia-Pacific 150, 151, 156
  internal consultation 130, 142, 152
  postwar role for 127, 129, 136
  redefining role of 139, 150
  regional organisation 139, 140
  regional security 9, 130, 139, 150
  relations with Asia 51, 159
  revival in Asia-Pacific 139, 150, 153
  role in ANZAC Agreement 128, 140
  status in Asia-Pacific 6, 127, 137, 140
  US cooperation 137, 167, 169
  US strategic partnership 10, 136, 142–3, 147, 172–4, 177
  see also Britain; British Commonwealth Far East Strategic Reserve; Imperial Conference
Commonwealth Foreign Ministers' Conference (1950) 165, 166, 167, 168
Commonwealth Prime Ministers' Conference
  (1944) 131
  (1946) 139, 142, 146
  (1948) 147, 157, 159, 160, 161
  (1953) 178
  (1955) 181, 195n.96
  (1956) 195
Conference on Eastern Trade 43, 44
Coombs, H.C. 150, 152, 155, 156, 190, 205
Crawford, John 189, 192

*Dalfram* strike 86
Dedman, John 147
Defence Review (1957) 196, 197
Dulles, John Foster 178, 186

East China Sea 16
Eggleston, Frederic 1, 24, 107
European Recovery Program (ERP) 156, 157, 158, 164
  see also Marshall Plan
Evatt, H.V. 145n.38, 149
  and ANZAC Agreement 123–5, 126, 128, 138
  and Cairo Conference 122–3
  and Commonwealth 128, 139, 147, 151, 157, 158
  and cooperation with British 110, 128
  and foreign policy 129, 130, 159–60
  and regional diplomacy 106, 139
  and US defence relations 142–3

and US support for war 107, 112
as Minister for External Affairs 106, 110, 129
championing importance of Australia 121, 122, 127, 138
criticism of US 110, 125, 126
on Asian nationalism 150, 151, 152
on regionalism 110, 115, 116, 120, 121, 122, 139, 150
strategic vision 116, 130, 135
visit to US 112, 120, 121
visits to Britain 120, 121, 147, 157, 158
wartime diplomacy 114–15, 121, 129

Far East Strategic Reserve, *see* British Commonwealth Far East Strategic Reserve
FESR, *see* British Commonwealth Far East Strategic Reserve
Five-Power Staff Agency 176, 177, 179
Five-Power Treaty 21, 22n.38
see also Washington Naval Conference
Forsyth, William Douglass 119, 120, 124–5, 136, 204
Four-Power Treaty 21, 22, 233
see also Washington Naval Conference

Gepp, Herbert 42, 43, 44, 205
Grant, Percy 27
Gullett, Henry 60, 61, 62, 69, 70, 73, 74, 75

Harding, Warren G. 20
Hodgson, William Roy 57
Hughes, William Morris 15, 18, 19, 22, 27
and Anglo-Japanese alliance 19–20, 22

and Australian vulnerability 16–17, 22
on lack of British consultation 30, 31–2
Pacific policy 16, 52–3
seeking US cooperation 16–17, 18
Hull, Cordell 42, 100–1, 105, 106, 119, 120, 125, 126

Imperial Conference 20, 28, 29
(1921) 19
(1926) 30
(1930) 31
(1937) 75, 76, 77, 82, 90
Imperial Economic Conference (1932) 38, 55n.79
Imperial Japanese Army 33, 45, 97, 98, 102, 103, 105
Imperial Japanese Navy (IJN) 16
India 30, 136, 139, 151–2, 155, 160
Indian Ocean 1, 16, 25, 149
Indonesia 114, 136, 149, 162, 184n.50, 199
see also Netherlands East Indies

Japan 16, 97, 114, 146
alignment with Axis powers 97, 98, 100
Allied occupation of 56, 136, 143–5
Allied strategy against 110, 111
and Colombo Plan 184, 185, 186
and Five-Power Treaty 21
and Four-Power Treaty 21, 22
and League of Nations 17, 33, 45–6, 50, 85, 97
and Netherlands East Indies 103, 104, 111, 112, 114
and Pacific pact proposal 76
and Philippines 112
and regional policy 162, 163, 164, 184
and SEATO 183–7

243

and trade diversion 60, 61–6, 74, 75, 77–8, 85, 88
army 33, 45, 97, 98, 102, 103, 105
as alternative market to China 163, 164, 184, 185
as bulwark against communism 6, 144, 146, 163, 164, 183, 184, 185
as challenger to Britain 4, 59, 66–7
as threat to Australia 4, 16, 19, 53, 75, 90, 114
attacks on US territory 108
Australian accommodation of 47, 51, 78
Australian appeasement of 82, 85, 86, 89, 92, 103, 104
Australian approval of peace treaty with 144, 146, 168
Australian change in attitude to 163, 183, 184
Australian declaration of war against 102, 107
Australian iron embargo 89–90, 91
Australian legation in 96, 97, 98
Australian markets in 35, 42, 43, 44, 53, 59, 163, 164, 199
Australian reluctance to act against 45, 46, 47–8, 66–8, 69, 88, 93, 203
Australian role in peace settlement 118, 122–4, 127
Australian role in postwar occupation 136, 143–4, 145, 146
Australian suspicion of 16, 23–4, 32, 163, 168, 183
Australian trade agreements with 68, 69, 88, 93, 104
Australian trade embargo 104
Australian trade war with 8, 60, 63, 64, 71, 72, 73–4

British interception of vessels 93, 94
British military vulnerability to 94, 95, 103, 108
Combined Japanese Fleet 98
competition with US 16, 19, 22
conditions of surrender 123, 127
'economic penetration' policy 77, 86, **87**, 90
economic rehabilitation 6, 144–5, 146, 163
in Burma 107
in Indochina 98, 101–2, 103, 104, 105
in Malaya 102, 107
in Singapore 102–3
in Southeast Asia 102
in Thailand 102, 104, 105, 107
in World War I 24
international relations 33, 50, 72, 75, 76, 85–6
international trade 144, 145, 164
invasion of China 33, 45, 76, 77, 89, 90, 97
invasion of Manchuria 33, 45–6, 50, 77, 97
Manchukuo 45, 46, 47, 48, 50–1, 52, 53, 91
military aggression 82, 85, 93, 94, 95, 97, 99, 103, 104, 105, 106
military superiority 84, 108, 114
naval power 16, 19, 21, 23, 25, 72, 98
navy 16
Pacific territorial expansion 16, 17, 19, 45, 53, 75, 86, 90
Pacific territories 17, 25, 123
peace negotiations 18, 106, 121, 143, 164, 168, 183, 202
peace settlement 116, 118, 123
peace treaty 144, 145, 146, 164, 168, 183, 201
post World War I 15, 16, 18

postwar constraints on military 144, 185
potential of war with Australia 81, 85, 91–2, 98
potential of war with British Empire 22, 26, 75–6, 91–2, 95–6
rebuilding of relations with Australia 184, 185, 186–7
regional economic integration 143–6, 183, 184, 186, 187
relations with Australia 1, 7, 16, 32, 33, 36, 42, 45, 46, 48, 49–51, 56, 66–9, 98, 203, 204
relations with Britain 13, 18–22, 47, 52, 85, 91, 93, 98, 184–5
relations with China 48, 51, 76, 85, 91
relations with Germany 91, 92, 98
relations with US 19, 89, 92, 93, 105, 106, 144–5
retreat from international treaties 72, 76
rise of 4, 13, 15, 57, 108
rupture in relations with Australia 74, 75, 85, 184
sanctions against 46, 47, 67, 68, 70–1, 85, 89, 92, 101, 103, 104, 105, 203
sinking of RN ships 82
trade with Australia 44–8, 49–50, 53–7, 66, 67–8, 74, 86, 93, 184
Treaty of Friendship, Commerce and Navigation with Australia 55, 61
US 'Reverse Course' in 144, 145, 147, 149
US claims on territories 116, 164
US dominance of occupation 143–6, 149, 153
US plans for occupation 121, 123, 127
US policy on 121, 123, 146, 163, 164, 168, 183, 184, 185–6, 202
US seizure of assets 104
war with China 77, 82, 85, 90, 91–2, 97, 105, 107, 203
war with US 104, 105, 112, 113
see also Allied Council for Japan; Anglo-Japanese; Australia–Japan Agreement on Commerce; Manchukuo; Manchuria; Manchurian Crisis; Second Sino-Japanese War; Tientsin incident
Jellicoe, Lord John 25, 26

Latham, John 35, 48, 49–52, 53–6, 97, 98, 202
League of Nations 15, 17, 18, 33, 45, 48, 50, 52, 53, 72, 85, 97
see also United Nations
Locarno Treaties 30, 72
London Naval Conference 72, 76
Longfield Lloyd, Eric 56, 57, 90, 98
Lyons, Joseph
and AEM 49, 53, 202
and Manchurian Crisis 47–8
and Trade Diversion Policy 60, 64–5, 67, 69–72, 73
Asia-Pacific policy 52–3, 76, 77, 202
at 1935 Leaders' Meeting 52–3, 69
at 1937 Imperial Conference 76, 77, 82
diplomacy with Japan 85, 89, 96
on Ottawa Agreements 39, 41–2, 67, 68, 69
Lytton Report 45, 48

MacArthur, General Douglas 112, 113, 143, 145
MacDonald, Malcolm 85
MacDonald, Ramsay 27

McEwen, John 189, 190, 191, 192
Macmahon Ball, William 56, 144, 145, 152, 153
Malaya 26, 49, 162, 182, 183, 193
  and US defence of 181–2
  ANZAM defence of 178, 181
  British defence of 148, 177, 182
  fall of 111, 112
  independence 192–3, 195
  Japanese advance on 102, 107
  nationalist agitation 152
  see also Australian, New Zealand and Malayan
Manchukuo 45, 46, 47, 48, 50, 51, 52, 53, 91
  see also Japan
Manchuria 45, 47, 48, 50, 123
  see also China
Manchurian Crisis 8, 32–3, 35–6, 45–8, 50, 68, 85, 88, 92
  see also China; Japan
Marshall, George C. 156
Marshall Islands 16, 17, 122
Marshall Plan 156, 157
  see also European Recovery Program
Melbourne, A.C.V. 42, 43, 44, 77, 78
Menzies, Robert 6, 10, 71, 99, 165, 166
  and ANZAM 176, 181, 182
  and ANZUS Treaty 171, 172, 176
  and embargo against Japan 93, 104, 105
  and SEATO 180–1, 182
  and Suez Crisis 194, 195
  and trade with Japan 86, 93, 187
  Asia-Pacific policy 6, 10, 97
  defence policy 100, 195, 197–8, 203
  foreign policy 5, 137, 168, 169, 171, 203, 204
  trade policy 71, 187, 189, 191
Murai, Kuaramatsu 61

National Security Council, see United States of America—National Security Council
NATO, see North Atlantic Treaty Organization
Nehru, Pandit Jawaharlal 160
NEI, see Netherlands East Indies
Netherlands 140, 150
Netherlands East Indies (NEI) 43, 49, 55n.83, 103, 114
  Australian desire for control of 114–15
  defence of 108, 112, 114
  fall of 112, 114
  war in 104, 111
  see also Indonesia
New Delhi Conference 152
New Zealand 96, 118, 124, 125, 178, 187, 193
  and ANZAC Agreement 123–4, 127
  and ANZAM 148–9, 175, 176–7
  and ANZUS 173–4, 175, 176
  and Pacific security 124, 125, 127, 128, 129, 141, 142, 172
  and SPC 139, 140
  and US encroachment in Pacific 124, 129
  foreign policy 20–1, 145, 151, 162
  zone of influence 122, 124, 125, 128
Nine-Power Conference 85, 86
Nine-Power Treaty 33, 85
  see also Washington Naval Conference
North Atlantic Treaty Organization (NATO) 173, 180

Ottawa Agreements (1932) 37–9, 41, 44, 53–4, 61, 67–9, 72, 189–92, 205

Pacific pact 76, 77, 202
Pacific War Council (PWC) 112, 126
Paris Peace Conference 17
Pearl Harbor 108

Roosevelt, Franklin D. 100, 101, 107, 115, 121, 123
Russia 13, 16, 18, 92, 108, 159, 163
  see also Union of Soviet Socialist Republics

San Francisco Conference (1945) 127
SEATO, see Southeast Asia Treaty Organization
Second Sino-Japanese War 77, 82, 85, 90, 91–2, 97, 203
Singapore
  calls for US support for 101, 102–3
  fall of 82, 108, 111, 112, 129
  Naval Base 13, 21n.37, 24, 47
  preparations for defence of 95, 105, 107
Singapore Strategy 24–8, 76, 81
South China Sea 2, 16
South Pacific Commission (SPC) 138, 139–40, 141, 156
South Seas Conference (1947) 139
South Seas Regional Commission 124, 138
South West Pacific Area (SWPA) 112, 113
Southeast Asia Treaty Organization (SEATO) 6, 172, 179, 180–6, 193, 196–7, 198, 206
SPC, see South Pacific Commission
Spender, Percy 165, 166, 167, 168, 173, 174, 178–9
Statute of Westminster 31, 32, 33
Sterling Area 4, 6, 37, 39, 155, 158, 160–1, 166
  and trade reform 117, 154, 157, 161, 187

and US 117, 154, 157, 160–1, 169
  as basis of British power 6, 9, 37, 154, 156–7, 160
  Australian retreat from 187–8, 199
  discrimination in 154, 155, 157, 187, 188
  members of 6n.16, 37, 151, 154, 159, 161, 167
  preferential treatment in 6, 37, 117, 154
  preservation of 9, 154–5, 158, 161, 167, 169, 188
  reserves 154, 158, 160, 187–8, 194
  threat to 117, 154, 157, 160
Suez Canal Company 193
Suez Crisis 192–9

Trade Diversion Policy 8, 59–78, 85, 86, 88, 206
Treaty of Friendship, Commerce and Navigation (Japan and Australia) 55, 61
Truman Doctrine 144
Truman, Harry S. 143, 163

Union of Soviet Socialist Republics (USSR) 121, 129, 136, 143, 144, 146, 149, 150, 156, 159, 163, 164, 176, 183, 194
  see also Russia
United Nations (UN) 120, 126, 127, 138, 139, 150, 152, 194
  see also League of Nations
United States of America (US) 1, 99
  alliance with Australia 6, 18, 24, 132, 137
  and ANZAC Agreement 125–6, 127
  and Cold War 136, 154, 156, 157, 159, 161, 162–5, 168
  and Five-Power Treaty 21, 22

247

and Four-Power Treaty 21, 22
and Indochina 178, 179
and League of Nations 15, 18
and SEATO 172, 180, 181–2, 186, 196
and Sino-Japanese War 77, 82, 85, 90, 91–2, 97, 105, 107, 203
and Washington System 22, 23, 24
antagonism with Australia 9, 118, 146
as creditor nation 14, 23, 36, 37, 70, 154, 187, 194
as global hegemon 9, 13, 15
Atlantic bases 102
Australian realignment with 171–99, 201, 203
Australian reliance on 5, 109, 132, 156, 196, 198
aviation 117, 118, 125
British economic reliance on 14, 24, 154–5
challenge to dominance of 2, 3
claims on Japanese territories 116, 164
Commonwealth cooperation 137, 167, 169
Commonwealth strategic partnership 10, 136, 142–3, 147, 172–4, 177
Commonwealth subservience to 127
competition with Britain 6, 174–5
competition with China 2, 3, 59
competition with Japan 16, 19, 22
declining interest in South Pacific 149, 153
disagreements with Australia 6, 131, 146
dominance of strategic outlook 3, 4, 176, 187, 205–6

economic policy 14, 23, 117, 160, 202
encroachment in Asia-Pacific 124, 125, 129, 131n.105, 146
Foreign Operations Administration 186
foreign policy 4, 18, 149, 154, 161, 164, 166, 169, 178, 196
growing influence in Japan 20
hegemony in Pacific 4, 8, 120, 125, 127, 131
in Asia-Pacific 9, 82, 108, 121, 144, 164, 168, 169, 178, 182, 183, 186, 198
in SPC 140
in World War II 15, 100, 101, 102, 103, 105, 108, 115
industry 14, 16, 23, 40, 41, 63
interests in Europe 100, 102, 156
interests in Pacific 99, 116, 117, 119, 121, 126, 127, 140, 164, 177
isolationism 4, 18, 99, 178, 202
Japanese attacks on territory 108
Joint Chiefs of Staff (USJCS) 173, 174, 182
lack of defence commitments 143, 147, 181–2
lack of interest in Singapore 101, 102–3
lack of military assurance 93, 94, 96, 101–3, 143, 203
markets 35, 36, 38, 40, 41
military cooperation with Australia 101, 112, 113, 163, 171, 172, 197, 198
military dominance 4, 6, 116, 118, 127, 172
military expenditure 19, 169, 196
Monroe Doctrine 17n.17, 53
National Security Council (NSC) 145, 164–5, 183, 184
naval superiority 20–1, 22
neglect of Pacific 114

non-aggression pact 76
nuclear policy 143, 195–6
occupation of Japan 121, 123, 127, 143–6, 149, 153
order in Asia-Pacific 6, 171, 172, 201
Pacific as 'American lake' 114–16, 119
Pacific bases 21n.37, 102, 112, 116, 118, 124, 125, 126, 141, 143
Pacific Command 175
Pacific Fleet 175
Pacific security guarantee 53, 82, 99, 106, 107, 108, 202
policy divergence from Britain 6, 104, 175
policy on Japan 121, 123, 144, 146, 163, 164, 168, 183, 184–7, 202
postwar planning 8, 108, 115–16, 117, 121, 123, 126, 127
power-sharing 120, 174–5
priorities 6, 22
recognition of Singapore's importance 102, 107
relations with Australia 4, 5, 9, 59, 103, 105, 186
relations with Japan 16, 19, 20, 22, 72, 76, 89, 92, 93, 105, 106, 144–5, 164, 202
reluctance to commit to Asia-Pacific 173–4, 177, 179, 180
resistance to joining war 96, 99, 100–1
'Reverse Course' in Japan 144, 147, 164
sanctions on Japan 89, 92–3, 103, 104, 105
security alliance with Britain 6, 24, 100–3, 107, 142–3, 144, 169, 172, 174, 181, 182
security relations with Australia 101, 122, 136, 181, 187, 197

seizure of Japanese assets 104
sphere of influence 172
State Department 101, 127, 143, 145, 163, 164, 167, 168, 173, 182, 186
strategic responsibility for Pacific 112
support for Colombo Plan 166, 167, 168, 186
territorial interests in Pacific 117, 126, 128, 142
trade 42, 59, 62, 117, 154–5, 156, 157, 160–1
trade with Australia 3, 40–2, 62–3, 70, 206
trade with Britain 14
unreliability of 6, 18, 24, 110, 118, 186, 203
war with Japan 104, 105, 112, 113
wartime strategy 8
withdrawal from Asia-Pacific 143
see also American–British–Dutch–Australian Command; Anglo-American; Australia, New Zealand, United States Security Treaty; Washington Naval Conference
USSR, see Union of Soviet Socialist Republics

Washington Naval Conference 8, 13, 20–3, 26, 33, 201
see also Four-Power Treaty; Five-Power Treaty; Nine-Power Treaty
Washington Naval Conference Treaty 45
Washington Treaties 72, 76
Welles, Sumner 100, 104, 107
Wilson, Woodrow 15, 17, 18

Yampi Sound 57, 89–90

www.ingramcontent.com/pod-product-compliance
Lightning Source LLC
Chambersburg PA
CBHW042043240426
43667CB00048B/2965